The Journal of Alexander Chesney

To my cousin Judy. I hope you enjoy learning about our Chesney ancestry, as I did. It's fascinating!

Love you

Pat Lewis (nee Scott)

The Ohio State University Bulletin

VOLUME XXVI OCTOBER 30, 1921 NUMBER 4

THE OHIO STATE UNIVERSITY STUDIES
CONTRIBUTIONS IN HISTORY AND POLITICAL SCIENCE NUMBER 7

The Journal of Alexander Chesney, a South Carolina Loyalist in the Revolution and After

EDITED BY

E. ALFRED JONES

of

London, England

WITH AN INTRODUCTION BY

PROFESSOR WILBUR H SIEBERT

THE OHIO STATE UNIVERSITY

INTRODUCTION

By WILBUR HENRY SIEBERT

THE JOURNAL OF ALEXANDER CHESNEY may be divided into four parts, namely, (1) the account of Mr. Chesney's family connections and of the migration of his father, Robert, with wife and children, from county Antrim, Ireland, to the Pacolet river, South Carolina (pp. 1 to 5) ; (2) Alexander Chesney's' experiences in the Revolution to April 5, 1782 (pp. 5 to 28) ; (3) his life, after his return to Ireland, as a loyalist applicant for relief and compensation (pp. 27 to 36) ; and (4) his career as a revenue officer at Mourne, Ireland, to about 1821 (pp. 36 to 56).

In many respects the vicissitudes through which Alexander Chesney passed are typical of the experiences of numerous other American loyalists His story, briefly sketched, is that of an adherent of the British crown who, as a youth, served as a guide for Tory refugees. For this he was imprisoned for a few days and then given the alternative of joining the Whigs or standing trial. As his father's family had been threatened with ruin for harboring some of these refugees, Alexander joined the Whigs in the hope, he says, of protecting his kindred. He served with them as a private from April, 1776, in campaigns against the Creek and Cherokee Indians and was at Augusta, Georgia, with them in the summer of 1779. Between these expeditions he engaged in conveying produce by team to Charleston, South Carolina, which was then in the possession of the Whig forces

When, at length, the British troops captured Charleston, May 12, 1780, and General Sir Henry Clinton issued a proclamation summoning the king's friends to embody, Mr. Chesney went within the lines, June 25, and became a lieutenant in the loyal militia. From this time on he served the crown faithfully in various capacities and quickly won the confidence of Major Patrick Ferguson, who was placed in command of Fort Ninety-Six. On August 9, 1780, Mr. Chesney was appointed captain and, after participating in a few minor engagements, was in the defeat and surrender of Ferguson's force at King's Mountain, October 9. Soon after this Chesney escaped and reached home, October 31. There he remained for the next

three weeks, concealing himself in a cave part of the time and stay-
ing with his father-in-law at intervals   Hearing that Lieutenant-
Colonel Tarleton had defeated Sumter at Blackstock's Hill, November 20, Chesney raised a company of militia and joined a strong
party of Tories under Brigadier-General Cunningham on Little
river.   In December Chesney was placed in command of the militia
guard at the jail of Ninety-Six, but went with Tarleton when the
latter came to that neighborhood and was with him in the defeat
and dispersion of his force at the Cowpens, January 17, 1781
Chesney again retired to his home, only to find it despoiled of all his
personal effects except two horses, with which he was able to bring
his wife and child to Robert McWhorter's place on the Edisto
river. Leaving them there, he proceeded to Charleston where he
was paid for some cattle and provisions he had supplied to Ferguson, and was assigned one of the sequestered houses and plantations
of the Whig proprietors of the Charleston district, together with
a quantity of provisions and the use of three negroes. Accordingly,
in March, 1781, he removed his family to comfrotable quarters on
the Ponpon river, a tributary of the Edisto, and, employing additional negroes, began to cultivate a crop of rice and Indian corn.

On his return to Charleston in May Chesney raised a troop of
horse by direction of Colonel Balfour and was stationed with it at
the British post at Dorchester, South Carolina, whither he now
brought his family. He promptly informed Lord Rawdon of the
activity of the Americans in that vicinity and accompanied a detachment to clear them out. During this skirmish he was wounded
in the thigh by one of the enemy   Early in July Chesney went with
Rawdon's force to relieve Fort Ninety-Six. The besieging Americans withdrew, crossed Broad River, and moved down the left bank
towards Charleston. Rawdon, fearing for the safety of the loyalist
inhabitants in the direction of Long Cane creek, sent his light
troops to bring them in and with the remainder of his men took the
road back to Charleston, but was soon cut off by the enemy. Under
these circumstances Chesney volunteered to carry a letter from
Rawdon to Balfour at Charleston, asking aid. In reply to this
appeal Colonel Balfour sent forward a detachment which enabled
Rawdon to advance.

After Lord Rawdon led his force from this section of South
Carolina, Chesney joined a corps of three companies raised for the
protection of the sequestered Whig estates by John Cruden, Esq.,

the commissioner "for the seizure, superintendence, custody, and management of captured property" in South Carolina. Meantime, the Americans had been rapidly regaining control of the Province and by December, 1781, the British found themselves confined to Charleston and its immediate vicinity. Chesney was now appointed to superintend the cutting of wood, which was made necessary by the winter season, and took pleasure in relieving the destitute condition of a number of refugee loyalists by employing them in this work Chesney had lost his wife at the close of November, 1781, and was compelled by ill health to give up the supervision of the wood cutters early in the following January. As he grew worse, instead of better, he sent his child to its relatives and sailed from Charleston, April 5, 1782, landing at Castle Haven, Ireland, May 19

By June 4 he was in Dublin, where he was introduced to a loyalist, Mr. Philip Henry, who had been exiled with others from South Carolina in June, 1778, and was now an officer in the Customs house at Dublin. Mr. Henry advised Mr. Chesney to seek a position in the revenue service and to file a claim for the losses he had suffered in the American war. After a short stay in Dublin Chesney paid a brief visit to his relatives in county Antrim and then proceeded to London, where he submitted a memorial, supported by testimonials, to the lords of the Treasury, August 3, asking for immediate relief. Having thus begun this negotiation, he took lodgings at 58 Crown street, Westminster. Through the kindness of his landlord Mr Chesney made the acquaintance of Mr. Lewis Wolfe, a clerk in the Treasury, who then or later acted as the agent in London for those American refugees who had returned to the north-east of Ireland. Mr. Wolfe proved to be helpful in various ways to our applicant.

Later Mr. Chesney attended a large meeting of the Association of American Loyalists in London at the *Crown and Anchor* tavern in the Strand, where it was determined to petition the king's ministers, Mr Chesney being named one of a committee of three to prepare the petition on behalf of those loyalists who had rendered services to Government and lost their property. After drafting another memorial and copying his testimonials for Lord North, arranging with two loyalists to send him any word from the Treasury, calling on Sir Henry Clinton and Lord Cornwallis about his personal affairs, and authorizing Mr. Wolfe to act for him in his absence, Alexander Chesney took his departure from London, August 16

On his journey homeward he waited on Lord Rawdon, from whom he received a letter soliciting the interest of General Burgoyne—now commander of the forces in Ireland—in having the bearer appointed to a position in the Irish Customs. At length, on August 30, he boarded the packet at Liverpool on his way to Dublin. Calling on Burgoyne in the latter city, he was given little encouragement in regard to the desired appointment. By September 7 he was back in county Antrim with his relatives. A few days later a letter from Mr. Wolfe asked for a sworn statement of his losses in America, accompanied by certificates from Cornwallis, Tarleton, and others. These documents he supplied promptly, his estimate of his losses totaling £1,998. 10s.

By the middle of December, 1782, Chesney heard from Lord Rawdon and, by the latter's direction, returned to Dublin to see about the Customs appointment   The outcome of this mission was an appointment as tide waiter at Waterford, whither the appointee betook himself to remain, as it turned out, only two weeks, for neither the location nor the duty pleased him   He, therefore, got himself removed to Belfast, and on March 1 married his second wife.

The honeymoon had lasted but little more than a fortnight when a letter from Mr. Wolfe called for the presence of the bridegroom in London, in connection with his claim as a distressed loyalist. Obtaining leave of absence from the Irish board of Customs, Chesney made his second journey to the British capital, arriving March 24, 1783   He spent the next week or more in getting his papers ready for the Treasury office. It was not, however, until May 6 that he was examined by the commissioners on Loyalist Claims   He also served as a witness for some of his fellow exiles when their claims were heard. Additional days were spent in calling on his own witnesses and in paying occasional visits to the Treasury. After spending two months in London and receiving a temporary allowance of £50 a year, he returned to Belfast.

On October 13, 1783, Chesney found it necessary to go to Dublin again to prepare a new memorial for the commissioners on Loyalist Claims. He did not overlook the opportunity afforded by this visit to apply for another appointment in the Customs. After returning to Belfast for a few days he, in company with two loyalist friends, journeyed for the third time to London, where he learned that he had been named coast officer at Bangor, a post that paid well and was not distant from county Antrim. Once more he wrote out his memorial, this time preparing copies for all the Commissioners. In addition he got his claim certified by other refugees from South Carolina, whose claims he certified in turn. He then returned to Belfast and removed his family to Bangor late in December, 1783. In the fall of the year following the commissioners put him to the further trouble of furnishing more proofs that his property had been confiscated.

On Christmas day, 1785, Mr. Chesney visited Mourne and effected an exchange with the coast officer at Annalong, which was a fishing village in county Down, where the new Customs officer was to have some exciting experiences with the nest of desperate smugglers harboring there. He brought his family from Bangor to Mourne, February 14, 1786, and in August received £133. 12s. in part settlement of his claim, the remainder of the award, namely, £255. 18s. coming to hand in November. Thus, it had cost our South Carolinian three visits to London, the repeated submission of memorials and testimonials, and much correspondence since August 3, 1782, to obtain an annual allowance of £50 and an award of less than £400 on a total claim of £1,998. 10s., which seems to have been later reduced to £1,564. 10s Either at this time or later Mr. Chesney's annual pension was cut down to £30. Needless to say the recipient of these sums was not pleased with the results of his efforts, and alleged that both his award and pension had been reduced by the commissioners on account of his employment in the Customs which, he said, they included as part compensation.

During the year 1789 the boatmen and smugglers at Annalong formed a combination to get Coast Officer Chesney removed from his place. However, he succeeded in thwarting them, clung to a position which was proving to be profitable, despite the risks of life and limb undoubtedly connected with it, and invested his compensation money in a town property. That smuggling was not declining at Annalong is indicated by the fact that Chesney reported to the lord lieutenant the arrival in Glassdrummond Bay on February 19, 1793, of five vessels engaged in the contraband trade. Accordingly, that official, in conjunction with the Irish board of Customs, sent several cruisers and two detachments of troops to protect the coast. By this time Chesney's personal affairs were prospering, and he thanked God "for health in the family and plenty of everything."

Already in 1791 the Association of United Irishmen had been formed, and in the fall of 1796 its members in county Down and several neighboring counties were secretly drilling in preparation for revolt This activity did not escape the notice of Mr. Chesney, who obtained a commission and embodied the Mourne Infantry at the end of January, 1797. His company was the first under arms in county Down, a circumstance to which he was inclined to attribute the prevention of a general insurrection in Mourne.

Despite the pressing nature of his official and military duties at this period, Captain Chesney was none the less attentive to the interests of his children. His oldest daughter, Eliza, was already thirteen and in a boarding school at Newry, and he was applying for a cadetship for his boy, Francis, who was only a few months more than nine years of age He was promised an appointment for Francis, but was informed that the boy would not be eligible until he was fourteen. Nevertheless, the ambitious father obtained a commission for this youth in the Mourne Yeomanry from Lord Castlereagh in May, 1798, attributing his success to that nobleman's ignorance of the appointee's age. At about the same time Mr. Chesney reluctantly became a justice of the peace

Late in May the Mourne companies, which had been put on permanent duty on account of the outbreak of the rebellion, were ordered to Newry. Early in the following month Captain Chesney returned to Mourne with part of the cavalry, surrounded the houses of the suspected leaders there during the night, and carried them off to Newry as hostages for the protection of the inhabitants, in case of a rising during the absence of the corps. After going with a detachment to Dundalk where, according to report, the rebels were under arms, Chesney and the Mourne Yeomanry marched back to Mourne, and half of the corps were released from permanent duty, but the order was rescinded, August 25, 1798, three days after the French had landed at Kallala Bay.

The closing pages of Alexander Chesney's *Journal*, which ends with the year 1820, is filled for the most part with items concerning his children. On March 24, 1803, his elder son, Francis, who was now fifteen, started alone on his way to London in the hope of being admitted to the Royal Military Acadamy at Woolwich. Being found deficient, he was placed successively in the Walworth and Diptford academies and the Royal Military College at Great Marlow, Bucks, a preparatory college for Woolwich. Eighteen months from the time of his first leaving home, Francis was gazetted to a second lieutenancy, to the evident satisfaction of his father who, in January, 1805, sent his younger son, Charles, to follow in his brother's footsteps, having obtained for him the promise of an East India cadetship. The expense of Charles's schooling, together with some trifling debts, proved somewhat embarrassing to his father during the year 1806; but the latter rejoiced in the thought that certain seizures he had made would "set him free." In 1807 Charles was in the Military Academy at Woolwich, and Francis was quartered with his company at Portsmouth, but was moved in the opening days of March, 1808, to the island of Guernsey. In the following June Eliza married Captain John Hopkins, and in October, 1809, Charles, now a lieutenant in the artillery, sailed for India, arriving at Madras, February 1, 1910. Jane visited with her sister, Mrs. Hopkins, who with her husband, spent part of this year in Dublin. Francis remained in Guernsey until November, 1813, when he resigned his staff position there and sought for military employment on the continent. Mr. Chesney, Sr., with the aid of Francis and several friends outside the family, tried to get an appointment in the Customs for his son Alexander, but within the limits of the *Journal* seems not to have succeeded. The birth of still another son, Thomas Crafer Chesney, is mentioned as having occurred on March 13, 1808, but no other entry appears regarding him. On February 13, 1814, Matilda died of a fever, which had attacked other members of the family. In the following September Francis, who had been on "an excurtion to France and along the ports of Holland," was assigned to a company at Woolwich. In 1815 he was promoted to a captaincy and in the next year was stationed at Leith Fort in Scotland. On November 22, 1816, Jane married the Reverend Henry Hayden, while Captain Hopkins retired from the service on a good pension. In the autumn of 1817 the fever again broke out in the Chesney family and left Mary, Anne, and Charlotte much debilitated. In February, 1918, Mr. Chesney was greatly surprised at receiving a letter from his eldest son, William, of whose survival he was not even aware, stating that he was living in the State of Tennessee, but was not in flourishing circumstances. The letter also referred to his grandfather, Robert Chesney, as being still alive

Meantime, Charles had married in the island of St. Helena and, being in poor health, had brought his wife to England and later to Ireland   Here they had taken a lodging at Rosstrever and were visited by Charlotte, Anne, and Mary, who had not yet fully recovered from their former illness.   In September, 1819, Charlotte married George Washington Bell. Three months later the Reverend Mr. Hayden lost his curacy in county Roscommon and brought his family to stay with his father-in-law until the following spring, when he was sent out as a missionary to St John, New Brunswick, by the Society for the Propagation of the Gospel in Foreign Parts.

In January, 1820, Mr Chesney was charged with neglect of duty by Customs officers at Newry, but was cleared by the surveyor-general who heard the case fully, and the matter ended with the approval of the defendant's conduct by the board of Customs.

During the previous dozen years at least smuggling had been going on at Annalong, as shown by occasional brief references in the *Journal*, and, according to Chesney, outside of Mourne where he had been able to hold it in check by the employment of a number of guards, the smuggling of tobacco into Ireland had been much stimulated by the close of the Napoleonic wars.   Naturally, Chesney's success in foiling the smugglers had aggravated them and led him into many quarrels with them.   The marked increase in the clandestine trade and the falling off in the import duties had aroused the lords of the Treasury to try their hand at the suppression of smuggling in the summer of 1820 by sending the royal naval inspector-general of the Preventive Water Guard to survey the Irish Channel with a view to establishing a preventive force. The Irish board of Customs instructed their revenue officers to co-operate in this project by supplying every assistance and information, an order which Mr Chesney appears to have complied with to the best of his ability, although he was to learn at the end of the year that the Water Guard, when established, would supplant his office.   However, he had made many seizures during the year, for which he had received a considerable amount of money, and he began at once to make arrangements for building on his farm at Ballyardle.

Not only is Chesney's record of thirty-five years in the Irish Customs highly creditable to him, as affirmed by the surveyor-general and the board of Customs in Ireland, but so also was Chesney's concern for the welfare of his children, including his son William, from whom he had been so long separated   In the closing sentences of the *Journal* Alexander Chesney notes that he has authorized

William to draw on Mr. Crafer and thinks it better that he should receive his portion of his father's estate and "turn it to account where he is," than spend money coming to Ireland "where he would find most things unsuited" to him.

The publication of this *Journal*, with it accompanying documents and its wealth of valuable notes, will add an important number to that small group of personal records by American loyalists which comprises the *Journal and Letters of Samuel Curwen;* the *Letters of James Murray, Loyalist;* Colonel David Fanning's *Narrative;* the *Correspondence of Thomas Barclay;* the *Recollections of a Georgia Loyalist; The Journal of a Voyage from Charlestown, S. C., to London, 1778;* Lieutenant Anthony Allaire's *Diary* (printed in Dr. Lyman C. Draper's *King's Mountain and Its Heroes*) ; the *Diary and Letters of Thomas Hutchinson;* Lieutenant James Moody's *Narrative of His Exertions and Sufferings in the Cause of Government since 1776; The Narrative of the Transactions, Imprisonment, and Sufferings of John Connelly, an American Loyalist and Lieutenant-Colonel in His Majesty's Service,* J. F D Smyth's *Tour in the United States of America; The Case of Ferdinand Smyth Stuart with His Memorials to the King, &c.; The Winslow Papers;* Joseph Galloway's *Letters to a Nobleman on the Conduct of the War in the Middle Colonies; The Examination of Joseph Galloway before the House of Commons;* C. Stedman's *History of the Origin, Progress, and Termination of the American War,* and Judge Thomas Jones's *History of New York during the Revolutionary War.*

It may be objected that some of the above named publications are not diaries, journals, or personal narratives; that at least one of them is a book of travels and that others are historical in nature. It would be futile in the space at command to attempt comparisons among the publications listed above. Suffice it to say that the authors of all of them were American loyalists and that even those publications which, according to their titles, are most removed from the autobiographical, will be found on closer inspection to contain not a little of the distinctly personal. All of these writings have their value for the student of American Revolutionary history and especially for the one who is interested in the Tory phase of the subject.

It is scarcely necessary to speak of the special qualifications of Mr. E. Alfred Jones for the task of editing *The Journal of Alexan-*

der Chesney, since the admirable results of his labors are manifest in this volume. The present writer can not, however, deny himself the pleasure of saying that Mr. Jones has long been familiar with the abundant materials relating to the American loyalists that are to be found in the Public Record Office, the British Museum, and other collections in London. Nor can he forbear to add that the Editor has greatly increased the value of this volume by his copious annotations, many of which contain information not easily available and some, information not accessible at all in print Mr Jones found Chesney's *Journal* in the British Museum (Additional MSS , 32627).

BIBLIOGRAPHY

COLLECTIONS OF SOURCE MATERIAL

American Archives, Series IV , Vols 3 and 4   Peter Force, ed
Audit Office Papers. (Public Record Office, London)
Historical MSS Commission, *Report on the American MSS. in the Royal Institution*, Vols I,
   II, III, IV
                        , *Report on the MSS of the Earl of Dartmouth*, Vol II
                        , *Report on the MSS of Mrs Stopford-Sackville*, Vol II
Second Report of the Bureau of Archives for the Province of Ontario, 1904, Part I   A Fraser, ed
State Records of North Carolina, Vol XIV , Journal of the House of Commons n, Vol XXVII
The Royal Commission on the Losses and Services of American Loyalists, 1783-1785   Roxburghe
   Club, 1915   H E Egerton, ed
Third Report of the Bureau of Archives for the Province of Ontario, 1905, A Fraser, ed
Treasury Papers (Public Record Office, London)

MEMOIRS, BIOGRAPHIES, AND LOCAL HISTORIES

Acadiensis, Vols I, VI, VII
Appleton, *Cyclopedia of American Biography*
A T Bethell, *The Early Settlers of the Bahama Islands*   1914.
R W. Bowers, *Sketches of Southwark, Old and New*   1905
Collections of the South Carolina Historical Society, Vol III
Col Charles Cornwallis Chesney, *Essays in Military Biography*   1874
John Cruden, *An Address to the Loyal Part of the British Empire and Friends of Monarchy
   throughout the Globe   (Report on the Management of the Estates sequestered in South
   Carolina, by Order of Lord Cornwallis in 1780-1782)* 1890   Pamphlet   Paul Leicester Ford,
   ed
J Watts DePeyster, *Local Memorials relating to the DePeyster and Watts and affiliated families.*
   1881
                        , "The Affair at King's Mountain," *Magazine of American History,*
   Vol V
Dictionary of National Biography
Lyman Draper, *King's Mountain and its Heroes.*
William Henry Drayton *Memoirs of the Am Rev as relating to South Carolina*, 1821, Vol II
H Jones Ford, *The Scotch-Irish in America*   1915
C C Jones, *History of Georgia*   1883
Gen Henry Lee, *Memoirs of the War in the Southern Department of the United States*, Vol I
S Lane-Poole, ed , *The Life of the late General F R Chesney*   1893
Lawrence and Stockton, *The Judges of New Brunswick and their Times*
E McCrady, *The History of South Carolina in the Revolution, 1775-1780*
.   , *The History of South Carolina in the Revolution, 1780-1783*
Lieutenant Roderick Mackenzie, *Strictures on Lieut, Col Tarleton's History*
William Moultrie, *Memoirs, 1802*, Vol II
E R O Callaghan, *Documents relating to the Colonial History of New York*, Vol VIII
Lorenzo Sabine, *The Loyalists of the American Revolution,* 2 vols
A S Salley, Jr , *History of Orangeburg County*, 1898
W H Siebert, "The Loyalists in West Florida and the Natchez District," *Mississippi Valley
   Historical Review*, 1916   Vol II
W B Stevens, *History of Georgia*, Vol II 1859
Colonel Banastre Tarleton, *History of the Campaigns of 1780 and 1781 in the Southern Provinces
   of North America*, 1787
Thornbury, *Old and New London*, Vols II and III
W. T Vincent, *The Records of the Woolwich District*, Vol I
Wheatley and Cunningham, *London Past and Present*, Vol. I

LETTERS, DIARIES, JOURNALS, AND NEWSPAPERS

Carleton's Correspondence (Public Record Office, London)
Chatham Papers, Bundle 220   (Public Record Office, London)
Clinton-Cornwallis Controversy. 2 vols , B F Stevens, ed
Colonel David Fanning's Narrative, A W Savary, ed , in *Canadian Magazine,* 1908
Correspondence of Charles, first Marquess Cornwallis, 1859, Vol I   C Ross, ed
Journal and Letters of Samuel Curwen, 4th ed , 1864
Journal of Rev John Wesley
Military Journal of Colonel John Graves Simcoe
Lieutenant Anthony Allaire's Diary in Draper's *King's Mountain and its Heroes*
Papers of Colonel Thomas Fletchall   (Public Record Office, London, A O 12 and 13)
Morning Chronicle and London Advertiser, April 1, 1786
Royal Gazette of South Carolina, Vol II, No 108
South Carolina and American General Gazette, June 25, 1778.

HISTORIES OF THE AMERICAN REVOLUTION

S G Fisher, *The Struggle for American Independence,* 1908, Vol II
Gordon, *American Revolution,* 1788
C Stedman, *The History of the Origin, Progress, and Termination of the American War,* 2
    vols , Dublin, 1794

MISCELLANEOUS

Col Charles Cornwallis Chesney, *Essays in Military Biography,* 1874
Alexander Garden, *Anecdotes of the American Revolution,* 1828
Alton and Holland, *The King's Customs,* 1910, Vol II
Fortescue, *History of the British Army,* Vol III
Notes and Queries, 8th Series, Vol III
Scots Magazine, Vol 43
South Carolina Historical and Genealogical Magazine, Vol 18
J Eardley Wilmot, *Historical View of the Commission for inquiring into the losses, services,
    and the claims of the American Loyalists at the close of the War in 1783, with an
    account of the compensation granted to them by Parliament in 1785 and 1788*   1815

CONTENTS

PART I

PAGE

THE JOURNAL OF ALEXANDER CHESNEY...... 1–56

PART II

ADDITIONAL NOTES·

LORD CHARLES GREVILLE MONTAGU 59
COLONEL JOHN PHILLIPS...... 60
INDIANS IN THE WAR 63
COLONEL THOMAS FLETCHALL 66
COLONEL AMBROSE MILLS... 72
LIEUTENANT-COLONEL JOSEPH ROBINSON 74
GENERAL ANDREW WILLIAMSON... 76
LIEUTENANT-COLONEL JAMES VERNON 78
COLONEL ZACHARIAS GIBBS 79
MAJOR PATRICK FERGUSON 82
COLONEL ALEXANDER INNES. 83
CAPTAIN ABRAHAM DE PEYSTER 84
THE BATTLE OF KING'S MOUNTAIN 86
BRIGADIER-GENERAL ROBERT CUNNINGHAM 87
COLONEL DANIEL PLUMMER 88
LIEUTENANT-COLONEL JOHN HARRIS CRUGER 89
THE BRITISH LEGION 90
JOHN CRUDEN 91
COLONEL ROBERT BALLINGALL 94
COLONEL ISAAC HAYNE 94
MAJOR JOHN ROBINSON 95
MAJOR MICHAEL EGAN 96
JAMES BARBER 97
PHILIP HENRY 97
JAMES SIMPSON 99
CAPTAIN JAMES MILLER..... 100
LIEUTENANT-COLONEL EVAN MCLAURIN 101
COLONEL RICHARD PEARIS 102
MAJOR PATRICK CUNNINGHAM 104
CAPTAIN MOSES KIRKLAND 105
LIEUTENANT-COLONEL JOHN FANNING 108
CAPTAIN JOHN SAUNDERS... 108
MAJOR THOMAS FRASER. 111
LIEUTENANT-GOVERNOR WILLIAM BULL 112
THE LOYAL MILITIA OF SOUTH CAROLINA 113
LOYALISTS' WARRANT 116

XV

SOUTH CAROLINA LOYALISTS IN NOVA SCOTIA AND ELSEWHERE   .   117
IMPORTANT CLAIMS AND AWARDS OF SOME SOUTH CAROLINA
    LOYALISTS   118

PART III

APPENDIXES·

  I   MINUTES OF THE EXAMINATION OF ALEXANDER CHESNEY BY THE
       COMMISSIONERS OF AMERICAN CLAIMS IN LONDON   125

  II. ALEXANDER CHESNEY'S MEMORIAL   126

  III AN ESTIMATE OF CHESNEY'S PROPERTY   .   127

  IV   EVIDENCE ON CHESNEY'S MEMORIAL .   .   .   130

  V   VARIOUS OTHER PAPERS RELATING TO CHESNEY:
       A   HIS ORDERS FOR WOOD CUTTING   .   138
       B   HIS COMMISSION AS CAPTAIN   .   .   138
       C   HIS COMMISSION AS LIEUTENANT OF INDEPENDENT
          SCOUTS   .   .   .   139
       D   TESTIMONIAL TO HIS SERVICES IN CONNECTION WITH
          SEQUESTERED ESTATES   139
       E   OTHER TESTIMONIALS TO CHESNEY'S SERVICES   140
       F   LETTER TO THE COMMISSIONERS FROM COLONEL JOHN
          PHILLIPS   140
       G   MAJOR JOHN DOYLE'S CERTIFICATE TO CHESNEY   141
       H   COLONEL ZACHARIAS GIBBS'S CERTIFICATE   .   141
       I   CHESNEY'S LETTER TO THE COMMISSIONERS   142
       J. LEWIS WOLFE'S LETTER TO THE COMMISSIONERS   .   144
       K   LORD CORNWALLIS'S LETTER TO THE COMMISSIONERS   144

  VI. RESOLUTION OF THE LOYALISTS ON PACOLET RIVER, SOUTH
       CAROLINA (1775)   .   144

  VII. PARTY DIVISIONS IN SOUTH CAROLINA FAMILIES   145

  VIII JUSTIFICATION OF TAKING THE OATH TO THE STATE BY THE
       COMMITTEE OF SOUTH CAROLINA LOYALISTS IN LONDON
       (FEBRUARY 21, 1785)   .   145

THE JOURNAL OF ALEXANDER CHESNEY

A SOUTH CAROLINA LOYALIST IN THE REVOLUTION AND AFTER

I was born in the townland of Dunclug near Ballymena in the County of Antrim Ireland the 16th or the 12th of September 1756[1] on Sunday; as appears by a register in my father's Bible.[2] My father Robert Chesney[3] or McChesney was only son to Alexander Chesney of Dunclug aforesaid, and of Jane Fulton his wife; His sisters were Ann married to William Purdy of Glenravil who was brother to my mother consequently my uncle before this marriage, they are now with their family settled in South Carolina. Second Martha Chesney married to Matthew Gillespey[4] who went to Carolina and died there shortly after their arrival about the year 1768; her husband is married again and lives near Enoree-River, South Carolina. Third Sarah Chesney who married James Archbold a pensioner and lives in County Antrim.

My grandfather Chesney had several brothers, I recollect to have seen some of their sons, who came from County Tyrone, and near the Bann-river.

My grandmother Fulton or Chesney had many Sisters and only one Brother named (I believe) George her sister Jenny was married to David Wilson of Dunclug County Antrim, Margaret was married to John Symonton near Lough-neagh; Sarah had been married to John Cook who died in Pensylvenna.[5] She removed to Pacholet-River[6] South Carolina where she died a few years ago and where her children are married and settled, Also Martha who had

[1] The date of birth is given as Sept 16 in *The Life of the late General F R Chesney*, ed by S Lane-Poole, 1893

[2] On his tombstone in the Mourne Presbyterian churchyard, Kilkeel, county Down, Alexander Chesney is stated to have died Jan 12, 1845, at the age of 88 years

[3] A contribution on the supposed origin of the name Chesney is in *Notes and Queries*, 8th Series, Vol III, pp 58, 135, 214, 296, 336, 490

[4] Query Was this the Matthew Gillespie who served in the American Revolutionary militia as a private in 1781 and 1782, and who resided in that part of South Carolina now embraced in Newberry county?

[5] The State of Pennsylvania

[6] The river Pacolet is in Spartanburg county and forms part of the boundary between Cherokee and Union counties in South Carolina, and flows into Broad river at the junction of those two counties with York county

been married to Niesbet [7] in the Waxhaws in South Carolina [8] they are both dead but they have left children who live there. My Grandmother had several other sisters.

My mother's name was Elizabeth Purdy youngest daughter of William Purdy and Martha his wife of Ballyreagh near Clough County Antrim. My father and mother were married about two years before I was born My grandmother Purdy's name was Martha Peden daughter of Thomas Peden and (I believe) of Jane Grier his wife of County Longford she was born the same year in which the conditions and capitulations of Limerick [9] were made. Lived to about to the year 1780 and died with her son William Purdy in Glenravil County Antrim

My Grandfather and Grandmother Purdy had twelve children, of which my mother was the youngest. I knew William who lived in Glenravil and went with his family to South Carolina, Robert who died in Killymorris near Clough; Jennie who married Alexander Wylie and lived in my Grandfather's farm in Ballyreagh; Jane had been married to John McCleland she died in a few years and left only one daughter Martha who since married John Barclay; Thomas and John went to Pensylvenia and live near Carlile [10] if alive. Margaret who married Pouge or Pogue lives near them I suppose the other children had died young for I do not recollect to have heard their names

My father's farm in Dunclug being too small for his family he removed to Kirkinreallough or Kirkmareally to one something larger, and having lived there about five years went to South Carolina in the Snow called the James and Mary of and from Larne; John Workman master James bold mate, Wilson second mate.

My father's family consisted of my father mother Alexander (myself) Ann, Martha, Jane, William,[11] Robert, John, and Peggy about 8 months old who died of the small pox on the passage; in all

---

[7] The Nesbitt family was prominent in the early history of Spartanburg county, South Carolina One member of the family, Wilson Nesbitt, owned and operated an iron plant there A loyalist named William Nesbitt, of South Carolina, was banished and his estate confiscated (See Sabine, *The Loyalists of the Am Rev*, II, 119) This loyalist was one of the 100 signatories to the petition that Alexander Constable of Boston, Massachusetts, might be given command of a loyalist regiment to be raised at Charleston, South Carolina He appears to have returned to South Carolina after the war

[8] Waxhaws was in the present county of Lancaster, near the boundary between North and South Carolina, and extended into Union county, North Carolina

[9] The city of Limerick capitulated to William III in 1691

[10] Carlisle, Pennsylvania

[11] William Chesney served in the Revolutionary militia, though a mere boy

eight children, my father and mother making ten, went on board & sailed from Larne the 25th. August 1772 and arrived safe in the Harbour of Charleston, South Carolina after a passage of seven weeks and three days which was I suppose about the 16 October 1772.

The small Pox having been very severe in the Vessel during the passage, when the Surgeon came on board an reported to the Governor[12] the state of the passengers we were obliged to ride Quarantine first three weeks and then a second three weeks and 8 days; making seven weeks and one day; nearly as long as we were on the passage

There is no disorder the Americans are so much afraid of as the small Pox, and with good reason as few of them have had it; We had a large house during the Quarantine allowed for the sick on Sullivan's Isle, which was kept for the purpose of an hospital; one Robinson has a salary from government for living there, We went back and forwards between the Ship and hospital which made a change, and beguiled the time a little; When the crew and passengers were recouvered we landed at Prichard's ship-yard on Town Creek,[13] a few miles above Charles-Town from whence the passengers proceeded to country as soon as they could respectively find Waggons destined for that part of the country where they meant to settle. My father and family agreed with John Miller of Turkey Creek[14] to leave his family &c at John Winns[15] old place (now Winnsborough) on Jackson's Creek with his waggon for which we paid one penny per pound Weight. When we came near Jackson's Creek[16] I went before and acquainted our relations (by marriage) Mr. John now Colonel Phillips[17] who with Mrs. Phillips his wife met them at Winn's old place, and brought them to their House. We got 100 Acres of land surveyed there, built a cabin and cleared some of the land; when my father received a letter from his Aunt Sarah Widow Cook (mentioned before as a sister to my grandmother) who resided Pacholet River about 60 miles higher up in the country, inviting them to settle there, on which I proceeded on foot in a right direction for that place, there being no direct road

[12] The governor was Lord George Greville Montagu   (See Additional Notes, p 59)

[13] Town creek divides Down island on the Cooper river from Charleston

[14] Turkey creek rises in York county, South Carolina, and flows into Chester county

[15] John Winn, founder of the town of Winnsboro in Fairfield county, South Carolina, was a colonel of South Carolina militia during the middle period of the Revolutionary war

[16] Jackson's creek was in the north of South Carolina

[17] Colonel John Phillips (See Additional Notes, p 60)

but I was to enquire for John Quin blacksmith on Sandy-River [18] about 20 miles off which was nearly the first house I called at; from thence to Ned Neils on Broad-River, but crossed the river something lower down on account of a Canoe being there, thence to Eliza Wells' on Pacholet where I crossed being then within 5 miles of my Aunt Cooke's, she had two sons Hugh, and John, and daughter Nancy who lived with her unmarried. Thomas and Sarah were both settled with their families in the neighbourhood; Sarah was married to Charles Brandon,[19] the whole family were remarkably civil to me, and the greater part of the settlers near them being their relations gave them weight, they soon found me a vacant track of 400 Acres which having got surveyed for my father I returned; and removed the family to Pacolet where we settled [20] on the north side near Grindall's shoal [21] about 12 miles from where it empties itself into Broad-River 50 miles below where the Indian line crosses that river, and 15 miles below the place where the Iron works [22] are now built, 60 miles north-east of Ninety-six;[23] and 250 miles [24] nearly north of Charles-town; to which place I went in 1774 to hurry the patent of my father's lands through the offices.

My cousins Cooke came back with me to assist in moving the family, bringing with them two horses which being put into a pasture of Col Phillips' on Jackson's Creek strayed away and were not found for 3 months after.

Our family lived at my Aunt Cooke's in the first instance whilst a Cabin was building by me and some land cleared which I did in part without any assistance; before planting time in 1773, when

---

[18] Sandy river is in Chester county, South Carolina

[19] One Charles Brandon served in the Revolutionary militia which was commanded during the last years of the war by Colonel Charles Brandon

[20] The Chesney plantation was apparently in the north of Union county, at its junction with Spartanburg and Cherokee counties The name is commemorated by the place called Chesnee in the north of Spartanburg county

[21] Grindal shoals, so-called from the family of Grindal, who lived on the north side and owned the shoal, which was a noted fishery It was on the north side of Pacolet river, at Grindal ford, that Morgan camped just before the battle of Cowpens The place is well described by John Kennedy in his novel, *Horse Shoe Robinson*

[22] These iron works were probably those on the southern side of Lawson's fork of Pacolet river, afterwards called Bivingsvil'e and known later as Glendale, which was half a mile higher up on the same bank The works were destroyed by the loyalists and never rebuilt (Draper, *King's Mountain and its Heroes*, pp 85 90, 91)

[23] The district of Ninety-Six, so named because it was 96 miles from Keewie, the chief village of the Cherokee Indians According to Lord Cornwallis, he had formed in this district, the most populous in the province of South Carolina, seven battalions of militia (C Ross, *Correspondence of Charles, first Marquess Cornwallis*, 1859, Vol. I, p 489) The present town of Ninety-Six is in Greenwood county

[24] The Chesney plantation was somewhat under 200 miles in a straight line northwest of Charleston

the family was established in the new residence and began the usual farming occupations increasing stock and clearing additional land without any particular occurrence save the birth of my brother Thomas and sister Eliza untill 1775 that resolutions were presented for signatures at the Meeting-house [25] by the congress party and I opposed them.

When the war broke out between England and America the congress party early in 1775 were sending a quantity of Ammunition and clothing as presents to the Indians;[26] On which the loyalists who had not joined them assembled and went to Ninety-Six a wooden-fort after besieging the place for some days took it,[27] and the stores; after distributing the Ammunition amongst the loyalists, both parties agreed to a Cessation of Arms for some weeks untill several of the leading men could go and return from Charles-town to receive Lord William Campbell's [28] directions on the business; Colonel Flechall [29] and Captain John Mayfield [30] were two of the delegates sent under the faith and sanction of a treaty; they were lodged in the goal of Charles-town, and the papers they had received from the Governor Lord William Campbell were seized. In the meantime the congress party sent to the neighbourhood of Ninety-Six an Army under the command of Colonel Richardson [31] who seized the leading men of the loyalists and put them in goal and disarmed the rest, all this was accomplished before the expiration of the truce.

---

[25] This was probably the occasion when the Rev William Tennent, the Congregational minister and member of the Provincial Congress, held a meeting and slaughtered a beast at a feast, about five miles east of the town of Spartanburg

[26] See Additional Notes, p 63

[27] For an account of the siege of Ninety-Six, see Colonel Thomas Fletchall in Additional Notes, p 69

[28] Lord William Campbell was appointed governor of South Carolina, June 8, 1773, and had married, April 17, 1763, a lady of that Province in the person of Sarah, daughter of Ralph Izard of Burton, St George's parish He did not, however, commence his duties until 1775 As a former officer of the Royal Navy, he served as a volunteer on board H M S *Bristol* in the attack on Charleston, June 28, 1776 He died, September 5, 1778, from the effects of a wound received in a naval engagement

[29] For Colonel Thomas Fletchell see Additional Notes, p 66

[30] Captain John Mayfield and other officers of Colonel Thomas Fletchell's loyal militia were brought as prisoners early in December, 1775, to the camp of Colonel Richard Richardson near Lieut -Colonel Evan McLaurin's store in Dutch Fork Among these officers were Benjamin Wofford, William Hunt, Daniel Stagner, and Jacob Stack (Drayton, *Memoirs of the American Revolution as relating to South Carolina*, 1821, Vol II, pp 125-126)

[31] Colonel Richard Richardson, the elder, of the South Carolina militia, who was promoted to brigadier-general in 1778 and died in September, 1780 His son, Colonel Richard Richardson, the younger, was subsequently a colonel of the South Carolina militia in Camden district

I went down to Jackson's Creek when Colonel Richardson's encampment was at Congaree [32] and piloted Cap⁺ James Phillips [33] and his company[34] to my father's and provided them a man (Charles Brandon) [35] as a guide to take them to Col¹. Mills' [36] in North Carolina who found guides through the Cherokee and Creek nations of Indians, on their way to St. Agustine in East Florida [37] where they were kindly received by the Governor [38] and continued there during the greatest part of the war, having been embodied in the South Carolina Regiment,[39] commanded by Major now Col¹ Joseph Robinson [40] a neighbour of mine, which Regiment distinguished itself throughout the war particularly at the seige of Savanah where by their meritorious exertions they saved the garrison. I piloted all the loyalists who came in my way and amongst Cap⁺ⁿ Buchanan supposed to be of the Royal Navy who endeavoured to keep up the spirits of the loyalists amongst whom a regular correspondence was kept up [1776] For which I was made a prisoner, my house ransacked, and Kept a prisoner [41] in the Snowy Camp on Reedy River [42] for about a week, Col¹ Richardson released me, but the congress party held me at enmity and forced me either to be tryed at Richardson's camp or to join the Rebel Army [43] which latter alternative I chose in order to save my father's family from threat-

[32] Congaree is about 16 miles southeast of Columbia Congaree river forms part of the boundary between Richland and Calhoun counties, South Carolina.

[33] Captain James Phillips, a brother of Colonel John Phillips

[34] Captain James Miller was of this party (see Additional Notes, p 100)

[35] See p 4

[36] Colonel Ambrose Mills (see Additional Notes, p 72)

[37] St. Augustine

[38] Patrick Tonyn, the able governor of East Florida He is remembered for his efforts to make that Province an asylum for the loyalist refugees from Georgia and the Carolinas and for his championship of the military abilities of the well-known loyalist, Lieut-Colonel Thomas Brown, the brave defender of Augusta, Georgia, in May and June, 1781 against the unjust attacks and criticisms of Brigadier-General Augustine Prevost Many of the letters and documents concerned with the controversy between Tonyn and Prevost are summarized in the *Report* of the Historical Manuscripts Commission on the American MSS in the Royal Institution

[39] The formation of the South Carolina Royalists, which is the correct title of this regiment, dates from July 20, 1778 Alexander Innes formerly secretary to Lord William Campbell, the governor, was appointed colonel and Joseph Robinson lieut-colonel It was to consist of eight companies of 50 rank and file, with one colonel, one lieutenant-colonel and other officers, whose names were submitted by Robinson A list of these names is in the Royal Institution (Hist MSS Comm, *Report on the American MSS in the Royal Institution*, Vol I, p 274)

[40] Lieutenant-Colonel Joseph Robinson (see Additional Notes, p 74)

[41] Alexander Chesney was made a prisoner early in 1776 by "a party of rebels under Col Steen," who was probably James Stein, an American officer who served with distinction in various actions under Sumter (*The Royal Commission on the Losses and Services of American Loyalists, 1783-1785*, ed by H E Egerton, Roxburghe Club, 1915, p 49)

[42] Reedy river is just west of Greenville in Greenville county, South Carolina

[43] Alexander Chesney rose to the rank of lieutenant in the "rebel army " (See p 8, n 56)

ened ruin, he had been made prisoner already for harbouring some loyalists;[44] and served from April 1776 untill June 1777 as a private during which time I was at Charlestown and Bolton's landing place opposite Long-Island whilst the British army was encamped there under Sir Henry Clinton, going on a reconnoitring party one day towards the British lines on Long-Island a gun with grape shot was fired, one shot of which was within a few inches of killing me having struck the sand close by where I had squatted down to avoid the discharge; I endeavoured with some others [45] to get to Genl. Clinton's Army but failed for want of a boat [46] and returned to the Americans

We then marched against the Indians,[47] to which I had no objection, helped to destroy 32 of their towns under General Williamson [48] with Col^l Sumpter.[49] We had a severe battle with the Indians near the middle settlements; in the course of the engagement five or six of them concealed behind a log fired at me as I ascended the hill before the others, and one of their balls struck a saplin of about six inches diameter opposite my breast; fortunately the young tree broke the force of the ball and saved my life

We were at this time on short allowance and my small portion having been put in the bag with the ammunition I threw it away to get at the powder &c and was nearly starved in consequence.

On returning towards Charles-town we were encamped at Tachaw near Nielson's ferry [50] on the Santee; from thence marched to Puriesburg [51] on the Savannah-river; then by water to Savannah-town which time we killed a number of Alligators with rifle guns;

---

[44] A few extracts from this Journal, with various interpolations and free renderings, and with several errors in the names of persons, have been published in *Essays in Military Biography*, by Colonel Charles Cornwallis Chesney, 1874, pp 135-153

[45] The others were Charles and Chr Brandon (see p 131)

[46] In evidence before the commissioners in London, Chesney said that the little party, having been discovered on the river, were obliged to return

[47] A map of the marches of General Andrew Williamson's force against the Cherokee Indians is in Drayton's *Memoirs*, Vol II, p 343 The Cherokees had 52 towns in Wesley's time (*Journal of Rev John Wesley*)

[48] General Andrew Williamson (see Additional Notes, p 76)

[49] Colonel Thomas Sumter, American partisan leader, (see Appleton, *Cyclopedia of American Biography*)

[50] Nelson's ferry on the Santee river was owned by one Reason Nelson, a loyalist and native of South Carolina, who died in August, 1781, leaving a widow, Ann, three sons, William, Ambrose, and Joshua, and two married daughters, Sarah, wife of John Martin Struden, and Frances The two elder sons died before 15 December, 1787, Joshua joined the New York Volunteers as a boy on 25 April, 1781, afterwards transferred as a driver to the Royal Artillery, and at the end of the war embarked with the 105th regiment for Ireland (A O 12/51, fos 409-414 A O 12/102, fo 110 , A O 13/133)

[51] Purysburg, Georgia, a place visited by the Rev John Wesley

then marched to Sunbury; thence to Fort Barrington [52] on the Altamaha near East Florida where we arrived the 25th March [1777] (trees then beginning to bud).

A total eclipse of the sun [53] happened when we were at Ogreechy-River [54] on our march to Sunbury.[55]

While at Fort Barrington we had several scrimishes with the Creek Indians, in which I was always a volunteer.

The Altamaha rose gradually (like the Nile) whilst we remained there.

Returned to Tacaw latter end of May and home in June 1777; when I purchased a tract of land on Pacholet River from Peter Howard where I remained some time. At a muster soon after I was chosen Lieutenant in Cap^tn Bullock's [56] company of Militia by my loyal friends. Went with a party to Bailis' fort [57] on the Indian line at the head of Pacholet River about 50 miles from home, and repaired the fort continued some months there—And was relieved the May following 1778 by the white inhabitants making peace with the Indians at Duet's corner.[58]

This winter I began to trade to Charles-Town with a waggon at which I had success and realized a good deal, the profits being with care 300 per cent.

In the summer I went out again after the Indians to Georgia in Cap^n McWhorter's [59] company of Volunteers as first lieutenant, the whole under command of Genl. Williamson; We were out as far

---

[52] Fort Barrington, on the Altamaha river in Georgia, was erected in the colonial period as a defence against the Indians   Early in March, 1778, it was the scene of the exploit of Lieut.-Colonel Thomas Brown of the King's Florida Rangers, when a detachment of that loyalist corps with a few Indians stormed the fort and took 23 Americans prisoners   Captain Andrew Johnston claimed the honor of being the first officer to enter it   (Hist MSS Comm., *Report on the American MSS in the Royal Inst.*, Vol I. pp 209, 221)   Captain Johnson afterwards lost his life at Augusta, in the siege of May and June, 1781, by Lieut.-Colonel Henry Lee   His father, Dr Andrew Johnston, of Georgia, was taken prisoner in this siege

[53] An annular eclipse of the sun on January 9, 1777, was visible in South Carolina, as was the total eclipse on June 24, 1778

[54] Ogeechee river in Georgia

[55] Sunbury in Georgia

[56] Captain Zachariah Bullock was not, as might be assumed from Chesney's statement, a loyalist, but an officer in the American militia of the district of Ninety-Six   (See p 9 footnote 62)

[57] Baylis Earle's ford on the North Pacolet river in North Carolina, so-called from Baylis Earle, father-in-law of Captain Edward Hampton a noted partisan leader on the American side   An action was fought at this spot on July 15, 1780   (See Additional Notes—Colonel Ambrose Mills—p 72)

[58] The Cherokee Indians signed a treaty of peace, May 20, 1778, at Duet's Corner, a place now known as Due West, in the north of Abbeville county, South Carolina

[59] This may be Captain Alexander McWhorter, deputy-commissary of Issues in the American militia of South Carolina.   Several men of this name were in the American service

as the Altamaha, during this excurtion I suffered greatly from an attack of the Flux, in about three months the whole party returned. Col. Phillips [60] was there also.

In the summer of 1779 I was at Augusta [61] under General Williamson again, who marched to join General Lincoln, I was down at Stono for some weeks, and returned home on business [62] before the attack was made on the British lines at Stono, by General Lincoln.[63] I continued to go frequently to Charles-town with the waggon laden with produce and returned with goods. One waggon and team were impressed last summer to Augusta & left there when we marched to join Lincoln the Waggon and Horses value 2000 currency were lost.

On the 3rd January 1780 I married Margret Hodge eldest daughter of Willm Hodge [64] and Elizabeth his wife who was a daughter of Widow Cook a sister to my grandmother Chesney my

---

[60] Colonel John Phillips, the loyalist (See Additional Notes, p 60)

[61] Augusta, Georgia, where a fort was built in 1787 *(Journal of Rev John Wesley)*

[62] This business would seem to have been the raising of a new division for the American service by Alexander Chesney

'State of S° Carolina) Whereas Alexander Chesney Lieutenant in Capt Zachariah Ninety Six District ʃ Bullocks company came before me and made Oath that on the 2d day of June last being Order'd home from the Camps at Stono, in Order to raise a new Division having his Waggon and Team then in the Service, and on the 3d of June he came by the Quarter House See his Team, which he was obliged to leave under the direction of his Brother, which Team being lost before his return with the Division, and have made diligent search has never found but one of the s Team which consisted of four Horses, and the remaining three he has never yet heard off, and he likewise says that about the middle of the Day his Brother informs him he went and see the Horses and that they were all there together, and in two or three hours after they were missing and could not be found, and that his brother is of opinion they were stole, and he also say that the Horse he got, he found with M Wetherford, who told him that he took the Horse from a Man who said he found him in an old field near the quarter House

Sworn before me this 6th September 1779 Wm Wofford J P " (From the Revolutionary Account Audited, Alexander Chesney, Office of the Historical Commission of South Carolina)

It may be said of William Wofford that he was lieut colonel of militia in 1779 and that he also served in the House of Representatives

The wagon and team mentioned in the above affidavit were appraised, August 4, 1779, by Robert McWhorter, William Hodge, who was Alexander Chesney's father-in-law, and Meshak Inman A claim was filed by Alexandere Chesney after the war, but there is no record of its payment. The Quarter House here mentioned was several miles out of Charleston, to the northward

[63] General Benjamin Lincoln's abortive attack on the British at Stono, June 20, 1779 (E McCrady, *The History of South Carolina in the Revolution, 1775-1780,* pp 382-391)

[64] William Hodge, father-in-law of Alexander Chesney, and his son, William Hodge, served in Colonel Thomas Brandon's regiment of South Carolina militia after the fall of Charleston This regiment was stationed in the county of Spartanburg William Hodge, the elder, and Alexander Chesney were joint debtors on a bond of £235 15s, dated 25 December, 1780, to one Edward Williams, a schoolmaster, of Ninety-Six district The original bond with signatures is with the papers of Colonel James Vernon, the loyalist, to whom all the assets of Williams were bequeathed (Public Record Office A O 13/123)

wife of Margret was born 30th 1759 [65] as appears by an entry in her Bible a part of which was torn by accident.

It was firmly believed in the beginning of the year that Charlestown would be reduced by the British, which happened accordingly on the 12th May following,[66] and Sir Henry Clinton having issued a proclamation commanding all His Majesty's faithful subjects to embody for the defence of his government, a number of loyalists assembled at Sugar Creek [67] and the waters of Fair Forest [68] under the command of Col¹ Balfour,[69] I took protection the 25th of June 1780 [70] from Isaac Grey [71] Captain South Carolina Reg[t]. And about the middle of June embodied with the Militia as Lieu[t]. I commanded in an affair at Bullock's' Creek [72] where the rebel Party was defeated in attempting to cross the ford, My father was present on this occasion and hearing the bullets whistle without seeing by whom they were fired, asked me where are they? I placed him near a tree until the affair was over, and resolved he should not be so exposed again

I then joined Col¹ Balfour and was in an affair at James Wood's house [73] above the Iron-works on Pacolet but not finding the opposition there that we expected, returned again to fair forest; Col¹ Balfour then returned to Ninety-Six, and Major Ferguson [74] succeeded to the command under the title of Col¹ and Inspector General of Militia. Shortly afterwards he marched to Thickety Creek [75] encamped, and requested me to carry an express to Cap[tn] Pat[k]

[65] The name of the month is not mentioned in Chesney's Journal

[66] Charleston capitulated to the British, May 12, 1780

[67] Sugar creek in Ninety-Six district The number of loyalists was 200   (See p 131)

[68] Probably Fair Forest creek in Spartanburg and Union counties, South Carolina, in a district so named by the first settlers, who exclaimed "What a fair forest is this!"   (Draper, *King's Mountain and its Heroes*, p 76)   Fair Forest has been made famous by the pen of William Gilmour Simms, the Carolina novelist

[69] Colonel Nisbet Balfour, of the 23rd Foot (Royal Welsh Fusiliers) was commandant at Charleston, and was succeeded in July, 1782, by Lieut -Colonel Isaac Allen, of the New Jersey Volunteers   His military secretary at this period was Captain Geroge Benson, of the 44th Foot, who married in 1781 a daughter of Dr Alexander Garden, of Charleston, an eminent surgeon and botanist and a loyalist   Colonel Balfour is in the *Dictionary of National Biography.*

[70] A certificate of allegiance to the British, dated June 27, 1780, and signed by Colonel Nisbet Balfour, is with the papers of John Hopton, loyalist, of Charleston, in the Public Record Office in London   (A O 13/129)

[71] Captain Isaac Grey's name cannot be found in the various published or unpublished lists of loyalist officers

[72] Bullocks creek is in York county, South Carolina

[73] This house has not been identified

[74] Major Patrick Ferguson   (See Additional Notes, p 82)

[75] Thicketty creek is a western tributary of Broad river, with which it unites a few miles above the junction with Pacolet river

Moore [76] then commandant at Anderson's fort [77] with a particular
private message to him to hold the fort till the last minute and before I could return the army had decamped about midnight and retreated towards Cap[tn] Lewis Boboes [78] on Tyger-River, where I
joined them, and we got an account that Col McDole [79] had without
opposition reduced Anderson's fort and made them prisoners, Moore
having shamefully surrendered it thus disappointing Ferguson's
scheme of bringing the Americans to battle whilst attacking it.
Major Gibbs [80] came to me in this situation of affairs, showed me a
paper containing instructions to go McDole's camp at the Cherokee
ford [81] on Broad-River and learn there numbers, their commanders
name what carriages they had how many horse and foot, and whenever they made any movement towards Col[l] Ferguson to return and
let him know, and that there would be a handsome reward. I told
Col[l] Gibbs that what services I could do were not with any lucra-
tive view and that I would undertake this difficult task for the good
of H M Service since he could not procure a qualified person to un-
detake it, I set out immediately and at Pacolet got a man to go with

[76] Captain Patrick Moore was of Irish descent and was born in Virginia Early in life
he settled on Thicketty creek, South Carolina. His force consisted of a sergeant of the American Volunteers and 93 loyalists and was surprised, 30 July, 1780, by a body of American militia,
600 strong, under Colonels Isaac Shelby, Elijah Clarke, and Andrew Hampton, and Major Charles
Robertson To the peremptory demand for the surrender of the fort, Moore replied that he
would defend it to the last extremity But when he saw the formidable force in front of him,
he relented and surrendered without firing a shot In surrendering Captain Moore was charged
by the officer second in command with cowardice and treachery Colonel Charles McDowell was
not present in person on this occasion, as Chesney states, Shelby s force having been detached
from the main force of McDowell at Cherokee Ford, about 20 miles distant Patrick Moore is
believed to have been captured by a party of Americans in 1781 near Ninety-Six and murdered,
as his remains were afterwards recognised by his great height, 6 feet 7 inches He left a
widow, a son and three daughters His brother, a noted loyalist partisan, was Colonel John
Moore (Draper, *King's Mountain and its Heroes*, pp 87-89, Anthony Allaire's "Diary," printed
in Draper's volume, E McCrady, *Hist of South Carolina in the Rev*, 1775-1780, pp 634-635)
[77] Anderson's fort, or Thicketty fort as it was more generally called, was originally built
as a defence against the Cherokee Indians and was a quarter of a mile north of Goucher Creek
and two and one-half miles above the mouth of this small water course, which empties into
Thicketty creek
[78] Captain Lewis Bobo was an officer in the militia on the Revolutionary side His residence was in the present county of Spartanburg Tiger river runs from Spartanburg county
and joins Broad river in the south-east of Union county, South Carolina
[79] Colonel Charles McDowell, the son of Joseph McDowell, an emigrant from Ulster in
1780 His brother, Major Joseph McDowell, led the militia from Burke and Rutherford counties,
North Carolina, at the battle of King s Mountain, where another brother, William, also fought
Major Joseph McDowell was in command of a force of mountainmen at the battle of Cowpens,
17 January, 1781, and in 1788 was a member of the North Carolina Constitutional Convention,
in 1792 he was elected a member of Congress (H Jones Ford, *The Scotch-Irish in America*,
1915, pp 509-510)
[80] Colonel Zacharias Gibbs, the loyalist   (See Additional Notes p 79)
[81] Cherokee ford is on Broad river in Cherokee county, near the junction of the present
counties of Union, York, and Spartanburg

me, who was acquainted with the North Carolina people; we went
to McDole's camp at night without being noticed counted all their
tents and waggons   found out who were their leaders, and that 500
horsemen were gone down to attack Nochols' fort,[82] with this news
I returned, and on my way found a loyalist in whom I could confide
and sent him off with the particulars by one route to Col¹ Ferguson
whilst I went by another and the Col¹ got intelligence time enough
to intercept them at the Iron-Works and defeat them,[83] in returning
I was taken at Grindall Shoal by a party of Rebels under Eusaw
Smith[84] and Desmond who took from me a Rifle gun borrowed of
John Heron   my brother in law, but as soon as they set out for the
rebel camp I made my escape joined Col¹ Ferguson at Culbered[85] and
received his thanks and friendship; on the 9th August I was appointed Cap[te] and assistant Adjutant General to the different Batalions under Col¹ Ferguson; and same day we attacked the enemy
at the Iron works and defeated them with little trouble to ourselves and a good deal of loss to the Americans in whose hands I
found some of our men prisoners whom I released.[86]

Our next rout [August 12] was down towards the Fishdam-
ford on Broad-River,[87] where there was a fight near the mouth of
Brown's Creek with Neale's Militia when we made many prisoners
amongst the rest Esaw Smith,[88] who had taken me so recently;
after this we crossed that River and formed a junction with the
troops under the command of Col¹ Turnbull[89] and the Militia under

---

[82] This fort is described as Nicholas's fort later (p 131)   Nicholas fort was on the Tiger
river, seven miles west of the present town of Spartanburg in South Carolina

[83] The old or Wofford's Iron Works situated on Lawson's fork of Pacolet river   At these
iron works a severe action was fought, August 8, 1780, between a force under Colonel Elijah
Clarke and Isaac Shelby and Major James Dunlaps detachment of loyalists, when Major Ferguson came up to the rescue of the loyalists and saved them from defeat   This action, which is
also known is the second battle of Cedar Springs, was claimed as a victory by both sides   Colonel
McDowell was not present in person   (Draper, King's Mountain and its Heroes pp 89-102,
E McCrady, The History of South Carolina in the Revolution, 1775-1780, pp 636-640)

[84] Captain Esaw Smith was in 1779 a member of Captain David Hopkins company of
the 3rd   South Carolina regiment of the Continental Line   In 1780 and 1781 he served in the
militia of the State

[85] Cullered, probably the plantation of Josiah Culbertson, a well known American partisan   According to Allaire's "Diary," it was at this plantation that Major Patrick Ferguson was
encamped, August 10, 1780

[86] This engagement apparently at the old or Wofford's Iron Works is not recorded in any
of the published histories of the war

[87] An action was fought at Fishdam ford on Broad river, below the present town of
Carlisle, near the junction of Fairfield, Union, and Chester counties, November 9, 1780, the
Americans being victorious

[88] Captain Esaw Smith   (See footnote 84 above)

[89] Lieutenant-Colonel George Turnbull (c 1734-1810), a Scotsman who had been lieutenant in 1756 and captain in 1765 in the Royal Americans regiment (now the 60th or King's
Royal Rifles) and had settled in New York   Early in 1777 he was appointed to the Loyal

Col. Phillips [90] and having received authentic accounts that Sumpter [91] had cut off our retreat to Lord Cornwallis' Army at Camden, we had it in contemplation to cross Broad-River and retreat to Charles-town at this time the halfway men (as those not hearty in the cause were called) left us, we then marched to the Rebel Col Winns' [92] and encamped there waiting for more authentic accounts. On the 16th we heard a heavy firing towards Camden, which kept us in the utmost anxiety untill the 18th when a letter was received from Captⁿ Ross [93] aid de camp to Lord Cornwallis informing us that his Lordship had attacked & defeated Gates' Army had killed or taken 2,200 men 18 Ammunition Waggons and 350 waggons with provisions and other stores. [94] This news made us as happy as people in our situation could possibly be, until the next night when we received an express that the rebels had defeated Col¹ Ennis [95] at Enoree; [96] this occasioned a rapid march that way The main

American regiment and was transferred, 7 October in the same year as lieut.-commandant of the New York Volunteers This corps distinguished itself at Fort Montgomery, 16 October, 1777, under the command of Major Alexander Grant, who was killed, in the gallant defence of Savannah in September 1779, at the capture of Charleston in May, 1780, at Rocky Mount, when Sumpter was defeated, in the battle of Camden, 16 August, 1780, at Hobkirk's Hill, 25 April, 1781, when Rawdon defeated Greene, and at Eutaw Springs, 8 September, 1781 Turnbull was not, however, present at the two last engagements, having been granted leave to proceed to New York, on account of ill health He married a daughter of Cornelius Clopper of New York and died at Bloomingdale, New Jersey, in October, 1810 (Carleton's Correspondence in the Public Record Office, Folio 41 B F Stevens, *Clinton-Cornwallis Controversy,* Index)

[90] Colonel John Phillips (See Additional Notes, p 60)

[91] Colonel Thomas Sumter (1734-1832) is in Appleton s *Cyclopedia of American Biography*

[92] Colonel John Winn (See p 3, footnote 15) Lieutenant Anthony Allaire was encamped at his plantation from August 17 to 19, 1780, while Colonel Winn was a prisoner on James Island

[93] Captain, afterwards General, Alexander Ross (1742-1827), the intimate friend and aide-de-camp of Lord Cornwallis It was Major Ross who, with Colonel Thomas Dundas, conveyed to Washington the determination of Lord Cornwallis to capitulate

[94] The defeat of Horatio Gates, former officer of the British Army, at Camden, 18 August 1780, was received with great enthusiasm McCrady quoting Bancroft, says that the American casualties are not known accurately Anthony Allaire, the loyalist, estimated the number of killed at 1200 and the prisoners at 1000 Tarleton's figures are 70 officers and 2000 men as the total American casualties Gates put the killed wounded, and missing at only 700 and the total loss of the British at 500 Lord Cornwallis gave the American loss as between 800 and 900 killed and 1000 prisoners (Tarleton, *History,* pp 104-9 131-5, Allaire's "Diary" E McCrady, *The Hist of South Carolina in the Revolution, 1775-1780,* pp 666-680, S G Fisher, *The Struggle for American Independence,* 1908, Vol II, 296-9 with a list of authorities Lord Cornwallis's report in the Stofford-Sackville MSS, Hist MSS Comm, *Report,* Vol II, 1910, pp 178-182)

[95] Colonel Alexander Innes (See Additional Notes p 83)

[96] The battle of Musgrove's Mills, the residence of the loyalist, Edward Musgrove, on the Enoree river, on 19 August, 1780, when the Americans were victorious The Americans, to the number of 500, were commanded by Colonels James Williams, Shelby, and Clarke, while the loyalists consisted of a company of New Jersey Volunteers a detachment of De Lancey's brigade and about 100 men of the South Carolina Royalists, under Major Thomas Fraser (Mackenzie, *Strictures on Lieutenant-Colonel Tarleton's History,* 1787, pp 24-6, Draper, *King's Mountain and its Heroes,* p 110, E McCrady, *The Hist of South Carolina in the Revolution, 1775-1780,* pp 690-4)

body having crossed the Enoree, I was left behind in command of the rearguard and being attacked in that situation [August 20] we maintained our ground untill the Main body re-crossed to our support; the Americans retreated [August 21] after suffering some loss [97]

We encamped for some time in the neighbourhood of Enoree, and then marched up to Fair-forest. Some particular business having called Col¹ Ferguson to Camden Captⁿ Depeyster who succeeded him to the command [September, 1780,] marched us up the Iron-Works and I obtained leave to see my home and family whither I went for about two hours and sent orders for those who had shamefully abandoned us some time ago to join us at the Iron-Works in order to do three months' duty in or on the borders of North Carolina, and returned to the camp that night, we continued some time at the Iron works and whilst there a party of Loyalists with whom I was, defeated Col¹ Brannan [98] destroyed some of his party and scattered the rest. I was present also at a small affair at Fair-Forest, the particulars of which, as well as numerous other skirmishes having escaped my memory, scarcely a day passed without some fighting.

Col¹ Ferguson having resumed the command and finding himself [99] pretty strong he marched us to the North Carolina line and encamped.

A dissatisfaction prevailed at this moment amongst the Militia founded on general Clinton's hand-bill which required every man having but three children, and every single man to do six months duty out of their province when required, this appeared like compulsion, instead of acting voluntarily as they conceived they were doing, and they were in consequence ready to give up the

---

[97] Alexander Chesney was unaware of Tarleton s surprise and defeat of Sumter at Fishing creek on August 18, 1780, when Sumter, asleep under a wagon, barely escaped with his life and in the confusion rode off without saddle, hat, or coat, reaching Major Davie's camp at Charlotte two days later, unattended by officer, soldier or servant (E McCrady, *The History of South Carolina in the Revolution, 1775-1780*, pp 690-694)

[98] Colonel Thomas Brandon (1741-1802), an American of Irish descent, of Union county, South Carolina, who shared in the action at Musgrove's Mills and was present at the battles of King's Mountain, Blackstocks Hill, and Cowpens (Draper, *King's Mountain and its Heroes*, p 469) He was a relentless foe of the loyalists

[99] Major Patrick Ferguson, described as colonel by Alexander Chesney in this *Journal*, marched on September 12 with 40 American volunteers and 100 militia to the head of Cane creek in Burke county, North Carolina to surprise a party of 300 of the enemy McDowell in command of this party, having received intelligence of the presence of Ferguson s force, deemed it prudent to remove, but was intercepted and routed (Allaire, "Diary")

cause;[100] but owing to the exertions of their officers a great part of which I attribute to myself, the tumult was happily appeased, and same night we marched with all the horse and some foot past Gibbert's town [101] towards Col Grimes' [102] who was raising a body of rebels to oppose us, whom we succeeded in dispersing taking many prisoners, and then joined the foot at Gilbert's town and encamped there for some time; sending away the old men to their houses, and several officers to raise men to supply their places and strengthen us. Col Ferguson soon after got intelligence that Col McDole [103] was encamped on Cain and Silver Creeks;[104] on which we marched towards the enemy, crossed the winding Creek 23 times, found the rebel party strongly posted towards the head of it near the mountains we attacked them instantly and after a determined resistance defeated them and made many prisoners, the rest fled towards Turkey-Cove [105] in order to cross the mountains and get to Holstein;[106] on this occasion I commanded a division, [September, 1780,] and took the person prisoner who was keeper of the records of the county which I sent to my father's as a place of safety. We then fortified Col¹ Walker's house [107] as a protection to the wounded, and

---

[100] Sir Henry Clinton s handbill stipulated service in the local militia by the married men with families and not elsewhere Young men without children were expected to serve six months out of the year, but were not required to march beyond North Carolina on one side or Georgia on the other (E McCrady, *History of South Carolina in the Revolution, 1775-1780,* p. 550)

[101] Gilbert Town is near the present town of Rutherfordton in North Carolina

[102] Colonel Grimes, in command of some American troops in the district of Catawba river in September, 1780 *(State Records of North Carolina,* Vol XIV, p 778) One Richard Grimes was appointed a commissioner, 7 July, 1781, to provide horses, by purchase or impressment, for General Greene's cavalry (Journal of the House of Commons in the *State Records of North Carolina,* Vol. XXVII, p 939)

[103] Colonel Charles McDowell

[104] Cane and Silver creeks are in Burke county, North Carolina Cane creek is so amazingly crooked that Captain Abraham de Peyster and Lieut. Anthony Allaire, with their loyalist force, were obliged to cross it nineteen times in a march of four miles (Allaire, "Diary") An indecisive action was fought on these creeks, 12 September, 1780, between Ferguson and McDowell (Draper, *King's Mountain and its Heroes,* pp 147-9, 199) According to a loyalist version of this action 80 prisoners were taken, one man killed, Captain White wounded, and all the American ammunition captured, the British loss being one man killed and two wounded (Allaire, "Diary")

[105] Turkey Cove is on the Catawba river, about six miles above the town of Marion, North Carolina

[106] The Holstein river district, at that time a portion of North Carolina, but now in east Tennessee

[107] Colonel Jacob Walker, whose house and plantation were in the fork of Cane creek and Second Broad river in Rutherford county, North Carolina Lieut Anthony Allaire was present on this occasion, on 13 September, at Colonel Walker's house, where he met Captain Ryerson, of the New Jersey Volunteers, and Lieut Duncan Fletcher, of the Loyal American regiment Allaire also alludes in his "Diary" on the 14th to the large number of "deluded inhabitants" who were coming in to proclaim their loyalty Two miles distant from the Walker plantation is Little Britain Church, where several loyalist soldiers are buried

proceeded in pursuit of the rebels to the Mountains [108] at the head of Cataba-River sending out detachments to scour the country and search the Caves; A fight happened in the neighbourhood between a detachment of ours and the Americans who were posted on a broken-hill not accessible to Cavalry, which obliged us to dismount and leave our horses behind, whilst employed in dislodging the Americans another party of them got round in the rear and took the horses mine amongst the rest; but it was returned by the person who was my prisoner in the last affair; about a week before he had been released as was usual at this time with prisoners   At this period the North Carolina men joined us fast.   Our spies returned from beyond the mountains [October] with intelligence that the rebels were embodying rapidly; other spies brought us word that Col¹ Clark had taken Fort Augusta [109] with its stores &c on which we marched towards white oak and Green River [110] to intercept him on his return from Georgia, Col Ferguson detached the horse in three divisions, one under my command with orders to proceed along the Indian line untill I could make out Clarke's route & join Captⁿ Taylor [111] at Bailis Earls fort, [112]   I proceeded as far as Tyger-river [113] and there learning that Clark was gone up the bushy fork of Seluda-river, [114] I took six of the best mounted men and got on his track untill I overtook the main body and one of the enemy prisoner within view of it, whom I carried to Col¹ Ferguson [October 4, 1780,] who thus obtained the information required

Our spies from Holsteen as well as some left at the Gap of the Mountains [115] brought us word that the Rebel force amounted

---

[108] The Blue Ridge Mountains in North Carolina

[109] Colonel Elijah Clarke had laid siege to Augusta from 14 to 16 September, but was foiled of success by the timely arrival of Colonel John Harris Cruger, of De Lancey's brigade, famous for his defence of the fort of Ninety-Six against Greene in May and June, 1781   Ferguson tarried long in North Carolina in the hope of intercepting Clarke, and left Gilbert Town for this purpose, 27 September, 1780   (Draper, *King's Mountain and its Heroes*, pp 199-200)

[110] White Oak is a creek tributary of Green river in Polk and Rutherford counties, North Carolina

[111] Captain John Taylor, of Shrewsbury, New Jersey, son of Thomas Taylor, was born 15 May, 1742, and was appointed lieutenant, 2 July, 1776, and captain, 26 August, 1780, in the New Jersey Volunteers   In July, 1776, he accompanied the British forces south and was in command of a small corps of cavalry until the battle of King's Mountain, where he distinguished himself   Captain Taylor married, 6 August, 1786, Eleanor Taylor, of Middletown, New Jersey, the marriage taking place there   He died, 13 November, 1822, leaving a widow, an unmarried daughter, and a son, Morris Taylor   (Public Record Office   W O 42/T3 , A O 12/14, fos 73-81 , A O 12/101, fo 258 , A O 12/85 , A O 12/109 , A O 13/109 , A O 13/109   A O 13/112 , Ind 5606)

[112] Baylis Earle's ford (see page 8, n 57)

[113] Tiger river (see page 11, n 78)

[114] Saluda river in South Carolina

[115] Gap of the mountains, probably in the Blue Ridge Mountains

to 3000 men, on which we retreated along the North side of Broad-river and sent the waggons along the South-side as far as Cherokee-ford,[116] where they joined us   we marched to King's Mountain and there encamped with a view of approaching Lord Cornwallis' Army and receiving support; by Col¹ Ferguson's orders I sent expresses to the Militia Officers to join us here; but we were attacked before any support arrived by 1500 picked men from Gilbert's-town [117] under the command of Col¹ˢ Cleveland,[118] Selby[119] and Campbell[120] all of whom were armed with Rifles, well mounted and of course could move with the utmost celerity; so rapid was their attack that I was in the act of dismounting to report that all was quiet and the pickets on the alert when we heard their firing about half a mile off; I immediately paraded the men and posted the officers, during this short interval I received a wound which however did not prevent my doing duty; and on going towards my horse I found he had been killed by the first discharge [October 9, 1780].

Kings Mountain from its height would have enabled us to oppose a superior force with advantage, had it not been covered with wood which sheltered the Americans and enabled them to fight in the favorite manner; in fact after driving in our piquets they were able to advance in three divisions under separate leaders to the crest of the hill in perfect safety untill they took post and opened an irregular but destructive fire [121] from behind trees and other cover: Col Cleaveland's was first perceived and repulsed by a charge made by Col¹ Ferguson: Col Selly's next and met a similar fate being driven down the hill, last the detachment under Col Campbell and by desire of Col¹ Ferguson I presented a new front which opposed it with success; by this time the Americans who had been repulsed had regained their former stations and sheltered be-

---

[116] Cherokee ford (see page 11, n 81)

[117] Gilbert Town (see page 15, note 101)

[118] Colonel Benjamin Cleveland   (See page 19, n 129)

[119] Colonel Isaac Shelby, a noted border leader and one of the commanders at the battle of King's Mountain, where he was conspicuous for valor   (Draper, *King's Mountain and its Heroes*, pp 411-416)

[120] General William Campbell (1745-81), of Scotch-Irish origin, who was ruthless in his methods with the loyalists, several of whom he condemned to death, e g, Captain Nathan Read, who elected to suffer death rather than submit to the demand that he should join the American forces   Draper gives other instances of his violence to the loyalists   At the battle of King s Mountain he was in supreme command, Shelby having magnanimously given way in his favor   Shelby and Sevier believed him to have shrunk from danger in this memorable victory of the Americans, but Washington, Gates, and Greene expressed their high sense of his merits (Draper, *King's Mountain and its Heroes*, pp 378-402)

[121] The expression. "an irregular but destructive fire," was apparently borrowed from Stedman's *American War*, Vol II, p 246

hind trees poured in an irregular destructive fire; in this manner
the engagement was mantained near an hour, the mountaniers
flying whenever there was danger of being charged by the Bayonet,[122] and returning again so soon as the British detachment had
faced about to repl another of their parties. Col Ferguson was at
last recognized by his gallantry although wearing a hunting shirt
and fell pierced by seven balls   at the moment he had killed the
American Col¹ Williams [123] with his left hand; (the right being use-
less [124]) I had just rallied the troops a second time by Ferguson's
orders when Capᵗ De Peyster [125] succeeded to the command but
soon after gave up and sent out a flag of truce, but as the Americans
resumed their fire afterwards ours was also renewed under the
supposition that they would give no quarter; and a dreadful havoc
took place until the flag was sent out a second time, then the work
of destruction ceased; the Americans surrounded us with double
lines, and we grounded arms with the loss of one third our numbers.[126] [October 9]

I had been wounded by the first fire but was so much occupied
that I scarcely felt it until the action was over. We passed the night
on the spot where we surrendered amidst the dead and groans of
the dying who had not surgical aid, or water to quench their thirst;
Early next morning [October 10] we marched at a rapid pace towards Gilbert's town between double lines of mounted Americans;
the officers in the rear and obliged to carry two muskets each which
was my fate although wounded and stripped of my shoes and silver
buckles in an inclement season without covering or provisions untill
Monday night [October 12] when an ear of Indian corn was served
to each; at Gilbert's town a mock tryal was held and 24 sentenced
to death 10 of whom suffered before the approach of Tarlton's
force [127] obliged them to move towards the Yadkin [128] cutting and

---

[122] The expression, "The mountaineers flying whenever they were in danger of being charged with the bayonet," is apparently borrowed from Stedman's *American War*, Vol II, p 246

[123] Colonel James Williams   (see page 20 n 139)

[124] Major Patrick Ferguson s right arm had been shattered at the battle of the Brandy-wine

[125] Captain Abraham De Peyster   (See Additional Notes p 84)

[126] The battle of King's Mountain   (See Additional Notes, p 86)

[127] Colonel Banistre Tarleton, who commanded the British Legion in South Carolina and was the author of a history of the campaigns of 1780 and 1781 in the Southern Colonies, wherein his military merits are much exaggerated   This history brought forth a book as a rejoinder, entitled, *Strictures on Lieutenant-Colonel Tarleton's History*, published in 1787 by Lieutenant Roderick Mackenzie   In this book the author accuses Tarleton of neglecting to mention the bravery of many South Carolina loyalists, "men, whose integrity was incorruptible, undismayed

striking us by the road in a savage manner Col¹ Cleveland [129] then offered to enlarge me on condition that I would teach his Regiment for one month the exercise practised by Col¹ Ferguson [130] which I refused, although he swore I should suffer death for it at the Moravian town; luckily his threat was not put to the test as I had the good fortune to make my escape one evening when close to that place; in the hurry to get off I took the wrong road and did not discover my error until I found I was close to the Moravian town:[131] I then retraced my steps until close to the pickets I had left and taking a fresh departure I crossed the Yadkin river before morning, proceeded through the woods toward home, John Weedyman one of my company had supplied me with a pair of shoes, which were of great use on this occasion, but as he remained a prisoner I never had an opportunity of making him a return

The first night I slept in the woods, next day I was supported by haws grapes &c as I could find them in the woods: The second or third day in pushing through the woods to get to a ford I heard a noise of some people (whom I knew to be Americans by white paper in their hats) on which I lay down and was so close to them that I could have touched one of their horses in passing; fortunately I was not observed, and soon after crossed the Creek after them. I then made for the Mountains in order to be guided by the Apalachian range [132] and get over the rivers with greater facility. After crossing Broad-river I met one Heron who had been with me in King's Mountain and who had with some others taken flight

in the hour of danger, who sacrificed their private interest to public good and who fought and bled with manly spirit and evinced a probity of mind under every reverse of fortune, which must endear them to posterity" (p 29)

[128] The Yadkin river rises in the Blue Ridge Mountains in North Carolina

[129] Colonel Benjamin Cleveland commanded the troops from the Upper Yadkin valley at the battle of King's Mountain In the annals of the war in South Carolina no officer on the American side treated his political enemies with greater severity The loyalists were regarded by him as so much game, or dangerous pests, worthy only of extermination At rare moments he was capable of generous instincts He it was who caused the execution of Zachariah Wells, on the plea that he was a dangerous Tory, as well as bringing about the executions of the loyalists after King's Mountain (Draper, *King's Mountain and its Heroes*, pp 425-454 S G Fisher, *The Struggle for American Independence*, 1908, pp 416-419) Colonel Cleveland s brutal treatment of Dr Uzal Johnson, of Newark, New Jersey, who rendered services to the wounded on both sides in this battle, was severely criticized (Allaire, "Diary", J Watts de Peyster, "The Affair at King's Mountain" in *Magazine of American History*, Vol 5, pp 402-423)

[130] The younger men were thoroughly drilled in military tactics by Major Ferguson (Draper, *King's Mountain and its Heroes*, p 73)

[131] Alexander Chesney says elsewhere that he was marched about 150 miles to Moravina Town (*The Royal Commission on Loyalists Claims, 1783-1785*, ed by H E Egerton Roxburghe Club, 1915, p 50) This town was probably the present Winston-Salem in North Carolina, a distance of about 100 miles in a direct line from King's Mountain

[132] The Appalachian Mountains, the general name for the great mountain system in the east of North America, called the Blue Ridge Mountains in North Carolina

early in the action, putting white papers in their hats,[133] by which disgraceful stratagem they got through the American lines: I passed a night at Heron's house and one before at another man's on whom I could depend, from both I took some provisions all the other nights I slept out; I do not remember the number exactly, but must have been nearly a fortnight [134] I reached home on the 31st October I found the Americans had left me little My wife had a son on the 20th whom I named William which was all the christening he had.

As I did not know where to find any British troops I continued about home some time [November, 1780,] and as the Americans were in possession of the country I was obliged to conceal myself in a cave dug in the branch of a creek under a hollow poplar with my cousins Hugh Cook [135] and Charles Brandon;[136] in which we were forced for want of room [137] to lie flat. Cooke's wife brought us food and news every night; I sometimes staid at my father-in-laws, untill I heard that Col¹ Tarlton had defeated Sumpter at Black-stocks fort [138] on Tyger-river on which I raised a company with great difficulty and joined a strong party at Col Williams' house on Little-river [139] where there was a strong party under General Cunningham.[140] Major Plumber [141] having been wounded at King' Mountain the command of our Regiment devolved on Jonathan Frost [142] as Major who directed me to assemble my company of Militia and join him at an appointed place on the Enoree. When I came to that place on the day and time appointed I found

---

[133] General Francis Marion distinguished his men from the Tories by placing white cockades on them, 12 August, 1780 (E McCrady, *The Hist of South Carolina in the Revolution, 1775-1780,* p 652) A similar method of identification may have been employed at King's Mountain

[134] The distance traversed by Alexander Chesney to his home on the Pacolet river would be about 120 miles in a straight line

[135] Hugh Cook (see p 4)

[136] Charles Brandon (see p 14, n 98)

[137] Room in the Journal obviously room

[138] The American and British accounts of the action at Blackstocks Hill on 20 November, 1780, differ Tarleton in his book (*Hist of the Campaigns of 1780 and 1781* pp 178 204) claims it as a victory, while MacKenzie *(Strictures on Lieutenant-Colonel Tarleton's History)* disagrees with this view, as does another British authority, Stedman (*American War,* Vol II pp 228-236) Compare Gordon, *American Revolution* 1788 edition, Vol III, p 471 Lee *Memoirs,* Vol. I, pp 213-220 Draper, *King's Mountain and its Heroes,* pp 376-377 , B F Stevens, *Clinton-Cornwallis Controversy.* Vol I pp 303 307, 315 E McCrady, *The History of South Carolina in the Revolution, 1775-1780,* pp 827-830 , and S G Fisher, *The Struggle for American Independence,* 1908 Vol II, p 370)

[139] Colonel James Williams was mortally wounded at King's Mountain

[140] Brigadier-General Robert Cunningham (see Additional Notes, p 87)

[141] Major Daniel Plummer (see Additional Notes p 88)

[142] Major Jonathan Frost was killed at the head of a party of loyal militia in an action against the Americans in December, 1780 He left a widow, Mary (Public Record Office T 50/2)

the Americans under Cap^tn then Major Roebuck [143] in possession of
it who immediately disarmed an marched us off, It was a great
blunder in Major Frost to alter the place of meeting: however he
did his best to remedy it; he pursued and overtook us about 12
miles higher up and having attacked Roebuck's party where they
were advantageously posted at a house   poor Frost was killed the
rest retreated.   Roebuck who was acquainted with me formerly.
paroled me to Ninety-six where I was exchanged for Captain
Clerk [144] a son to Col' Clerk who had been taken after the attack on
Augusta in Georgia.   I was then sent to garrison the goal of Ninety-
Six [December, 1780,] which I fortified and had the command of
the Militia stationed there.   Col^ls Allen [145] and Cruger [146] commanded the fort near the goal; where I continued until Tarleton came
into Ninety-Six district to go in quest of General Morgan [January,
1781,] and sent to the garrison for guides acquainted with Morgan's
situation which was then convenient to my house on Pacholet, [147]
I joined Col Tarleton and marched to Fair-forest having failed to
get intelligence of Morgan's situation   he sent me out [January
16,] to endeavour to do so and to make the mills grind for the Army:
when I reached Pacholet-river I swam my horse over a private ford
not likely to be guarded, leaving the man behind me to go on more
quietly & reconnoitre the samp   I found the fires burning but no
one there, on which I rode to my father's who said Morgan was
gone to the Old-fields about an hour before; my wife said the same
and that they had used or destroyed my crop & took away almost
every thing.   I immediately returned to Col Tarleton and found he
had marched towards the Old fields.   I overtook them before 10

---

[143] Benjamin Roebuck rose from the rank of lieutenant to that of lieutenant-colonel in the
American service during the Revolutionary war   He served in the actions at Hanging Rock,
Musgrove's Mills, and at King's Mountain, where he commanded a company   He distinguished
himself at the battle of Cowpens   (Draper, *King's Mountain and its Heroes,* p 470)

[144] Captain John Clarke, son of Colonel Elijah Clarke

[145] Lieut.-Colonel Isaac Allen, (1741-1806) lawyer, of Trenton, New Jersey, who commanded a battalion of the New Jersey Volunteers and served in the campaign in the South with
singular good conduct, gallantry and reputation   In the siege of Ninety-Six he was in command of a body of about 200 New Jersey Volunteers, and in 1782 he was lieutenant-colonel commandant at Charleston   At the peace he removed to New Brunswick in Canada, with his wife
Sarah, daughter of Thomas Campbell of Philadelphia, and was appointed a member of the
Council and a puisne judge of the Supreme Court   His only son, John, was prominent in the
history of that Province, as was also his grandson, Sir John Campbell Allen, chief justice
(*Second Report of the Bureau of Archives for the Province of Ontario,* 1904, Vol. I, pp 248-
251 , Lawrence and Stockton, *The Judges of New Brunswick and Their Times,* pp 3, 59, 77,
141, 507 , Public Record Office   Ind 5604-5605-5606 , Sabine, *Loyalists of the American Revolution,* Vol I, p 159)

[146] Lieut.-Colonel John Harris Cruger (see Additional Notes, p 89)

[147] General Daniel Morgan had camped at Grindal ford, on Pacolet river, just before the
battle of Cowpens   (See page 128, footnote 2)

oclock near the Cow-pens on Thickety Creek where we suffered a total defeat by some dreadful bad management.[148] The Americans were posted behind a rivulet with Rifle-men as a front line and Cavarly in the rear so as to make a third line, Col Tarleton charged at the head of his Regiment of Cavalry called the British Legion [149] which was filled up from the prisoners taken at the battle of Camden; the Cavalry supported by a detachment of the 71st Regt under Major McArthur [150] broke the Riflemen without difficulty, but the prisoners on seeing their own Regt opposed to them in the rear would not proceed against it and broke: the remainder charged but were repulsed this gave time to the front line to rally and form in the rear of their Cavalry which immediately charged and broke the 71st (then unsupported) making many prisoners: the rout was almost total I was with Tarleton in the charge who behaved bravely but imprudently the consequence was his force disperced in all directions the guns and many prisoners fell into the hands of the Americans

The men being dispersed I desired them to meet me at General Cunningham's,[151] I proceeded towards home to bring off my wife and child on the 17 Janry [,1781,] and found there was nothing left not even a blanket to keep off the inclement weather; or a change of garments; then leaving a pleasant situation in a lamentable state without a shilling in my pocket; proceeded for General Cunningham's, sleeping encamped that night at Fair-forest;[152] As we could not preval on General Cunningham to use any exertions to embody his brigade of Militia we went to Edisto river [153] in order to settle there having nothing but two horses and our clothes left, everthing else being in the hands of the Americans and by them confiscated.[154]

I have not been at Pacholet since nor am I likely to be.

I continued at Robt McWhorter's [155] on Edisto for some days and leaving my wife and child there proceeded to Charles-town

---

[148] The battle of Cowpens, January 17, 1781, when the British under Tarleton were defeated

[149] British Legion   (See Additional Notes p 90)

[150] Major Archibald McArthur had been transferred from the 54th Foot as major of the 71st Foot, 16 November, 1777 He was promoted to lieut -colonel of the 3rd battalion of the 60th Foot, 24 April, 1781

[151] Brigadier-General Robert Cunningham (see Additional Notes, p 87)

[152] Fair Forest (see p 10, n 68)

[153] Edisto river ? North or South fork of Edisto river, or Edisto river

[154] The name of Alexander Chesney is not found in any published lists of confiscated property

[155] Robert McWhorter was one of the appraisers of Alexander Chesney's wagon and horses (See p 9, n 62)

where contrary to my expectations I met with several of the British officers who had been taken at King's Mountain;[156] and who very readily assisted me to get pay for some cattle and provisions I had furnished Col Ferguson with for the use of his detachment, and not satisfied with this they introduced me to Col Balfour commandant of Charles-town who hearing from them of my great activity and that I had lost my all gave me an order to Mr Cruden commissioner of sequestered estates [157] to have me accomadated with my family on some one of them; this produced an order to Coll Ballingal [158] and Mr Kinsay [159] at Jacksons-borough [160] who ordered me a house and provisions with the use of three negroes to attend my family   thus was I at once introduced to a new set of loyalists and I immediately removed my wife and child and Charles Brandon [161] with his family to Fergusons Riverside plantation [162] near Parker's-ferry [163] on Pond-Pond-river [March] where I soon fixed myself very comfortably having purchased in Charles-town some bedding &c to set up house-keeping a second time.

I joined the negroes allowed me for my family with others on the Plantation and began to make a crop of Indian corn and rice.

The Rebels increased much in the neighbourhood of Pond-pond and a general rising being expected I sent express to Col Balfour the commandant of Charles-town to acquaint him of it who detached 100 men to bring off the Militia from Pond-Pond· by his desire I sent to communicate confidential intelligence to Capto McKinnon [164] at Motte's house [165] near Nelson's ferry [166] on the Santee River which journey of 120 miles I performed in 24 hours: I then returned to Charles-town, [May] and at the wish of Col

---

[156] All the officers and men at King's Mountain, except Major Patrick Ferguson, were loyalists

[157] John Cruden (see Additional Notes, p 91)

[158] Colonel Robert Ballingall (see Additional Notes, p 94)

[159] The name of Kinsey cannot be traced

[160] Jacksonsborough, now Jacksonsboro, is in Colleton county

[161] Charles Brandon (see p 14, n 98)

[162] This plantation in St Paul's parish, in Charleston district, was that of Thomas Ferguson, a wealthy planter, who was a member of the South Carolina Provincial Congress and of the Council of Safety

[163] Parker's ferry is on the Ponpon river, a tributary of the Edisto river, and is in the south-east of Colleton county, a few miles north of Jacksonsboro

[164] Captain John McKinnon, deputy quartermaster-general at Charleston at this time, and who was one of the directors of the lottery raised for the benefit of the poor loyalist refugees at Charleston in February, 1782   (Royal Gazette of South Carolina, Vol II, No 108)

[165] Motte's house was the summer residence in Calhoun county of a well known planter, Jacob Motte, who was a strong adherent of the American cause   At this place was Fort Motte, well known in the history of the Revolutionary war   Lee in his Memoirs gives a charming picture of Rebecca Motte the widow of Jacob

[166] Nelson's ferry (see p 7, n 50).

Balfour raised a troop of horse and was stationed at Dorchester [167] a strong British-post and moved my wife and child thither   We had not been at this place long before I ascertained that Major Snipes,[168] Col[ls] Haynes [169] and Marrion [170] had returned, crossed Pond-Pond river and were embodying troops [June, 1781,] which intelligence I communicated to Lord Rawdon [171] and His Lordship immediately ordered out a detachment of which I was one   we crossed Pond-Pond river at Parker's ferry,[172] and the boats having been removed to impede our march I swam my horse over accompanied by others and procured feather-beds to transport those who could not swim across the River; we then proceeded rapidly and reached Snipe's plantation [173] by day-light, which we soon cleared of him and his party driving them out with loss: on this occasion I was wounded in the thigh with a spear by a man concealed in a Ha-Ha [174] whilst in the act of leaping my horse over it; but I made him prisoner and took him with the others made on this occasion to Dorchester. About this time a detachment was sent and succeeded in taking Col[l] Hynes,[175] who soon after deservedly suffered for Treason; as it was discovered that he had communicated with the rebels whilst a British commissary.   There were daily skirmishes at this period, the Americans constantly contracting our posts in every direction.

In the beginning of July I joined the Army under Lord Rawdon then marching towards Ninety-Six to relieve the place;[176] on our approach the Americans who were besieging it broke up, crossed Broad-river, and proceeded along the left bank towards Charles-town· Lord Rawdon finding that the country must be abandoned, detached his light troops towards Long-canes [177] (a branch of Savanna River to bring away the Loyalists and their families; taking himself with the main body the route of Charles-

---

[167] Dorchester is in the county of that name in South Carolina

[168] William Clay Snipes was captain of the Horse Shoe company of the Colleton county regiment of South Carolina in 1775 and was afterwards promoted major of that regiment

[169] Colonel Isaac Hayne (see Additional Notes, p 94)

[170] General Francis Marion

[171] Lord Rawdon was born in 1754 and was a peer in the Irish peerage   In 1783 he was created an English peer under the style of Baron Rawdon of Rawdon, and in 1793 succeeded his father as 2nd earl of Moira (see Dict of Nat. Biog)

[172] Parker's ferry (see p 23, n 163)

[173] William Clay Snipes (see note 168 above)

[174] Ha ha is a sunk fence (Oxford English Dictionary)

[175] Colonel Isaac Hayne (see Additional Notes, p 94)

[176] Lord Rawdon went to the relief of Colonel Cruger's force in Ninety-Six in June, not in July (see pp 16, n 109, 90)

[177] Long Cane creek is in Abbeville county, South Carolina, where it joins Little river, a tributary of the Savannah river

town as far as Congaree;[178] where the Americans had recrossed the river & made a fruitless effort to oppose his march by preventing our crossing the creek which we did without difficulty and proceeded to Orangeburgh;[179] where we expected to meet reinforcements from Charles-town and be joined by the light troops and Loyalists, but were disappointed in both and soon after surrounded by the Americans who pressed us so closely that we had nothing but 1 lb of wheat in the straw served out to each man every 24 hours. The parties going out daily to forage had constant skirmishes with the enemy and one day Major Doyle [180] sent out with what mounted men he could muster (about 20 or 30) to cover the foraging; which he did effectually driving off the Americans with some loss: on this occasion Lord Edward Fitzgerald [181] having broken his sword on the back of an American I supplied him with another to continue the attack for which he felt greatly obliged.

A day or two afterwards Major Doyle [182] came to me with a message from Lord Rawdon to know if I could find any one well acquainted with the road to Charlestown and willing to go thither with a message of great importance; as all the expresses sent hitherto had either been killed of taken prisoners: being perfectly acquainted with the whole of the neighbouring country I immediately went and offered my services to his Lordship; which were readily accepted; I was offered any horse in the camp I might think better than my own, but I thought myself the best mounted officer there, and found before many minutes use for every muscle of the

[178] The Congaree river in South Carolina

[179] Orangeburg, in the county of that name, in South Carolina

[180] John Doyle (1856-1834) served throughout the American war of Independence   In 1778 he was attached as captain to the Volunteers of Ireland, raised in America in that year and later as major of that corps, which afterwards became the 105th Foot, reduced in 1784   He appears to have been in command of South Carolina militia early in 1782   In 1805 he was created a baronet, and died a general

[181] Lord Edward Fitzgerald, soldier, politician, and conspirator (1763-1798), was at this time, at the age of 18, lieutenant in the Volunteers of Ireland, to which he had been appointed in 1778   As commanding officer of the 54th Foot, in 1791 he signed the discharge of the celebrated politician, William Cobbett, who had served in the army from 1784 to 1791, and who went to Philadelphia in 1792 and was fined for his attack on American institutions   In 1796 he joined the United Irishmen and was discovered as a participator in organizing the Irish rebellion   On this occasion he was an enemy of Alexander Chesney, who fought on the opposite side in this rebellion   (See *Dictionary of National Biography*)

[182] This officer was probably Captain William Brereton, who was in command of a detachment of the 17th Foot (Grenadier company) at Charleston   In his order book, preserved in the officers' mess of the 1st battalion of this regiment, he mentions under date of 20 January, 1782, that a sergeant and four privates of the British Legion had been found guilty of quitting their posts in search of plunder and of plundering the house of an American and ill-treating his family   Such conduct met with no mercy at Captain Brereton's hands, he sentenced the sergeant and one private to death, and the other privates were punished with the lash   (E A H. Webb, *The Leicestershire Regiment*, 1912, p 82)

good animal that carried me   I set out instantly for Charles-town
and was scarcely past the sentries when I found myself pursued
by 4 or 5 of the enemy two of whom kept it up about 20 miles
through the woods; my intention was to come into the Charles-
town road where it crosses the Cypress-swamp at Cunningham's
house 2 miles above Dorchester, but by cance I kept too much to
the right and crossed the swamp by another path a little lower
down, and soon after I saw a picket of the enemy on the Charles-
town side of the swamp; who must inevitably have taken or killed
me, had I not by good fortune missed the common path, which they
were carefully guarding   I passed through Dorchester, and remained with my wife whilst a fresh horse was saddled, and I could
give Cap[t] Brereton a message from Lord Rawdon for Col Coates [183]
at Monk's Corner [184] of the 19th Reg[t] desiring him to be on the alert
as the Americans had crossed Broad and Santee Rivers in great
force; this was forwarded by express to the Col[l] and I set out for
Charles-town wher I delivered my letter to Col Balfour (the commandant at 4 oclock P M twelve hours after I received it from
Lord Rawdon at Orangeburgh; a distance of 80 miles.   The Col[l]
was walking under D[r] Frazier's [185] piazza; the detachment was
instantly turned out and marched immediately to relieve Lord
Moria [186] from his uncomfortable situation.   On reaching Dorchester I found to my grief that the Americans had visited that
place during my short absence and taken away my horse with 300
others out of Major Wright's [187] pasture.   So soon as we joined
Lord Rawdon he found himself strong enough to force his way

---

[183] James Coates was appointed brevet lieutenant-colonel of the 19th Foot, 26 October, 1775, and was promoted colonel of that regiment, 16 May, 1782   He reached the rank of general, 19 April, 1802

[184] Moncks Corner is the county seat of Berkeley county South Carolina

[185] Dr Frazier was probably Dr James Fraser of Beaufort in South Carolina, where he had settled in 1765 as a medical practitioner   In 1773-74 he was a captain-lieutenant in the Granville county militia, but in 1775 his resignation was demanded because of his suspected Toryism   By his marriage to Mary Ash he formed an alliance with a prominent family in South Carolina Dr Fraser's loyalty took a practical form early in February, 1779, when he joined the British forces on board H M S Vigilant (Captain R Christian) on duty off the coasts of South Carolina and Georgia In March 1780, he was appointed commissary of captures at Charleston and held other military appointments during the war   Dr Fraser's estate was confiscated and sold and in the list of "unjust charges" against it was that of Governor John Rutledge At the end of the war he went over to England, and in 1788 he was living with his large family at East Greenwich   (Public Record Office A O 12/51, fos 174-182, A O 12/72, fo 381, A O 12/109, A O 13/83, A O 13/96, Hist MSS Comm, Report on the American MSS in the Royal Institution, Vol II, p 100) See page   for his certificate to Alexander Chesney

[186] Lord Rawdon did not succeed his father as 2nd earl of Moira until 20 June, 1793

[187] This officer was perhaps Major James Wright (who was born in America in 1748) of the Georgia Loyalists and the King's Florida Rangers until the latter was absorbed in the King's Carolina Rangers He died in 1816   (Ind 5605-5606)

through the enemy which he did immediately, marching towards Charles-town, and encamped without opposition near Monk's corner: where we had some trifling skirmishes without any event of importance.

The Americans by degrees got possession of all the country except the small part inside the quarter House where I was posted.

Lord Rawdon having moved his force to some other part of the country, I then joined a corps of three companies raised for the defence of the sequestered estates by John Cruden Esq.[188] In one of our excurtions up Cooper's River [189] to procure a supply of rice, the schooner in which I was upset and 12 men were drowned the greater part belonging to my company; being on deck I saved myself by swimming and 6 or 7 others had the same good fortune The Schooner turned keel up, and not being quite filled with water immediately, the men could exist for a little time; we heard them crying for assistance and did all we could to afford it but unfortunately only one man could be got out in time to save his life and this was effected by cutting a hole in the vessels bottom. I lost my watch, sword and several other things.

Soon after this the troops were obliged to abandon the neighbourhood of the quarter house and confine themselves entirely to Charles-town neck [190] [December, 1781]; and a quantity of wood being required for fuel I was appointed to superintend the operation in which a vast number of people must be required and having full power to employ any persons; I chose a number of loyalists whom I found within the lines in a destitute condition; and this gave them immediate relief; preventing numbers by that means from starving They were continued whilst I had the charge which was a great satisfaction to my feelings, but ill health coming with the affliction I gave up the charge to Cap[tn] McMahon [191] early in January [1782], soon after the death of my wife who died 28th Nov[r] 1781 and is buried near Gillen's Gen's landing not far from Stuart's house on James Island.

---

[188] John Cruden (see Additional Notes, p 91)

[189] Cooper river emptes itself at Charleston

[190] When the year 1781 began, the British were in possession of almost the entire State of South Carolina At the end of the year, British rule was practically confined to Charleston and its immediate vicinity

[191] Captain McMahon was Captain John McMahon (son of John McMahon, comptroller of the Customs at Limerick), who was an officer in the Volunteers of Ireland and barrackmaster at Charleston in 1781 He became an intimate friend of George IV when prince of Wales and was keeper of the prince's privy purse In 1817 he was created a baronet

My illness continued without much hope of recovery: I was induced to send the child to my relations, in order to return to Europe. I took my passage in a transport called the Lady Susan John Cumming master and sailed from Charles-town the 5.th April under convoy of the Orestes sloop of war commanded by Sir Jacob Wheate.[192] The fleet consisted of 52 sail and we had a pleasant passage. My companions were Major Robinson [193] late of the Camden Militia Major Michal Egan,[194] and Lieut James Barber [195] of the Royal Militia. We made Mizen head on the Coast of Ireland the 19th of May [1782] and put into Castlehaven next day in a hard gale of wind when we landed and proceeded to Cork by land: I got my baggage landed, bought a horse and proceeded to Dublin accompanied by Charles Philip Campbell [196] and Soloman Smyth [197] both from Charlestown; & their society not only beguiled a long and tedious journey but was the means of forming a lasting friendship with M[r] Campbell; we took lodgings together on reaching Dublin, the 4th of June in Peter's row. I had brought a letter of introduction from Cap[tn] McMahon to his father [198] and by his advice I drew up a memorial to the Lord Lieu[t].[199] stating my services and requesting some situation; but the then Lord-Lieu[t]. being of the party which was unfavourable to the Americans I was refused   M[r] Campbell introduced me to Philip Henry [200] also a loyalist who had obtained a good situation in the Custom-House and by him I was advised to turn my thoughts to obtain something of that kind, as well as to establish a claim for compensation in lieu of property lost or confiscated; but being anxious to see my few remaining

---

[192] Sir Jacob Wheate, 5th baronet, commander in the Royal Navy, who married in December, 1782, Maria, daughter of David Shaw of New York After his death in 1788, his widow married Admiral the Hon Sir Alexander F I Cochrane (G E C, *Complete Baronetage*)

[193] Major John Robinson (see Additional Notes, p 95)

[194] Major Michael Egan (see Additional Notes, p 96)

[195] James Barber (see Additional Notes, p 97)

[196] The name of Charles Philip Campbell cannot be found in any list of loyalist claims for compensation

[197] Solomon Smyth was a prosperous upholsterer at Charleston and the owner of a plantation of 300 acres fifty miles from that city Banished from South Carolina because of his loyalty, he went first to Bermuda, thence to the West Indies, and to Georgia According to certificates of Lord Cornwallis and Sir Henry Clinton, Smyth served with the British Army and "rendered essential services" during the war From 1783 he was granted a pension of £50 a year until his death early in 1824 in England or Ireland His son, born about 1766, was an apothecary and appears to have gone to the West Indies (Public Record Office A O 12/99, fo 176, T 50/8 T 50/27)

[198] Captain McMahon's father, (see p 27 or 191)

[199] The lord lieutenant of Ireland was the 3rd duke of Portland, who was appointed, 14 April, 1782, and was succeeded by Earl Temple in September following The duke was prime minister in 1783 and again in 1803

[200] Philip Henry (see Additional Notes, p 97)

relations in the Co Antrim, I went thither before I had matured my plans for the future.[201]

My health having improved a good deal since I left Charlestown I found myself able to proceed to Ballymena [202] after a short stay in Dublin: I found my aunt and uncle Purdy in good health, she was my father's sister her name Anne, and perceiving that I was much cast down in consequence of my great losses and bad prospects she told me to take courage and that all might be well adding that the family once had been very rich and were entitled to an estate situated in one of the Northen Counties of England. I paid but little attention to he story at the moment and did not make even an entry at the time: but as well as I can remember she stated in substance that the above estate belonged to a person called Richie or Ritchie who raised a company on it and came over to Ireland in the command and died leaving an infant daughter whose name was said to be Anne, & she married my paternal great-grandfather Robert Chesney of Grange near Toom-ferry who appears to have neglected establishing his right probably in consequence of the troubles then existing both in England and Ireland: but his eldest son John (my grand uncle) went to Dublin to make searches and found most satisfactory records respecting the claim but pursued it no farther nor has anyone taken up the business since until this moment when it is probable from the lapse of time that the holders of the lands in question coult not be disturbed after being so long in peacable possession, by the real heirs   By way of making up for my neglect in not committing to writing what my aunt said, I have collected in a book all the particulars which came in my way from time to time likely to throw any light on the subject; but I have never been able to hear what records it is likely my grand uncle searched in Dublin: nor did he follow the advice he then received of proceeding to England on the business.

The family must have been of Norman extraction originally; and probably came to England with the Conqueror; the derivation of the name 'Cheney formerly de Chesnoye from the Fr: G. Chesnoye, a place where the oaks grow, this from Chesne an oak; which Menag again draws from the Latin Quercius, skin · from Quernicus oaken, made of oak'. I presume the stock was derived from Ralph de Caineto (id est Cheney) who came into England with the Con-

---

[201] For notes on the life of Alexander Chesney in Ireland, see *The Life of the late General F R Chesney*, ed by S Lane-Poole, 1893, pp 20-54

[202] Ballymena, a town in county Antrim It was the scene of an obstinate battle between the yeomanry and the United Irishmen of the district, in the rebellion of 1798

queror and had large possessions given him by that King, whose
decendants were very numerous and high in rank having peerages,
Bishopricks &c; the succeeding branches extended to the north
of England and Scotland from whence my greatgrandfather is said
to have removed to this country during the religious troubles; at
least such is the belief of one of the branches of the family now
residing in County Tyrone.

After a short stay with my relations and friends in Co Antrim
I proceeded to Dublin to go to London and try what could be done
with the Ministry, to which step I was urged by friends Henry
and Campbell:[203] on the 28th [July, 1782,] sailed from George's
quay for Liverpool in the Prince of Orange packet; next day we
saw Holly-head [204] and on the 30 landed in Liverpool, this was my
first visit to England, and I was gratified the day of the 31st in
viewing the town the docks and a 64 gunship lying there. In the
afternoon I set out by the stage for London and arrived at the
Bull and Mouth inn [205] on the 2nd [August] and proceeded to the
golding cross, Charing Cross [206] in a hackney coach

On the 3rd [August, 1782] I went to the War-office, and to
Mr Townsend's secretary of state office for the American department, where I left my papers and the following memorial

To the Right Honourable the Lords Commissioners of His
Majesty' Treasury.

The humble petition of Alexander Chesney, late of Charles-
town in the province of South Carolina,

Humbly Sheweth,

' That your Petitioner for several years prior to the present American war, resided on Broad-river in Ninety-six district in
South Carolina aforesaid· that at the commencement of the Rebellion in that province your petitioner took an active part in
favour of the British government, and rendered the loyal subjects
in that country, as well as His Majesty's army essential services.

That soon after the reduction of Charles-town by Sir
Henry Clinton your petitioner was appointed Captain of a company

---

[203] Philip Henry and Charles Philip Campbell (see p 28)

[204] Holyhead, North Wales

[205] The Bull and Mouth inn, situated in St Martin's Le Grand was a celebrated London
office for coaches to all parts of England and to Scotland   An illustration of this picturesque
inn, as it stood about 1520 is in Thornbury's *Old and New London* Vol II, p 217   See also
Wheatley and Cunningham, *London Past and Present,* 1891, Vol I, p 300

[206] The Golden Cross inn Charing Cross was a famous inn and coach office, and is illustrated in Thornbury's *Old and New London* Vol III, p 127   See also Wheatley and Cunningham, *London Past and Present,* Vol I, p 300

of Militia, and Adjutant of the different batalions of militia, under the late Major Ferguson of the 71st Regt; in which capacity he served until the defeat of that officer on King's Mountain, where your petitioner was wounded and taken prisoner. That your petitioner after he obtained his liberty again acted in his military capacity, until the out posts were drove into the garrison of Charlestown.

That your petitioner has lost all his lands and other property the same being confiscated by the rebels.

That your petitioner's ill state of health brought on by fatigue of service in defence of his King and Country, is now in London in hopes to recover strength to return & render government every assistance in his power.

That your petitioner relying on the certificates hereunto annexed to corroborate his loyalty, begs to submit his case to your Lordships consideration to grant him such relief as to your Lordships shall seem meet

And your petitioner as in
duty bound shall ever pray
Alex Chesney

to which I was promised an answer the following morning at 11 Oclock in the afternoon I took a lodging at Mrs Crisfields No 58 Crownstreet Westminster: this circumstance was beneficial to me as Mrs Crisfield introduced me to Mr Lewis Wolfe [207] a clerk in the Treasury who kindly offered to render any assistance in his power to further my claims; from which moment he was essentially useful in many ways, and through me he afterwards became agent for all the Loyalists: a place now held by his Brother in law Mr Crafer [208] my particular friend.

On the 4th August called at Mr Townsend's [209] office but did not receive any answer to my memorial afterwards at Lord Cornwallis' [210] 8 Albemarle Street and found that his Lordship is gone

---

[207] Lewis Wolfe acted as agent in London for the American loyalists who had returned to the north-east of Ireland

[208] One Thomas Crafer was paymaster of pensions and allowances to the American loyalists and their children who were living in 1833-36

[209] Thomas Townsend (afterwards 1st Viscount Sydney) was secretary for war in 1782

[210] Lord Cornwallis was ever ready to help the loyalists who had sought refuge in the British Isles, especially those who had fought under him in America, by giving them certificates certifying to their loyalty In many cases he appeared in person to urge claims before the commissioners for American Claims in London

to Norfolk; then to Lord Huntingdons [211] St James place to enquire for Lord Rawdon who is gone to the country for two months· also Lord Shelburnes [212] with the same bad success. after dinner I went to see Westminster Abbey and wah highly gratified by a sight of that venerable pile, and hearing an Anthem sung; I also viewed Westminster-Hall and the bridge before my return to the lodgings.

Sunday 5th attended service at Westminster Abbey; I dined with M[rs] Crisfield and two ladies   The person who travelled from Liverpool with me under the assumed title of a Russian Major, and who said he had been taken prisoner by some of the native powers in India, paid his lodging and took his departure having got assistance from the Russian Ambassador.[213]   It appeared afterwards that this man was but a Serjeant Major in the Russian Army so that he rather disgraced himself by assuming a title which did not belong to him

Monday 6th on my way to M[r] Townsend's office I saw the guard relieved in the park; I was told to memorial M[r] Townsend in order to get his assistance in forwarding my application to the Treasury. I gave my papers to M[r] Rose,[214] who told me the Board are to sit tomorrow but will not enter into the merits of claims, as there is to be a gentleman appointed expressly for that purpose   I called at the Archbishop of Canterbury's [215] to enquire for Lord Cornwallis and ascertained that his Lordship will not be in town for 5 weeks.

About this period there was a general meeting of loyalists at the Crown and Anchor Tavern,[216] General Arnold [217] and almost every one who had a claim attended; after some conversation as to the best plan to be pursued it was determined to draw up a general petition to the Ministers to take our case into consideration for which purpose three of the number were pitched upon viz Lieu[t] Governor Ball [218] and M[r] Simpson [219] to represent those who had lost property or rendered services to the government; and myself

[211] Hans Francis, 10th earl of Huntingdon, whose sister, Elizabeth, was the mother of Lord Rawdon

[212] William, 2nd earl of Shelburne, secretary of state for Foreign Affairs, prime minister, 1782-83, and 1st marquis of Landsdowne

[213] The Russian ambassador in London at this time was Monsieur Jean Simoline

[214] George Rose, secretary to the Treasury

[215] Frederick Cornwallis (1713-83), archbishop of Canterbury, uncle of Lord Cornwallis

[216] The Association of American Loyalists in London in 1779 first met at Spring Gardens coffee house, and afterwards at the Crown and Anchor tavern in the Strand, a historic tavern which is described by Wheatley and Cunningham in *London Past and Present* Vol I, p 480

[217] General Benedict Arnold

[218] Lieutenant-Governor William Bull (see Additional Notes, p 112)

[219] James Simpson (see Additional Notes, p 99)

to act for those who had been actively engaged in the war, besides losing property the petition was speedily presented to Ministers, and on it was found the act of restitution:[220] also the resolutions of the first Lord of the Treasury classing the Loyalists.[221]

August 7th employed in preparing a Memorial with copies of testimonials for Lord North; after dinner went to the Treasury and met two gentlemen (loyalists) who promise to communicate to me any intelligence they may receive from the Treasury; next day I called there myself but did not see M[r] Rose nor was there any answer; further than there would not be anything decided for some time; and that I might appoint some one to act in my absence: I ascertained where Major Ross [222] Aid de Camp to Lord Cornwallis lives also the address of Col[l] Tarlton.[223]   On the 9th Major Ross accompanied me to Sir Henry Clinton's,[224] and took my papers to consult Lord Cornwallis as to the best steps to be pursued.

11th or 12 my papers were returned from Lord Cornwallis by Major Ross' hands with a message that his Lordship would do everything to assist my vews; and as my farther stay would be expensive without any immediate utility, I empowered M[r] Lewis Wolfe [225] to act in my absence and he kindly promised to write to me whenever any thing interesting should occur respecting the claims.

Aug[t] 16th Left London in a coach from Lad-Lane [226] having taken my place for Loughborough [227] which I reached next day and got to Cavendish,[228] near Lord Huntingdons' seat at Dannington Park [229]

---

[220] The acts of Parliament of 1788 and 1785, awarding compensation to the American loyalists

[221] The loyalists were divided into several classes for the purpose of the above acts   In the first were those who had rendered exceptional services to Great Britain   The second was composed of those who had borne arms against the Revolution. Loyalists who were zealous and uniform were in the third   In the fourth were loyalists resident in Great Britain   The fifth embraced those who took the oath of allegiance to the Americans but afterwards joined the British, while the sixth class consisted of loyalists who bore arms for the Americans, but later joined the British forces

[222] Major Alexander Ross (see p 13, n 93)

[223] Colonel Banistre Tarleton (see p 18, n 127)

[224] Sir Henry Clinton (He is in the *Dictionary of National Biography*)

[225] Lewis Wolfe (see p 31, n 207)

[226] Lad lane is now Gresham street. In this lane was the old tavern, The Swan with two Necks, the headquarters of coaches to Chester and Holyhead and to Liverpool, through Coventry and Lichfield   An advertisement of the coaches from this tavern is in the *Morning Chronicle and London Advertiser* for 1 April, 1786

[227] Loughborough in Leicestershire

[228] The parish of Cavendish, in Leicestershire

[229] Donington park, in the parish of Cavendish, was once the home of the celebrated Selina, countess of Huntingdon, foundress of the religious sect known by her name   It was enlarged in 1795 by Francis Rawdon, 2nd earl of Moirn and 1st. marquis of Hastings

18th Waited on Lord Rawdon [230] who gave me a strong letter of recommendation to General Burgoyne,[231] soliciting his interest to get me appointed to some Revenue situation in Ireland.

On the 19th set out for Manchester by the stage and slept at the Bell Inn Derby,[232] next night at the former place and on the 21st at Liverpool; but could not get to sea until the 30th when the packet sailed for Dublin with a fair but very light wind; so that we made little way towards Dublin where we arrived late the evening of the 3rd of Sep[tr] I took up my quarters where I had been formerly (in Peter's Row).

On the 4th I waited on General Burgoyne with Lord Rawdon's letter but as I received little or no encouragement from him I determined to go to Ballymena and endeavour to engage in some business or other until the result could be ascertained of the London business: this day I called on M[r] Henry [233] at the Custom House and gave him an account of my proceedings in London; which were interesting to him as had also lost property.

Sep[tr] 7th set out at 4 oclock in the morning by the Coach for Newry [234] where I slept; and proceeded on horse-back to Antrim [235] next day, thence to my uncle Purdy's.

About the 10th [October, 1782] I received a letter from M[r] Wolfe requiring me to send a sworn account of my losses in America accompanied by certificates from Lord Cornwallis Col[l] Tarlton &c &c which I did soon after; the amount being £1998 10s in which all the losses were included that could be substantiated with facility before the commissioners. I received a flattering letter from Lord Cornwallis some time in Nov[r] [1782] inclosing one for Col Eustace [236] the Sect[y] in Dublin to facilitate my views either by obtaining a commission in a Fencibble Reg[t] but of this letter I made no use for some time except consulting M[r] Henry, by whose advice I sent it some time afterwards: when it appeared the com-

[230] Lord Rawdon became 2nd earl of Moira in succession to his father in 1793

[231] General John Burgoyne, of Saratoga fame, was commander-in-chief of the forces in Ireland from June, 1782, to December, 1783

[232] The Bell inn, Derby, was a noted coaching house and opens on Sadler Gate   In the early 19th century it was a conspicuous meeting place of the Whig party   Washington Irving describes a wet day there in his story of the stout man in *Bracebridge Hall*

[233] Philip Henry (see Additional Notes, p 97)

[234] Newry, a seaport in county Down

[235] Antrim, in the county of that name

[236] Colonel Charles Eustace became a member of the Irish Parliament and a major-general on the staff in Ireland in 1798, he died in 1803

missions were all given away. I made arrangements with Mr Miller [237] to purchase and open a shop in Ballymena.

I remained about Ballymena until the middle of Dec [1782] when Major Robinson [238] brought a message for us to wait on Lord Rawdon at Montalto.[239]

On the 23rd [December] Robinson and I called at Montalto, where we did not find his Lordship but received a message to go to Dublin and call on Counseller Doyle the Major's brother [240] who would endeavour to assist our views in the Revenue: that night we slept at Widow Flinn's near Rathfuland,[241] next at Dundalk the third within 20 miles of Dublin; and on the 26th reached Dublin by 12 oclock, the whole of which journey we performed on foot· the day of our arrival we called on Mr Campbell,[242] took our lodgings in Pill-lane, and amused ourselves by going to the play.

27th [December] called at Counseller Doyle's who was gone to the country; I then waited on Col^l Eustace with Lord Cornwallis' letter who said the Fencible Regiments are full of officers.

Robinson [243] and I on the 30th called at Counsellor Doyle [244] who gave us hopes of success, and said he would call on the Lord Lieut;[245] next day he told us he had seen the Lord Lieut; but had not received an answer to his application.

On the 2nd Jany 1783 Counsellor Doyle told us that the Lord Lieu^t had acceded to the request would give us places in the Revenue and required our names; which we gladly furnished to the Sect^y Mr Scrope Bernard,[246] who had been a loyalist also.

Jan^ry 3rd [1783] called and left copies of my papers at the Castle [247]; and on the 6th Robinson and I received a letter 5 Jany

[237] Captain James Miller (see Additional Notes, p 100)

[238] Major John Robinson (see Additional Notes, p 95)

[239] Montalo was afterwards sold by the 2nd earl of Moira to David Ker

[240] William Doyle, K. C, master in Chancery, father of Lieut-General Charles W Doyle, K C B, and of Captain Sir Bentinck C Doyle, R N, and brother of Major John Doyle (afterwards General Sir John Doyle, baronet) (See p 25, n 180)

[241] Rathfriland in county Down

[242] Charles Philip Campbell (see p 28, n 196)

[243] Major John Robinson (see Additional Notes, p 95)

[244] Major John Doyle (see p 25, n 180)

[245] The lord lieutenant of Ireland was Earl Temple

[246] Scrope Bernard, son of Sir Francis Bernard, baronet, (governor of Massachusetts, 1760-69) was born, 1 October, 1758, at Perth Amboy, New Jersey, while his father was governor of New Jersey He was educated at Harrow and at Christ Church, Oxford, private secretary to the lord lieutenant of Ireland in 1782 and 1787, member of Parliament, and under secretary of state for the Home Department He became fourth baronet and assumed the additional name of Morland

[247] Dublin Castle.

1783 from Scrope Barnard from the Castle notifying our appointments to Tide waiters places—his at Larne and mine at Waterford
until something better should offer: trifling as this appointment
was I was truly grateful for it, and found it in my present situation and circumstances a most timely relief from idleness and perhaps the fear of want; not knowing that I should ever receive any
thing else from government.

On the 7th went to the Custom-House and received my commission for which I paid the fees; and immediately set out by the
Kilkenny Coach, from whence I got a conveyance to Waterford in
a return chaise: I remained about a fortnight, and not liking the
duty or situation, I took an opportunity of getting myself boarded
on a vessel for Dublin and on arriving at the Custom House I applied to M[r] Morgan [248] who got me immediately removed to Belfast whither I soon moved by land: I was back and forwards to
Ballymena until the 1[s] of March; which was the day I was happily
united to Jane Wilson [249] eldest daughter of John Wilson [250] and
Elizabeth Kirkpatrick his wife   she has but one sister (Molly) and
six brothers viz James, John, Samuel, William, David and Charles:
my wife was born the first Sunday in April 1763 and consequently
in her 19th year at the time of our marriage. I continued at the
Birney-hill until the 12th of April, then removed to a house in Her-
cules-lane Belfast.[251] I was scarcely fixed in my residence when a
letter arrived from M[r] Wolfe requiring my presence in London
about the American claims, and having through my friend Henry [252]
obtained the Board's leave I set out for Dublin,[253] and on the 15th

[248] Probably Francis L Morgan, who was promoted first clerk in the secretary's office of
the Irish board of Customs

[249] Jane Chesney died June 13, 1822, and was buried with her husband in the Mourne
Presbyterian churchyard at Kilkeel, county Down

[250] John Wilson was the son of John Wilson, a Scotsman, and his wife Jennet Brown,
who was a conspicuous beauty of the time   John Wilson, the elder, was a strict Covenanter
refugee from Scotland and settled at Birney Hill in the parish of Skerry or Braid, near Ballymena, and took part in the defence of Carrickfergus in 1690 and was present at the landing
there of William III   His sister, Margaret Wilson, at the age of 18, suffered death in the Solway
at the hands of her persecutors, rather than subscribe to the hated prelacy   (The Life of General F R Chesney, ed by S Lane-Poole, pp 20-23)

[251] Hercules Lane is believed to have been named after Sir Hercules Langford   (Benn,
Hist of Belfast, 1877, p 258).

[252] Philip Henry (see Additional Notes, p 97)

[253] The experiences in Dublin at this time of an American-born officer in the 26th, Foot,
Lieut George Inman, of Boston, Massachusetts, are quoted in his journal, in the possession of
the Cambridge (Massachusetts) Historical Society, under date of 10 April, 1783   Joining his
regiment, then stationed in Ireland, he complains of having had "a great deal of trouble and
greatly imposed upon by the Custom House people"   He was very glad to quit Ireland and his
regiment, which had been exceedingly expensive, and where he had been "meeting with the
greatest imposition from every person whom I had anything to do with "

took my lodging in Pill lane; next day I saw my friends Henry & Campbell [254] who both advised me strongly to proceed to London: Mr Winder [255] also promised me his support and friendship; a thing of great importance as being Secretary to the Board.

20th Sailed in the Fly packet at 10 o'clock in the morning for Liverpool, and reached our destination the evening of the 22nd; I slept at the Bull Inn, Dale-street, and next day at 2 oclock set off by the Coach for London, and got there in the evening of the 24th.

On the 25th I took a lodging at Mr Wolfe's, and began to copy my papers; next day I called at the Treasury and at Col Phillip's [256]: I was employed about a week at the papers, and having finished them, I obtained certificates of their truth from Lord Cornwallis Col^{ls} Balfour and Phillips; and returned them to the office.

May the 6th I was examined by the commissioners for American claims who appeared to be well satisfied with the result; next day I was again at the Treasury to give evidence for some of my loyal friends, and saw Lords Cornwallis & Rawdon there on the same good errand also Cap^{tn} Guest.[257]

On the 10th Mr Wolfe informed us it would be necessary to attend at the Treasury again on Monday; which accordingly happened and we saw Messrs Wilmot & Coke the commissioners,[258] afterwards called on Lord Cornwallis for a frank.

14th Called again on Lord Cornwallis with Col^l Phillips and Cap^{tn} Miller [259] also at Lord Rawdon's we took a walk in the park afterwards and saw their Majesties going to St James': it gave me great pleasure to see our beloved Monarch in whose cause I had sacrificed my all.

Called at the Treasury and found that the Board had not yet taken up Messrs Wilmots and Coke's report on our claims; wrote by post to inform Mr Henry [260] of the state of our affairs at the Treasury; also to obtain leave of absence for me: I sent at this

---

[254] Charles Philip Campbell (see 28, n 196, 30, 35)

[255] Thomas Winder, secretary to the Irish board of Customs

[256] Colonel John Phillips (see Additional Notes, p 60)

[257] Edward Guest, cornet in the 1st Regiment of Horse, 21 May, 1774, and lieutenant, 4 October, 1777

[258] John Eardley Wilmot and Daniel Parker Coke, commissioners of American Claims (See *Hist View of the Commission for inquiring into the losses, services, and the claims of the Am Loyalists at the close of the War* .. *in 1783 with an account of the compensation granted to them by Parliament in 1785 and 1788*, by J Eardley-Wilmot, 1815; *Second Report of the Bureau of Archives for the Province of Ontario*, ed. by A Fraser, 1904, pp 13-25, 1314—76, *The Royal Commission on Loyalists' Claims, 1783-1785*, ed by H E Egerton; The Roxburghe Club, 1915, pp xxx-xxxv)

[259] Captain James Miller (see Additional Notes, p 100).

[260] Philip Henry (see Additional Notes, p 97).

time a small sum of money but all I could spare to Mrs Chesney at the same time encouraging her to hope for better times; and that from the appearance of things it would not be necessary to return to America as some were doing on chance thinking they could not be worse off: which was partly my intention before I came to London

I remained in London until about the 24th of May receiving many acts of friendly attention from Col Phillips [261] and Mr Wolfe [262]: I had obtained a temporary allowance of £50 a year and having put matters in a favourable train for the commissioners' report, I set out for Bristol with Col Phillips [263]; & after passing a day or two with his family I took a passage in a Brig for Strangford [264] on the 2nd of June we put into Dublin by contrary winds, and next day I proceeded to Belfast, where I remained until the 13th of Oct^r [1783] in much anxiety about my London business; and constantly hearing from Mr Henry [265] on this subject equally interesting to him

Octr 13th proceeded to Dublin to make out a new memorial for the Commissioners; also with a view of getting something better, or at least a removal to the West of Ireland; the journey was performed; partly on foot the rest in carriages of different kinds: I failed in getting removed, and whilst employed in preparing my papers I heard of the death of Mr Harman Coast officer at Bangor; for which situation I immediately applied through Major Skeffington and Mr Winder [266] with little hopes of success: and rather thought of getting placed on the list of guagers—General Luttrel [267] exerted himself personally in my favour, and I was every day at the Castle or with some friend trying to make interest.

Novr 4 my papers being ready I set out for Belfast leaving things in an uncertain state as to the Coast Officers place: soon after I embarked with Col Phillips and another loyalist at Donghadee [268] for Liverpool which we reached about the 9th; Mr Miller [269] and I took an inside and an outside place between us for London

[261] Colonel John Phillips (see Additional Notes, p 60)

[262] Lewis Wolfe (see p 31, n 207)

[263] Colonel John Phillips (see above)

[264] Strangford, a seaport in county Down

[265] Philip Henry (see Additional Notes, p 97)

[266] Thomas Winder (see p 37, n 255)

[267] General Henry Lawes Luttrell (1743-1821), soldier and politician, an opponent of John Wilkes, and afterwards 2nd earl of Carhampton (Dict of Nat. Biog)

[268] Donaghadee, county Down.

[269] Captain James Miller (see Additional Notes, p 100)

which plan was both pleasant and oeconomical—On arriving in London I found that General Luttrel had obtained the Coast-officers place for me at Larne or rather Bangor,[270] and that Mr Henry [271] was about to set off to establish his claims before the commissioners; on the 18th he arrived with the pleasing news of my appointment which placed me at once near County Antrim and above want two most agreeable circumstances. I prepared a memorial for each of the Commissioners and also the secretary; and so soon as I had got my claims certified by the other loyalists and had performed the like service for those whose claims were known to me I set out for Belfast by way of Dublin; and a few days after removed my family to Bangor where we took a lodging at Mrs Scott's on the 30th Dec^r [1783].

Continued at Bangor without any particular event all this year [1784] improving myself in writing & Arithmetic; the claims before the commissioners being still undecided and causing constant correspondence with London, as well as with Col Phillips Mr Henry &c.

No particular event until the 14th June [1785] when Eliza Chesney [272] was born at half past 6 oclock in the morning and was called for Lady Moira as well as her two Grandmothers. In autumn the commissioners required more proofs that my property was confiscated [273]; in consequence of this I obtained certificates from Lords Cornwallis and Rawdon: I also referred the commissioners to an act of the provincial congress of Jackson's burgh inserted in the Charlestown papers; which act confiscated the property of every person under Arms; and was passed soon after the reduction of Charles-town in 1780 by the British.[274]

---

[270] Reference is made to this appointment by a later addition to the Journal in these words "W J Skeffington's letter of 4 Novr 1783 and Mr Henry's of 10 Novr 1783 to Mrs Chesney at Belfast"

Written across page 40 of the Journal in later handwriting is this note "Zach Gibbs one of the Loyalists writes on the 30 August 1784 that he is setting out for Nova Scotia to occupy a Grant of Land there "

[271] Philip Henry (see p 38, n 265)

[272] Eliza Chesney, eldest daughter of Alexander and Jane Chesney, married Captain John Hopkins and died in April 1822.

[273] The commissioners of American Claims in London required reliable evidence of confiscation of loyalists' property

[274] An incomplete list of loyalists whose property was confiscated by the State of South Carolina is printed in the *Statutes at Large* of South Carolina, Vol 6 (Cooper's edition), Appendix, pp 629-633 Another list was printed by Miss Mabel L Webber in *South Carolina Historical and Genealogical Magazine*, Vol 14, p 40.

22^d August 1785 My Grandfather John Wilson writes to make known the death of his son John.[275]

A letter of 17 July 1785 from Robert Lusk gives news of my grandfather Chesneys family and that my brother William [276] had been taken to them from the Hodges.[277] But Robert Harper's letter of 10 April 1785 mentions that the Law gave him back to the Hodges. 29 August this was reversed by the Magistrates who gave him to his grandfather.[278]

On Christmas-day [1785] I visited Mourne [279] on my way to Dublin to see how I should like an exchange with the Coast-officer at Annalong [280] Mr Williams [281] who was obliged to leave the country; in consequence of having killed John Atkinson with a stone in return for a blow he gave with a stick; this exchange being effected [282] without trouble I proceeded to Dublin to try to get an allowance of £14 per Annum which my predecessor had enjoyed; but did not succeed; & returned to Bangor in order to prepare for a removal.

Fb^r 14th [1786] removed my family to Mourne & was placed in a house called the barrack situated in Ballymaiveamore [283] nearly 3 miles from Annalong; there were two families in the house John McDowell and James McCrumb [284] a Tide waiter; but at May I got the whole house to myself and began to put in some crop: at this time I was very low in cash the consequence of my repeated journeys to and from London. The same anxiety continued about the claims until August when I received £133.12.0 as a dividend; and in Nov^r £255.18 being the remainder of my small allowance [285] which appeared to have been reduced by the commissioners in consequence of having received a Revenue employmnt.

---

[275] This paragraph in the Chesney Journal occurs on page 41.

[276] See page 2, n 11

[277] Robert Hodge, father-in-law of Alexander Chesney

[278] This paragraph occurs in the Chesney Journal on page 41

[279] Mourne, county Down.

[280] Annalong, county Down, a fishing village and the headquarters at that time of a desperate band of smugglers.

[281] James Williams

[282] Alexander Chesney's exchange with James Williams is recorded in the Minute Book of the Irish board of Customs to take place as from 25 December, 1785.

[283] Ballyveamore, Ballymacveaghmore or Ballyvea, where stood the old "Barracks," pulled down a few years ago, which was the birthplace of Alexander Chesney's son, General Francis Rawdon Chesney

[284] or McCrum

[285] The total amount of Alexander Chesney's claim for the loss of his property in South Carolina was £1,564 10s., and the award was £394 (Public Record Office A O 12/109) Included in this claim are the wagon and four horses, impressed into the American service (see page 129) The following additional entry is made in the Chesney Journal on page 41, "The property not as yet confiscated though retained for that purpose" [?1785]

7th March [1787] a daughter born about at 7 Oclock P M called for the mother (Jane)[236]. The communications with Lady Moira [237] by letter commenced this year and she expressed anxiety to give me a lift.

Continued at Ballyvea [1788] under Mr Savage [238] and going frequently to Dublin in the Barge to look for something better. Went to Babbriggan [239] to look at Straw Hall engaged it and as the Board would not allow me to remove in consequence of the combination formed against me; I lost nearly a year's rent.

1788 Mr. Savage wrote a kind letter of adieu regarding the account he had received of my drinking with low people. I determined to avoid all that might have this bad appearance in future.

On the 16th of March Francis Rawdon Chesney [290] was born at 2 Oclock called after my kind patron Lord Rawdon which I made known by a letter on the 29 July 1789.

In May the American claims were finally settled by the Commissioners, who most unexpectedly and unjustly took into account the Revenue employment I obtained through my personal friends Lords Cornwallis and Rawdon, and adjudged it to be part compensation: this arrangement reduced my annual pension to £30.

During this year there was a combination of the Boatmen backed by Mr Savage [291] and the smugglers to get me removed and although they perjured themselves to gain their ends I foiled them at Rosstrevor [292] in presence of a Commissioner Col Ross,[293] whose friendship I gained by their attack.

This year I bought Brackany from James Purdy. Was at Dublin after the tryal endeavouring might and main to get removed or get something better or rather more quiet as to employment An

---

[236] Jane, who married the Rev Henry Hayden, M A, of Trinity College, Dublin, who went out as a missionary of the Society for the Propagation of the Gospel to Foreign Parts, at Grand Lake in 1820, and in 1822 was transferred to Rawdon, Nova Scotia.

[237] Lady Moira, wife of Francis Rawdon, 2nd earl of Moira

[238] Francis Savage was surveyor at Newcastle, county Down In a letter to the Irish board of Customs, 20 February, 1789, he refers to the growth of refractoriness among the people of Mourne and to the frequency of their attacks upon the Revenue officers when seizures of smuggled goods were made. The board decided in consequence to send a detachment of military to Newcastle to assist the officers in the execution of their duty

[239] Balbriggan, a seaport in county Dublin

[290] Francis Rawdon Chesney, (1789-1872), afterwards general, the explorer of the Euphrates and founder of the overland route to India. (See *Dict. of Nat. Biog.* and *The Life of the late General F R. Chesney*, ed by S Lane-Poole, 1893)

[291] Francis Savage (see above).

[292] Rostrevor, on Carlingford Lough

[293] Robert Ross, a high officer in the Irish board of Customs

exchange to Balbreggan was partly arranged in Dec[r] but afterwards given up.

Col Ross' examination took place end of July and in September 1789 The Atkinsons M[r] Savages [294] relatives & the M[c]Neillys [295] were censured and affidavits were taken privately from the boatmen against me by M[r] Savage.

The Board of Customs decided that in the case of Seizures made by the Barge, the Surveyor when at sea should have $\frac{3}{8}$: The Mate or Deputy acting under him $\frac{1}{8}$ and the remaining 4/8 equally to the   [?]   & crew. The Surveyor when out at Sea to have $\frac{1}{8}$ and the Deputy $\frac{3}{8}$—The crew as before when present.

[1790] Still wishing to get removed out of Mourne either to an equal, or better place; and felling the ill effetcs in a pecuniary way of my journies to Dublin with that view.

Tords the end of Jan[y] 1791 I had a bad fall from my horse & my collar bone broken.

May 14th a son born at 11 Oclock at night whom I named Charles Cornwallis,[296] as a small token of gratitude to my patron

Nov[r] I bought Ballymacveamore [297] from M[r] Robert Norman which appeared likely to prove a good way of employing the American compensation money there being at that time a fair interest and a strong probability of more by endeavouring to improve this Townland.

On the 4 Dec[r] 1790 The famous Smuggling Lugger Morgan Rattler being anchored in Glassdrummond Bay with a number of Yawls alongside and astern with goods in each preparatory to landing the Revenue pinnace was sent out, and a part of officers stationed on land to prevent a landing. In order to effect this purpose 16 men were despatched in the Lugger's boat to chive off the Revenue land party and take the pinnace also—The Revenue party now opned a fire on the assailants who were not only deterred from their purpose when landed but cut off from their own boat. The Lugger now fired a Gun to cover her Men and she sent at the same time a reinforcement of 12 men who landed about half a mile north of the Revenue party and attacked them by firing in their rear. I moved towards the latter party leaving some of my people to protect our boat. During this movement, the Smugglers got their first party

[294] Francis Savage (see p 41, note 288)
[295] Probably Henry McNully, coast officer, Mourne
[296] Captain Charles Cornwallis Chesney, of the Bengal artillery, who died in 1830
[297] Ballymacveamore (see p 40, n 283)

and boat to sea and the Revenue party being obliged to retreat before the 2^d party of the Lugger's men the landing was effected. My party fired some 10 or 12 rounds. The Smugglers were heard to say fire at the man on horseback meaning myself. I stated these particulars and suggested that a Military party should be stationed in Mourne to prevent such outrage in future.

Towards the end of 1791 I received an account (also previously from my Father) from I Purdy on reaching S Carolina of the nominal Sale of my property which in fact made a debtor. I also found that it would be very difficult to get my son William brought over as I had hoped to arrange.

Jan^{ry} 17th [1793] Alex^r McDowell preventive officer was murdered at Turlogh-Hill, which event created a great sensation; and a large reward was offered by Government, the officers and inhabitants of Mourne for the conviction of the person or persons concerned in this atrocious act: but nothing certain transpired. The Board at my recommendation gave a pension of £6 a year to his widow.

Smuggling was so extensive at this period, that on the 19 Feb 1793 Five vessels namely 3 Cutters 1 Lugger and 1 Wherry anchored in Glassdrummond Bay during the day. Having made this fact duly known the Lord Lieut caused Capt Drury to sail immediately in quest of them with His Majestys Ship Squirrell. The Board ordered the Ross, the Breech and Mary cruisers to proceed to that part of the Coast and with reference to the possibility of some of them being privateers with Arms, the Lord Lieut ordered a Troop of Dragoons to proceed (through Newcastle) to Mourne, and a party to proceed from Rathpebuid [298] to 8 Mile Bridge to act in conjunction with the Company at Kilkeel [299]: also that the Revenue party at Rostrevor should be strengthened from Newry.

24 June [1793] removed to Prospect &c &c

1794 Feb^{uy} 3 A kind letter came from Lady Moira offering my son Francis a Commission in Col Doyle's Regiment [300] if he is old enough to be appointed

The Brig Surprise was wrecked near Annalong

---

[298] Rathfriland.

[299] Kilkeel, county Down, where the Chesney family worshiped in the Mourne Presbyterian Meeting House, and where Captain Alexander Chesney and his wife and nine of his children are buried

[300] Colonel John Doyle (see page 25, n. 180)

July 26   A daughter born at 3 Oclock in the morning named after her aunts Molly and Anne.[301]

My friend M[r] Wolfe joined partnership with his brother in law M[r] Crafer [302] in the Agency to the American loyalists.

M[rs] Chesney took Francis to Dublin on Oct 17 18 1794 with reference to his future and presented him to Lady Moira who was all kindness, even wishing her to stay in the House

Feb[ry] [1795]   Letters passing between Mess[rs] Wolfe and me whose advice I asked about placing my son Francis at the Royal Military Academy.

July 6 1795 Col. Skeffington [303] advises an application to Lord Moira who was about to proceed to the Continent in command of an Army.[304]

During this summer we had a fever in the house which attacked M[rs] Chesney, Eliza, Francis (slightly) and Mary Anne who thank God all recovered: this was not the only trouble, for some malicious person having sent a general charge to the Coll[r] of Strangford against me and the party for neglect of duty; an investigation took place before the Surveyor General M[r] Cuthbert. He pronounced it to be founded in malice—The Board afterwards granted a reward of £50 to the party for their exertions the two preceeding years which showed how well they were satisfied.

Still making enquiries about the Woolwich Academy [305] during the year [1796] the country was a good deal disturbed by designing persons who appeared to have deep designs in view

Lord Cornwallis had declined on the 24 Feby 96 asking a direct commission on account of the age [306]

And Mess[rs] Wolfe & Crafer 3[d] March 1796 recommended the Mil Academy,[307] and to obtain the Master Gen[ls] nomination thro Lord Cornwallis, age 12 to 16. £20 a year to be given in addition to the Gov allowance

---

[301] His daughter, Marianne, who married John Shannon Moore, and died October 31, 1858, aged 65

[302] Thomas Crafer, paymaster of pensions to the American loyalists, 1815-1827

[303] Major the Hon W. J Skeffington was the second son of Clotworthy, first earl of Massereene, and was appointed constable of Dublin Castle, 19 November, 1784 He died in 1811

[304] Francis Rawdon-Hastings, 2nd earl of Moira, was appointed, 15 July, 1795, to command the force ordered by Pitt to proceed to Quiberon and to act as auxiliary to the army of the count of Artois

[305] Royal Military Academy, Woolwich (see W T Vincent, *The Records of the Woolwich District*, Vol I).

[306] A commission for Alexander Chesney's eldest son, Francis Rawdon

[307] The Royal Military College at Great Marlow, Bucks, a preparatory college for Woolwich.

Thank God my affairs are in a most prosperous situation; health in the family with plenty of everything.

Jan[r] [1797] I raised a company, called the Mourne Infantry,[308] in order to put down the turbulent spirit manifested all through the Country last Autumn; by my own exertions they were embodied on the 30th; but Mess[rs] Henry M[c]Neilly [309] and Thomas Spence (formerly a quarter master of Dragoons) having refused commissions; I got Jack Kilpatrick and Henry M[c]Neilly son to the former appointed in their room. Several disturbances in the County and several houses of those who would not join burnt one of mine amongst the rest: Mine was the first company under arms in the County; which probably prevented a general insurrection in Mourne. A guard was mounted agreeably to a letter from the Castle [310] E. Coote 9 Feb. 1787, The augmentation which I proposed subsequently was declined (10 April 1797); and a later offer of a part of the corps to serve permanently was left in abeyance Welbrace 7 July 1797. I had sent my Daughter Eliza to Miss Thompsons Boarding School in Newry where her progress was satisfactory.

In April [1797] applied to the Master general of the ordinance for a cadetship for Francis;[311] and in June I received a notification of that appointment but he cannot be admitted until 14 years of age· which will be 6 years hence. I thought it might be a useful preparatory step to put him in the yeomanry for a little time therefore got him appointed to a Lieutenancy I had also obtained the appointments of . . . .[312] in the Revenue at Annalong which was afterwards cancelled. I had rather hopes at this period that the Mourne Yeomanry [313] might have been made part of a Fencible

---

[308] Although Alexander Chesney was commissioned, 31 October, 1796, to enrol and command the Mourne infantry, the force was not actually embodied until the end of January following As the first company under arms in county Down, it was mustered at a moment when the Association of United Irishmen, formed in 1791, were drilling secretly and actively in the counties of Down, Antrim, Derry, and Donegal The people of Ulster, proud in the recollection that theirs was the first Province to raise the standard of rebellion, issued an address in 1797, exhorting their fellow-countrymen to revolt (*The Life of the late General F R Chesney*, ed. by S Lane-Poole, 1885, pp 39-40)

[309] Probably Henry McNully, coast officer at Mourne.

[310] Dublin Castle

[311] Alexander Chesney's eldest son, Francis Rawdon Chesney

[312] The word is not clear in the text

[313] Yeomanry were first established in Ireland in 1796 The rebellious inhabitants of Belfast, mostly Presbyterians, opposed their establishment as vehemently as the Roman Catholics in Dublin. (Sir Richard Musgrave, *Memoirs of the different Rebellions in Ireland*, 1801, pp 228, 290)

Captain Alexander Chesney was in November, 1821, commanding officer of the Mourne

Corps in which I could have had the rank of Major but this was declined. Pelham's [314] letter 29 Jan\[^y\] 1798.

Although not 10 years of age, and therefore far too young I had obtained a Commission for my Son Francis, who accompanied the Corpe to Newry although quite unfitted for such Service, Lord Castlereagh who could not have known his age had given him a Commission. 19 May 1798.

Accepted a commission of the peace in consequence of a wish expressed at the Castle; I had declined this before when the Marquis of Downshire [315] asked me through Rector Warring [316]

Jan\[^y\] [1798] Some trouble about a stranded Sloop the New Loyalty of Belfast; Mess\[^rs\] Matthews Beers, and Jerry Atkinson supporting M\[^r\] H McNeilly in his claim as principal Salvager: this business was settled satisfactorily in April: about this time I felt that I had rather done injustice to my family by spending money for the Yeomanry business thereby creating envy, a less active part would have preserved more friends with less need of them.

The Corps put on permanent duty and arrangements were made for this purpose by Gen Nugent's [317] letters The Rebellion having broken out. Mourne being chiefly through my exertions pretty well disarmed and quiet, the corps was ordered to do duty at Newry. A few days after our arrival there early in June I came back to Mourne with a part of the Newry Cavalry and surrounded the houses of the suspected people during the night, I thus seized and carried off the supposed leaders of the disaffected and kept them as hostages in Newry for the safety of the Mourne people in case of a rising in our absence Major Porter [318] of the Argyle Fencible Regiment Commanded and his arrangements appear to have been very judicious.

A detachment being ordered to go to Dundalk in consequence of an express from thence mentioning that the Rebels were under

---

Yeomanry—a corps which had volunteered to serve out of its own district during the war with the French in 1815 Chesney, in November, 1821, applied for leave of absence from his official Customs duties to serve with the Mourne Yeomanry out of his district, if required

[314] Thomas Pelham was appointed a principal secretary of state in Ireland, 24 June, 1796, and was created earl of Chichester in 1801

[315] Arthur, 2nd marquis of Downshire

[316] Rev Lucus Waring, rector of Kilkeel

[317] Field-Marshal Sir George Nugent, baronet, who served during the American Revolutionary war, was in command of the north-eastern district of Ireland He married, 16 November, 1797, Maria, daughter of Brigadier-General Cortlandt Skinner, who raised the well-known loyalist regiment the New Jersey Volunteers, in the American Revolutionary war

[318] Captain John Porter was promoted major, 1 October, 1797, in place of Lieut.-Colonel John Campbell (resigned) of the 2nd battalion of the Argyll (or Clavering) Fencible regiment, commanded by Colonel Henry M Clavering (W O 13/3803)

Arms in that neighbourhood I volunteered to go; and on our march: having pointed out to Capt Campbell the commander, the roads by which we could be attacked, as well as the general situation of the country: as this convinced him I had some knowledge of Military matters, he consulted me afterwards on all occasions, and appointed me to do staff duty, issuing orders: paroles countersigns &c &c one day we took several hundred pikes near the town, and the Rebels having dispersed; soon after we were ordered back to Newry by the commandant Major Porter of the Argyle fencibles [319] who gave us a welcome home dinner and had the Right Honb^le Isaac Corry [320] to meet us.

The Corps ordered to return to Mourne [in July] the town of Newry having become tranquil by the rebels losing the battle of Ballynakinch [321] the day on which Mrs Chesney (then all alone at Prospect) was confined of a daughter Matilda.[322]

Some of their leaders who were forming plans in the neighbourhood of Newry taken and executed there.

A further increase of the Mourne Yeomanry was declined altho passed. [Herbert Taylor's letter, 21 July, 1798] I caused the Boats throughout Mourne to be numbered and Registered.

Aug. 7th [1798]. half the Corps ordered off permanent duty. 25th The whole corps put on permanent duty again in consequence of the French landing in Killala-Bay.[323] Major Matthews [324] obtained an order from the Brigade Major Gethen to command both corps, as the right of Major in the Army; I applied to the Castle and gained my point: Lord Castlereagh [325] decided that I am the senior Yeomanry Officer

Sep^t 9th I transmitted an address from the Roman Catholics of lower Mourne to the Lord Lieu^t and received a favourable answer.

16th Mr Moore and I forwarded a similar one from the Dissenters to Lord Castlereagh to be also laid before the Lord Lieu^t.

---

[319] Major John Porter (see p 46, n 318)

[320] Isaac Corry (1755-1813), Irish politician, represented Newry in the Irish Parliament, 1776-1800, chief Government speaker in favor of the union, 1799-1800, fought a duel with Henry Grattan in 1800 (*Dict of Nat. Biog*)

[321] The battle of Ballynahinch, where the rebels were defeated (W H Maxwell, *Hist of the Irish Rebellion in 1798*, p 204)

[322] Matilda Chesney died in 1814

[323] The French landed on the shore of Killala Bay, four miles from Killala, 22 August, 1798

[324] Joseph Matthews, captain in the 8th (or Kings Royal Irish) regiment of Light Dragoons from 1793 to 1796

[325] Viscount Castlereagh, the statesman, was keeper of the Irish privy seal in 1797-8, and chief secretary for Ireland, 1799-1801

President [in 1799] of a Court Martial to try Major Matthews for Mal conduct as a yeomanry officer of which charge he was acquitted

July [1800] Mrs Chesney went to see her mother in County Antrim taking with her Eliza, Francis and Charles; they got back safe notwithstanding the still disturbed state of the Country—At this time I applied to Lord Cornwallis to have me superannuated: in August saw his Lordship on the business at Dundalk who acceded to my wish and desired a Memorial to be made out stating the value of my employment; which was done and referred to the commissioners [in December] stating the wound I got in the Ballagh: but so many difficulties occurred that I was sorry I had applied: being uncertain about the result and whether to take a farm or not.

Feb [1801] went to wait on the commissioners about my application; found that their report was not favourable to my wishes on account of short service

March 8th A Son born at 3 Oclock in the morning, called him Alexander [326] after myself

April 6th Took a deed of a farm in Ballyardle [327] from James Carr for which I paid £145.

[June] Finding I could not be superannuated on eligible terms, I determined to give up all further idea of it for the present: which gives me an opportunity of pursuing my usual avocations, without further interruption

In Octr. [1801] Francis paid a visit to Lady Moira at her particular request going each morning to Moira House [328] and returning to sleep at Mr Normans

Febr [1802] James Purdy [329] having refused to go the post-office he was on my representation suspended, and a tryal took place before the Collector at Newry; which ended in his being

---

[326] Alexander Chesney, the younger, died in 1832, unmarried

[327] General Francis Rawdon Chesney built a house at Ballyardle for his mother, Jane Chesney, and called it "Pacholet," in memory of his father's home in South Carolina Here Captain Alexander Chesney died, 12 January, 1845 The house is still standing (1917)

[328] Moira House, Dublin, was visited by Rev John Wesley, who describes it in his *Journal* it is now the "mendicity institution" (see *Memorable Dublin Houses*)

[329] James Purdy, Customs boatman at Annalong, in succession to John Boyd, who had been maltreated in an attempt by an armed mob to rescue a seizure of tobacco from three of the Customs' boatmen

obliged to take his turn of duty: although Mr Beers,[330] Purdy and Wallace swore everthing that malace could dictate to injure me

April 7 Received a letter from Lord Chatham [331] and another on the 5 May saying he would appoint my son Francis to a cadetship when of the proper age and possess the other qualifications requisite: he will not be old enough until next March, in the meantime he must apply diligently to latin grammar and the other studies.

Lady Moira expressed her willingness to receive him in Dublin to acquire French & Latin &c or else at Belfast.

Mr Crafer 5 May 1802 agreeably to what is required in Col Haddens [332] letter recommends that Francis should apply diligently to Latin & other studies for the Academy

13th March [1803] received a letter of the 9th to send my son to Woolwich; and on the 24th he went off by himself by way of Liverpool to London, where I hope he will meet every kind assistance from Messrs Wolfe and Crafer. [April 19th] Francis being found deficient in height and English grammar was placed by Mr Crafer at an Academy near Walworth kept by a Revoult a Frenchman.[333]

In May I sent Charles to Dublin to wait upon Lady Moira with the hope that something might turn up for him.

[June] Francis went to Woolwich again with two gentlemen sent by Lady Mora: recommended by Major Phillips to go to Dr Towne"s Academy at Deptford [334] whither he went immediately

1803 Lugage taken by Archbold

---

[330] An enquiry was held by Francis Carleton, collector at Newry, into the allegations of William Beers, surveyor at Annalong, and James Purdy, Customs boatman at the same place, that Alexander Chesney had been guilty of corrupt connections with smugglers The board of Customs, as a result of Carleton's report, dated 24 March, 1802, informed Chesney that the circumstances of the spirits being sent to his house at an unseasonable hour was open to suspicion, and cautioned him as to his future conduct respecting smugglers James Purdy's suspension was cancelled (Minute Book of the Irish board of Customs, No 278, p 126, in the Public Record Office in London)

For an account of the laxity in the Irish Customs early in the nineteenth century, see Atton and Holland, *The King's Customs*, 1910, Vol II pp 11-14

[331] John Pitt, earl of Chatham, was master-general of the Ordnance at this time

[332] Colonel James Haddon, Royal artillery, afterwards major-general

[333] John Revoult, M A, master of Walworth Academy His portrait was painted by Sir William Beechey, R A, and was presented to him "by the gentlemen who had been educated under him as a token of their high respect and affectionate regard towards him—1798 " This portrait cannot now be traced. A mezzotint of it was done by James Ward in 1798 He is shown holding up a book, entitled *Introduction to the Arts and Sciences, 1798.* (R W Bowers, *Sketches of Southwark Old and New*, 1905, p 488)

[334] Alexander Mark Kerr Hamilton, son of Colonel Archibald Hamilton, the loyalist, of Flushing, Long Island, New York, and his American wife, Alice Colden, was at Rev Dr Towne's Academy at Deptford in 1785, at the age of 18 He subsequently became a major-general in the British Army

On the 2ᵈ July 1803 Mʳ Revoult sent to me a satisfactory letter about Francis who is now gone to Dʳ Townes at Deptford. Mʳ R says he found ın hım a great ingenuity, much natural good sense and such a degree of docılıty as made me wısh that he had come to me sooner. I am sorry he staıd so short a tıme because I was ın hopes he would have profited much

[July 13] Francis finally admıtted a cadet, warrant made out, but he is to remain at Deptford untıl there shall be a vacancy at Marlow.

[September 21ˢᵗ] Francıs went to the Mılıtary College at Marlow ³³⁵ was examıned and admitted.

[December 1ˢᵗ] Vacatıon at Marlow commenced Francıs came home for a month & ıs to joın at Woolwich 12 Janʸ.

The Brıg Brıstol from Lısbon for Lıverpool havıng on the 16ᵗʰ Decʳ been stranded at Annalong and the entıre of her cargo 301 Bags of cotton 21 Chests of fruıt havıng been saved by me got the business amıcably settled and every charge thereon paıd, every person concerned paıd off and hıghly pleased   I got in all about £300 for my exertıons, thank God not an accıdent nor any person hurt or ınjured at her.

Francis set out for the Point [January 3, 1804] to go to Woolwıch

Joıned the Academy on the 12ᵗʰ Mʳ Crafer went down wıth hım.

[Aprıl] Francıs has got ınto the Medium Academy good accounts of his progress. He ıs acquaınted with Oldfields mother who is kind to him

[November 9ᵗʰ] Francis gazetted to a 2ᵈ Lieutenancy just 18 months after he left this house; but wıth a heavy expence, for travellıng back and forward and being placed at the Walworth and Deptford Academies, to whıch must be added his outfit. Much ıs due to Mʳ & Mʳˢ Crafer for their unremıtting kındness to Francis

26 Nov 1804 I sent a very partıcular letter of advıce to Francis about hıs future conduct as an Officer and success in lıfe

Determined on sendıng Charles to Mʳ Revoults Academy to qualify him for any situatıon which mıght offer: he set out ın Janʸ & went to Revoults ın Febʸ [1805] at Walworth. Francıs at Woolwich doing duty and no sıtuatıon havıng been obtained for Charles, I determined on bringing him home at the end of the quarter.

---

³³⁵ A proposal was made by the supreme board of the Royal Mılıtary College at Marlow ın 1806 that the college should be removed from Marlow to Wınchester   The proposal was, however, negatıved (W O 40/37)

[June] Wrote to Gen¹ Lloyd [336] and obtained leave for Francis to visit us, and bring Charles—

[June 29ᵗʰ] Francis and Charles set out from London for Prospect.[337]

[September 29ᵗʰ] Francis left us for Woolwich to join his company at Portsmouth, as a 1ˢᵗ Lieut of Major Merediths [338] Compy; he remained at Mʳ Crafer's a while and proceeded to Portsmouth 23ʳᵈ Octʳ—His company is under orders for service—my son is much respected as far as I can learn, he is a dutiful good son though an expensive one.

[1806] Having obtained the promise of an East India cadetship for Charles, I send him to Revoults: I hope he will be successful as the expence will be great, and heavy on me: but I have great hopes from him as a scholar and an oeconomist: My lands much improved now yielding a clear profit rent of £100 per Annum. This with good health in the family ought to silence all murmurs and discontent; during this year somewhat embarrassed with trifling debts and Charles' schooling; but the seizures I have luckely made will abundantly set me free, so that I have every reason to be thankful.

[1807] Charles at the Woolwich Academy, Francis still quartered at Portsmouth and come home by way of Bristol and Milford Haven to see us in Decʳ after a bad passage. Anxious inquires were made in Dublin and answered by Mʳ Norman 26 Nov 1807.

Francis set out on 26 Jany [1808] and proceeded with his company to Guernsey on the 1ˢᵗ March and arrived on the 4ᵗʰ.

13 March a Son Born whom I afterwards named Thoˢ Crafer [339] after my kind friend in the Treasury.

[June 16] Eliza married to Capᵗ Hopkins [340] with every pros-pect of happiness.

[October, 1809] Charles sailed for Bengal being made a Lieut fire worker in the Artillery; which appointment has been expensive but I hope it will turn out well.

[November 16] Francis came home to see us from Guernsey. Fixed as Surveyor with the increased Salary of £120 which I owe

---

[336] Lieut.-General Vaughan Lloyd, Royal artillery

[337] "Prospect," the residence of Alexander Chesney, was six miles from Kilkeel, and has since been used as the Annalong Coastguard Station

[338] Major David Meredith, Royal artillery

[339] Thomas Crafer Chesney was accidentally drowned in 1825

[340] Captain John Hopkins

to my friends Sack & J. White [341] with Frank Morgan's [342] exertions, tho being placed under Newry instead of Strangfor^d from 18 Dec^r

[1810]Finding myself more at ease on account of the encreased salary: Cap^{tn} and Mrs Hopkins part of the year at Dublin; Jane with them   No news from poor Charles since his arrival in Madras 1st Feb^{ry} last.

I had the pleasure of succeeding with regard to a Boatmans appointment for Francis McDowell whose Father was murdered in 1793.

The two Smuggling cutters Matchless & Jno [343] (as supposed) were met by the Resolution [344] Cruiser but she did not attempt to engage them or either of them.

April 1811 The Hardwicke [345] came to action with the Matchless [346] and was eventually beaten off by her.   The Matchless was afterwards taken by the Bat Revenue tender of 4 Guns.

Francis still in Guernsey and in June appointed Aid de Camp to Major General S Albert Gledstanes [346] which I hope will continue and prove very beneficial to him; in addition to the many blessings we have received from Almighty God it would be desirable to have my pension at the Treasury continued to my wife in case of my death; on which I have written to my friend Mr Crafer—

A particular object with me shall be to get a situation for my son Alex^r either in the Army or Revenue· and as all the family like and wish for Prospect I ought to see whether the promise made by Mr Needham [347] can be realized by Lord Kilmorey.

[1812] Writing to the Custom House and sending a Memorial to the Lord Lieu^t to see if my son Alex^r could be joined in the same commission with myself, also spoke to Lord Killmorey on the subject and received a favourable answer.

---

[341] Probably John White, who was principal surveyor of Customs at Ringsend in 1813

[342] Francis L Morgan, who succeeded Madden as first clerk in the secretary's office of the Irish board of Customs

[343] *Juno*

[344] The *Resolution* was stationed at Strangford in 1813

[345] Alexander Chesney in his letter of 28 August, 1813, to the board of Customs claims that he was the first person to give information to Captain Thomas Lacy, commanding the *Hardwick* cruiser at Rostrevor, of the arrival on the coast of the *Matchless* smuggling cutter   The board accordingly recommended Captain Lacy to pay him 50 guineas as the informer's share of the money paid to Captain Lacy and his crew   (Minute Book of the Irish board of Customs, Vol 334, p 133, Vol 335, p 14)

[346] Major-General Albert Gledstanes was promoted lieut -general in 1814 and knighted in the same year   Francis Rawdon Chesney married in 1822 his (Gledstanes') niece, a daughter of John Forster

[347] Francis Jack Needham, only brother of Robert, 11th viscount Kilmorey

[April] Francis visited us from Guernsey; numerous applications to Lord Moria now going to get something better for myself also my sons; writing to Sir John Doyle [348] on the same subject.

[1813] Applications for Alex[r] to Lord Castlereagh also occupied with the idea of getting him joined with me in the commission as he is unfit for an appointment by himself. I contemplated thro Lord Castlereagh a rise for myself to the post either of Collector or Comptroller of the Customs.

[November] Francis resigned his staff in favour of Sir Alberts [349] nephew, in a handsome manner he is now in London trying to get employed on the Continent.

[December] A bad fever got into our house and attacked several of the family. Francis came to see us.

[1814] The fever still in the house and of course in an uncomfortable state a servant girl Mary Fitzpatrick died of it.

[February 13] I lost poor Matilda—The rest recouvered: occupied in preparing a Memorial about the Matchless [350] which Francis takes with him [April] to London. Francis joined his company in Guernsey. Still occupied with Alex[r] business but no success.

19 May The Treasury referred the question to the Commissioner of Customs once more and one half of the King's share £862.6.11½ having been awarded to Cap Lacy & crew I am trying to get the same sum for my exertions instead of the pittance of £50 received by me from Cap[t] Lacy.[351]

[September] Francis is gone on an excurtion to France and along the ports of Holland. Francis company ordered to Jamaica[352] and he to another at Woolwich.

[1815] Francis still at Woolwich in Aug[t] he came to see us being promoted to be a 2nd Cap[t] at Gibralter; He as well as myself much occupied about Alex[r], making applications to Lords Killmorey Castlereagh &c &c.

Jack Morgans letter of 20 Nov 1815 mentions the Capture of the .... Smuggling Schooner by the .... near .... [353]

[November] Francis is gone to France to try to be stationed there instead of Gibralter.

---

[348] General Sir John Doyle, baronet (see p 25, n 180)
[349] Lieut -General Sir Albert Gledstanes (see p 52, n 346).
[350] The *Matchless,* smuggling cutter (see p 52, n 345)
[351] Captain Thomas Lacy (see p 52, n 345)
[352] Jamaica, West Indies
[353] The words omitted are illegible

[March, 1816] Francis exchanged to Leith-fort [354] which is preferable to Gibralter.

[October] Francis came from Scotland expressly to assist me in applying to Lord Castlereagh received a favourable answer from his Lordship and the papers sent to Lord Killmorey.

[November 22] Jane married to the Rev[d] Henry Hayden soon after Hopkins [355] retired from the service on a good pension by which he is clear of much trouble under the Navy.

In March Francis company ordered from Leith-fort, fixed at Island Bridge [May, 1817]. He and I much occupied about Alex[r] but no answer from Lord Killmorey or Lord Castlereagh.

[October] The fever again attacked us brought by M[r] Hopkins who as well as several others severely attacked Francis in England trying to see Lord Castlereagh about Alex[r].

[November and December] Mary Anne and Charlotte weak and sickly after the fever.

In Feb 1818 I received by a letter from himself of 24 Oct 1817 the most unexpected intelligence that my eldest Son William [356] is still alive and residing though not in flourishing circumstances in the State of Tenessee. Through our former neighbour the Rev James McMechan William obtained news of me. His letter mentions that my aged Father was still alive in 1817.

[September 16] Charles and his wife Sophia Cauty whom he married at S[t] Helena reached Weymouth poor Charles in bad health.

[October] Charles and Sophy in London Francis at home making out a Memorial for my resignation.

[November] Lord Killmorey died just as I was about to resign; I have therefore great reason to be thankful to God for his mercy as I do not know what his successor will do.

[January 1819] Charles & Sophy came over from Carmarthen and have taken a lodging at Rosstrevor to which place Mary Anne & Charlotte are gone hoping the change of air will do them good:

---

[354] Leith, Scotland

[355] Captain John Hopkins (see p 39, n 274)

[356] William, only son of Alexander Chesney and his first wife, Margaret Hodge (see p 20) Alexander Chesney in his will of 1813 recommended his son, William in America, to the humanity of the British Government, as he was left without parents or support in infancy by the Revolutionary war, and hoped that the Government, to whom he (Alexander Chesney) had rendered many services during that war, would be pleased to continue his pension of £30 as a loyalist to his said son, William.

busy sending estimates to get the house raised in order to make more room.

[March] All came home.

[April] Francis went to Scotland

[June] began to unroof the house   Charles and Charlotte in Roscommon   Sophy at Strangford.

[July 12th] Busy at the house.

Charles Crafer came over for a few days & goes to Scotland with Francis Charles and Sophy.

[September] Charlotte married to George W. Bell [357] at Castlerea.[358]   Busy with the house and applying to Lord Killmorey for Alexr   no great hopes.

[November and December] Busy about smuggling, the House finished all tolerably well.   In the latter end of this year Mr Hayden [359] lost his curacy in Co Roscommon, and as he could not get another he & family came to live with me.

In January of this year [1820] Peter West a walking Officer of Newry and sent some time ago with a party to Kilkeel made a complaint against me for dereliction and neglect of duty in which charge he was strongly supported by Mr Thompson Collector of Newry who after a partial enquiry made a strong report against me; But on my requesting for a rehearing of the case a Surveyor General (Major Crampton)[360] was sent down to investigate   The consequence was that Mr Thompson was obliged to acknowledge the inaccuracy of his report and acquiece in Mr Cramptons which was very strongly in my favour—The business ended in Board's approval of my conduct.

Owing to the peace the smuggling of Tobacco into Ireland is increasing to a very considerable extent; tho' from my exertions and the number of persons I have employed it is considerably checked in Mourne.

---

[357] Charlotte, fourth daughter of Alexander Chesney and his second wife, married George Washington Bell, a surgeon, and died at "Pacholet," 27 April, 1857, aged 62

[358] Castlerea, county Roscommon

[359] Rev Henry Hayden (see p 54)

[360] John Crampton, surveyor-general of the Customs in Ireland   His report of his exhaustive investigation into Chesney's alleged negligence not only exonerates Chesney from all blame but adds that it was with infinite satisfaction that during a service of 35 years in the Revenue, perhaps unparalled in activity, no sensible grounds of belief in the rumors concerning Alexander Chesney could be found   This report, dated 18 March 1820, was supported by the board of Irish Customs, which completely cleared him of every imputation of neglect of duty (Minute Book of the Irish board of Customs, Vol 427, pp 34-35, in the Public Record Office, London)

In consequence of my so frequently foiling the smugglers in their attempts; I find them extremely irritated and consequently have had many quarrels with them.

From the serious falling off in the import duties and the well known increase of smuggling the Government seem determined to put an effectual stop to smuggling in this country for that purpose (in the summer) the Lords of the Treasury directed Lieu^t James Dombrain R N Inspector General of the Preventive Water Guard to survey the Irish Channel for the purpose of establishing a Preventive force: Previous to M^r D's surveying the coast   the Board of Customs directed all their Officers to give him every assistance & information in their power—Consequently I made a general statement of the extent and nature of smuggling, and a proposed plan for its abolition on the Mourne coast.   In July Mr Dombrain arrived and I handed it to him for which he was obliged and I have since reason to know it was of essential use to him.

Some time in the Spring Mr Hayden received an appointment as Church Missionary in New Brunswick and in the latter end of Summer he went out from Portaferry to S John's N: B: in the Brig Dorcas   Savage Andrew Pollock   Master.

In the latter end of the year [1820] I ascertained that on the establishment of the Water Guard this establishment would be done away with and that I would be turned out of the Revenue House I occupy; I therefore began to make arrangements for building on my farm in Ballyardle.

Francis at home during a great part of the Year.

During the year made considerable seizures for which I received a good deal of money.

My Son William has been authorised to draw on Mr Crafer. I mean to give him a child's portion of what I have, and it is obviously better that he should receive this and turn it to account where he is rather than spend money in coming hither where he would find most things unsuited.

ADDITIONAL NOTES

ADDITIONAL NOTES

Lord Charles Greville Montagu

Lord Charles Greville Montagu, second son of Robert, third duke of Manchester, was appointed governor of South Carolina in 1766 While in the enjoyment of that office he acquired extensive tracts of land in that Province, amounting to 18,138 acres, of which a detailed list has been preserved. (A.O. 13/133.) Of this land he sold 7,198 acres for £3,331.12 4, the purchasers' names being recorded in the list just mentioned.   The large sum of £36,830. 10s. was claimed after his death by his brother, the fourth duke, for compensation for the loss of these lands in South Carolina, but the commissioners of American Claims in London rejected the claim because of the absence of satisfactory proof of loss by confiscation by the State of South Carolina or by other causes. (A.O. 12/109.)

In 1780, Lord Charles Greville Montagu, although no longer officially connected with South Carolina, prepared a scheme for raising a regiment of 500 men in that Province, for service in the Revolutionary war. The scheme was not, however, accepted until 1782, when he was appointed to the command, with the rank of lieutenant-colonel. The regiment, which was called the Duke of Cumberland's (and also the Loyal American Rangers), was destined for service in the West Indies. A second battalion was, in December, 1782, authorized to be raised, and Lord Charles G. Montagu proceeded from Jamaica for that purpose. (Hist. MSS. Comm. *Report on the American MSS. in the Royal Inst.* Vol. II. pp 209, 245; Vol. III pp. 108, 273; Vol. IV. p. 79.) A list of the officers at the end of the war is in the Public Record Office. (Ind. 5606.)   At the end of the year 1783 Lord Charles G. Montagu set sail with over 300 men of his regiment from Jamaica for Halifax, Nova Scotia, where the men proposed to settle. Here he died, 3 February, 1784, at the age of 45, and was buried in the historic church of St. Paul's, Halifax, where many American loyalists have worshiped and have been buried. The inscription on his monument in the church states that he was employed in settling in Nova Scotia a brave corps of Carolinians whom he had commanded during the late war between Great Britain and Spain (*Acadiensis*, Vol. 5, pp. 81-82). By his will, Lord Charles Greville Montagu bequeathed the two brigs, *Montagu* and

Industry, to his son and daughter, and made bequests to these four officers of his regiment: Lieutenants Angus McDonald and Brian Meighan (or Meighlan), Ensign Robert Barrett, and Thomas Caldwell. A clause in the will directs that the command of the three divisions of the Duke of Cumberland's regiment should devolve on the above Lieutenant Brian Meighan, Ensign Robert Barrett, and one Cunningham, who may have been Captain Andrew Cunningham or Captain Ralph Gore Cunningham, both of whom were on the half-pay list of the regiment.

Lord Charles Greville Montagu was on terms of friendship with General Moultrie, to whom he offered the command of his own regiment if he would accompany him to Jamaica, when Moultrie was a prisoner on parole (Moultrie, *Memoirs,* Vol II, pp. 158, 166-7, E. McCrady, *Hist. of S. Carolina in the Revolution, 1780-1783,* pp. 350-354.

COLONEL JOHN PHILLIPS

John Phillips emigrated with his wife and seven children from Ulster to South Carolina in 1770 and settled at Jackson's creek in Camden district.

The first manifestation of his loyalty was in July, 1775, when he prevented by his influence at a meeting held at the meeting house in his district all the people except two from signing the association to support the American cause. In the same year he refused an offer of a commission as lieutenant-colonel in the American militia. *(The Royal Comm. on Loyalist Claims, 1783-1785,* ed. by H. E. Egerton; Roxburghe Club, 1915, pp. 48-9.) From this time John Phillips was a marked man and suffered imprisonment for his attachment to the crown. Two sons were also imprisoned for loyalty, one of whom died in the jail at Orangeburg.

In 1780 when Lord Cornwallis inaugurated the loyal militia in South Carolina, Phillips was one of the first officers selected and was given the command of the Jackson's creek militia, with the rank of lieutenant-colonel. His two sons, just mentioned, and a brother, Robert, joined his regiment.

Shortly after Tarleton's defeat at Cowpens on January 17, 1781, Colonel Phillips and a party under the command of Lieutenant-Colonel John Fanning were detached from the main force to escort to Camden the British officers who had been wounded in that battle. Four days later, however, this party was surrounded by a superior force of Americans, which outnumbered the loyalists by four to one, and in the skirmish several of the loyalists were killed or wounded, Colonel Phillips, with his son David, and his brother, Robert, being taken prisoners. In March of the same year Colonel Phillips was exchanged for Colonel David Hopkins and his brother (A.O. 13/133) was also exchanged and forthwith rejoined the loyalist forces.

This Irish loyalist was ordered by Lord Rawdon to accompany him to Charleston in August, 1781, when the command of his regiment devolved temporarily upon his son, David, who had the misfortune to be captured by Colonel Hampton and was "inhumanly murdered" by his captors. Soon afterwards, Colonel Phillips' wife and eight children were turned off his plantation and obliged to seek shelter in Charleston.

Colonel John Phillips received 150 acres of land on "Crocky creek," Catawba river, by the death of his widowed sister, Mary Dunsketh, in 1775, and of her only son in 1777.

Robert Phillips, his brother, first bore arms on the side of the Crown in 1775. He was banished from South Carolina and took refuge in East Florida, where Governor Patrick Tonyn appointed him lieutenant in the East Florida Rangers Anxious to see his family again, he resigned his commission in this corps and joined the force of Brigadier-General James Patteson, proceeding from Savannah to join Sir Henry Clinton at Charleston in March, 1780. On his arrival in South Carolina he joined his brother's regiment, the Jackson's creek militia, and was appointed lieutenant. The original petition of Robert Phillips bears his autograph signature; he died August 25, 1782, at Charleston. (T 50/2, fo. 85; T. 50/4; T. 50/5)

Captain James Phillips, mentioned on page 6, was another brother of Colonel John Phillips.

At one time in his military career Colonel Phillips was sentenced to be hanged for sedition and loyalty, and was defended at the trial by one Thomas Phepoe, an Irish lawyer who had emigrated in 1771 to Charleston, but was acquitted. (A O. 13/132.)

Colonel Phillips was given the appointment of muster-master of the loyal militia and refugees at Charleston in 1782, when the Americans had virtually overrun the Province of South Carolina and the loyalists had left their homes in large numbers without food or clothing and sought shelter at Charleston, taxing the resources of the British to provide them with the necessaries of life.

During this anxious time, the refugee hospital, crowded with unhappy loyalists, was in charge of **Dr. Charles Fyffe**, with **Dr. Nathaniel Bullein** as assistant surgeon. (T. 50/2; T. 50/4.) Some effort was made to provide the refugee children with education by a schoolmaster, one John Bell; some of these children's names have survived   (T. 50/5.)

The original memorial of Colonel John Phillips is endorsed by his fellow-countryman, Lord Rawdon, that no man in South Carolina had exerted himself more in his station for the support of government. (A.O. 13/79; *The Royal Comm. on Loyalist Claims, 1783-1785*, ed. by H. E. Egerton; Roxburghe Club, 1915, pp 48-9.) With this memorial are (1) a letter from Lord Cornwallis to the commissioners of American Claims, introducing his as "my friend Col. Phillips of South Carolina, who has as much merit as any man on the Continent of America, & whom I beg leave very particularly to recommend to your favor"; and (2) Colonel Nisbet Balfour's certificate of 1 July, 1782, that "in his rank of life I have known none more worthy of it [an allowance] or a family who have suffered more from their fidelity to their King and country." Colonel Balfour also gave evidence in person before the commissioners and spoke highly of the services of Colonel Phillips in procuring intelligence of enemy movements, describing him as "honest and humane," and adding that he "never knew an instance of any of his reports which did not prove strictly true" Lords Cornwallis and Rawdon also gave personal evidence in support of the claim of Colonel John Phillips and expressed their appreciation of his services in the war, concluding with the testimony that they were more obliged to him than to any other person in his district in South Carolina.

Colonel John Phillips died in the country of his birth in 1809, and in his will, dated 4 May, 1807, he is described as of Ballyloughan in the parish of Ahogill, county Antrim. In this will are mentioned his wife, Elizabeth, otherwise Lurkan; two daughters, Rachel and Mary Phillips; and four granddaughters, Lilly and Ann McCrearys, Rachel Phillips and Lilly Jean Kirk. To his son, Robert, "if he comes home" (being presumably in America) he bequeathed his watch. His executors were Captain James Miller (see page 100), his daughter, Rachel Phillips, and Thomas Phillips of Ballyloughan.

Jane, mother of Colonel John Phillips, was a close family connection of the Chesneys

The sum of £860 was granted to Colonel Phillips by the British Government as compensation for the loss of his property in South Carolina from his claim of £1,874 He also received a pension of £84 from 1784 until his death. (A.O. 12/109; A.O. 463/24; T. 50/8; A.O. 12/46, fos. 171-184; A.O. 12/101, fo. 283; A.O. 13/133.)

INDIANS IN THE WAR

Both sides in the American Revolutionary war in the Southern Colonies attempted to secure the support of the Indians

The attention of the Colonial Congress was very early drawn to the importance of securing the alliance, or at least the neutrality, of the Indian tribes during the conflict. (E. B. O'Callaghan, *Documents relating to the Colonial History of New York*, Vol. VIII. p. 605.)

Colonel Thomas Fletchall, the loyalist, fearing an incursion by the Indians into his district in South Carolina, recommended the governor, Lord William Campbell, by letter of 19 July, 1775, to protect the frontiers against them It was perhaps to this letter that the governor replied, ordering Colonel Fletchall to hold himself and his militia in readiness to suppress any opposition to Government, and if necessary to seek assistance from Alexander Cameron, deputy superintendent of the Creek and Cherokee Indians (Hist. MSS. Comm. *Report on the MSS. of the Earl of Dartmouth*, Vol. II. p. 355.)

The powerful influence of Cameron with the Indians was recognized by the Council of Safety of South Carolina, who in 1775 offered him many inducements to join the Americans. (Sabine, *Loyalists of the American Revolution*, Vol I, p 287). It was probably after this failure to secure Cameron's influence that William Henry Drayton held his conference with the chief of the Cherokees on 25 September, 1775, when he attempted to wean them from their loyalty by promising them supplies of ammunition and other gifts, both for trade and their personal comfort, as he naively describes it. (Drayton, *Memoirs of the Revolution*, Vol. I, pp. 407-8.) Drayton at this conference pictured the future condition of the Indians under royal Government in the most lurid colors, accusing the king and the English of claiming to make laws by which they would "have a right to take all our money, all our lands, all our cattle and horses and such things, and not only all such things, but our wives and children, in order to make servants of them; and beside all these things, to put us in strong houses, and to put us to death, whenever they please." (Drayton, *ibid.*, p. 421.) Drayton had taken with him a man of great influence and popularity among the Cherokees, the father of a natural son by a Cherokee squaw, in the person of Richard Pearis, a considerable trader among them, who was afterwards the chief witness against Drayton's denial of his intention to persuade the Indians to fight against the loyalists.

A vain attempt was made in October, 1775, to rescue Captain Robert Cunningham (atferwards a brigadier-general) from the hands of his captors by a party of loyalists commanded by his brother, Captain Patrick Cunningham (see page 104). The party was, however, compenscated in some measure for this failure by their seizure of the ammunition destined for the Indians, mentioned above. (Drayton, *ibid.*, pp. 64, 66-7.) The Provincial Congress resolved, 8 November, 1775, by 51 votes to 49, to assemble a force under the command of Colonel Richard Richardson to seize Captain Patrick Cunningham and the other leading loyalists of that party, Henry O'Neal, Hugh Brown, David Reese, Henry Green, Nathaniel Howard, and Jacob Bochman. (E. McCrady, *The Hist. of South Carolina in the Revolution, 1775-1780*, p. 88.)

It is stated that Richard Pearis was so disappointed in failing to receive the military command to which he is said to have aspired that, in a spirit of malice and vengeance, he had spread a false report abroad among the loyalists of Drayton's intention to employ the Indians in fighting against them. Pearis went so far as to make a solemn affidavit accusing Drayton of endeavoring to persuade the Indians for this purpose. (Drayton, *ibid.*, pp. 116-7) Drayton's denial of such intention has been published. (Journal of the Council of Safety, 6 December, 1775, in *Collections of the South Carolina Hist. Society.*, Vol. III. pp. 55-6; see also Force, *American Archives*, Series IV., Vol. 4, p. 29).

A loyalist version of Drayton's transaction of the gift of ammunition to the Cherokees is furnished by Colonel David Fanning, at that time a sergeant in the loyal militia of South Carolina. He asserts that it was the intention of Drayton that Pearis should bring down the Indians to murder the loyalists, and that when captured, Pearis confessed his guilt to the charge of attempting to engage the Indians for that purpose (Colonel David Fanning, "Narrative," ed. by A. W. Savary, in the *Canadian Magazine*, 1908.)

Reference is made elsewhere to the allegiation that the fear of the loyalists of an attack by the Indians at the instigation of Drayton's party was largely responsible for the conflict at Ninety-Six in November, 1775. (Page 63.)

In the summer of 1776, Major Andrew Williamson organized an expedition against the Cherokees, in the belief that they had been encouraged to hostility by Colonel John Stuart, superintendent of the Indians, and by his deputy, Alexander Cameron. Several loyalists, including Alexander Cheseny, Colonels John Phillips and Ambrose Mills, joined this expedition, whether in ignorance of this rumor or in the expectation of an attack on the white inhabitants in general, it is impossible to hazard an opinion. Chesney himself offers no reason for joining Williamson, except that he had no objection to fighting against the Indians. It must, however, be remembered that he was at this time a conscript in the American forces

By November, 1777, the revolutionists in Georgia had already seduced the northern Creek Indians from their allegiance to England, and were now, through the agency of Galphin, threatening the Cherokees with destruction for their attachment to Great Britain. (W. H. Siebert, "The Loyalists in West Florida and the Natchez District," in *The Mississippi Valley Historical Review*, 1916, Vol. II, p. 467.)

Later attempts were made by the British to encourage the support of the Indians. Lord Cornwallis, writing to Sir Henry Clinton under date of 29 December, 1780, says that when the men from the mountains had come down to attack Major Patrick Ferguson he directed Lieutenant-Colonel Thomas Brown to encourage the Indians to attack the settlements of "Watogea, Holstein, Caentuck and Nolachuckie, all which are now encroachments on the Indian territories." The mountaineers, fearing an attack, were obliged to abandon their projected march to join an American force near King's Mountain. A report seems to have reached Lord Cornwallis that the humanity of the Indians was in "striking contrast to the barbarities committed by the mountaineers." (Hist. MSS. Comm., *Report on the American MSS. in the Royal Institution*, Vol. II., p. 225.)

Moultrie in his *Memoirs* mentions the efforts made to secure the services of the warriors of the Catawba Indians on the side of the Americans. (Vol I. p 81.)

The activities of the Indians in South Carolina had virtually come to an end early in January, 1782, when Benjamin Thompson, better known later as Count Rumford (the Massachusetts loyalist), wrote that very little was to be expected from the Indians as friends and that as foes they would not be by any means formidable. (Hist MSS. Comm , *Report on the Stopford-Sackville MSS.*, Vol. II. p. 251.)

Both Burke and Lord Chatham condemned the employment of Indians in the war by the British.

Colonel Thomas Fletchall

Colonel Thomas Fletchall was probably born in South Carolina, where he was the owner of a large plantation in the district of Ninety-Six. He was already a justice of the peace and a coroner when in the year 1769 he accepted the appointment of colonel of a militia regiment of over 2,000 men, from the governor, Lord Charles Greville Montagu.

Sabine in his *Loyalists of the American Revolution* states that Colonel Fletchall was of much consideration in the Colony before the war and that he was regarded as undecided in his political views, though the Whig party made him a member of an important committee, raised to carry out the views of the Continental Congress (Moultrie, *Memoirs*, Vol. I.). Colonel Fletchall, however, describes himself as a loyalist from the outbreak of the Revolutionary troubles in South Carolina, a description which is confirmed by his letter of 19 July, 1775, to Lord William Campbell, the governor, assuring him of the loyalty of about 4000 men in his district   In this letter Colonel Fletchall informs the governor of the seizure of Fort Charlotte on the Savannah river by the "rebels," as he calls them, Major James Mayson, Captain John Caldwell and others, and of the subsequent capture of the leaders by the loyalists. In this same letter he suggests that the frontiers should be protected from incursions not only from the "rebels" but also from the Indians, thus anticipating William Henry Drayton's alleged attempt to secure the services of the Cherokee Indians for the Revolutionary party (see page 64). This letter brought forth a reply, 1 August following, expressing the governor's appreciation of the capture of the rebels at Fort Charlotte, authorizing Fletchall to fortify that fort by militia and requesting him to avoid giving offence to the inhabitants of his district and generally to preserve peace (Hist. MSS.

Comm., *Report on the MSS. of the Earl of Dartmouth*, Vol. II., p. 355). The seizure of Fort Charlotte by order of the Council of Safety, on 12 July, 1775, was the first overt act in the Revolutionary war in South Carolina. An important omission from Colonel Fletchall's letter was that one of the officers who had participated in this seizure was Captain Moses Kirkland, who was soon to turn over to the loyalist side (see page 105). While alluding in this letter to the capture of Major Mayson and others, who had proceeded with the powder and stores from Fort Charlotte to Ninety-Six Court House, he concealed the fact that Kirkland, who is stated to have had an old grudge against Mayson, had now joined Colonel Fletchall and had disclosed a scheme for capturing Mayson and the stores. Fletchall, on the authority of an enemy (Drayton, *Memoirs*, Vol. I, pp. 321-3) is said to have declined to appear publicly as a supporter of Kirkland's scheme, but those more active loyalists, Robert and Patrick Cunningham and Joseph Robinson, joined by Major Terry (a deserter from the Revolutionary party who afterwards recanted and became animated in the American cause, *ibid*, p. 384), rode off with 200 mounted men to Ninety-Six. Here they took Major Mayson prisoner on 17 July and committed him to jail on a charge of robbing the king's fort, but after some hours confinement admitted him to bail.

Colonel Thomas Fletchall claims, in support of his loyalty, to have impeded with the help of Robert Cunningham and Joseph Robinson, the raising of the levies of American horse in the back country of South Carolina and to have influenced many waverers against signing the association of the Revolutionary party. The articles of this association were read, 13 July, 1775, by Major Terry at Fletchall's plantation to the men of his regiment by his orders, but not one would sign it, a decision of which he approved. His men then agreed to sign an association of their own, expressing loyalty to the king, which had been drawn up by Major Joseph Robinson, and which was generally signed from Broad to Savannah rivers. (Drayton, *Memoirs*, Vol. 1, p. 312; Hist. Mss. Comm *Report on the MSS. of the Earl of Dartmouth*, Vol. II, pp 341, 351.)

At this psychological moment Lord William Campbell, the governor, had he been a man of greater initiative and of a more adventurous spirit, would have seized the opportunity to support Colonel Fletchall and the loyalists, by his personal presence among them. The exercise of his high position and influence would have assured the raising of a strong armed force, which he could have employed in what would probably have been the overthrow of the proceedings of the Provincial Congress (E. McCrady, *The Hist. of South Carolina in the Revolution, 1775-1780*, pp. 38-39).

Colonel Thomas Fletchall came into conflict with two ardent spirits of the Revolutionary party on 17 August, 1775, in the persons of William Henry Drayton and Rev. William Tennent, the Congregational minister and member of the committee of the Provincial Congress, who in private conversation with him for nearly three hours, humored him, laughed with him, remonstrated and entreated him to join his country, America, against the mother country, without shaking his loyalty in the slightest. The entreaties of Drayton and Tennent were met by this influential loyalist with the answer that he "would never take up arms against his King or his countrymen and that the proceedings of the Congress at Philadelphia were impolitic, disrespectful and irritating to the King." (*Ibid*, pp. 44-46, Force, *American Archives*, Series IV, Vol. II, pp. 214-217.)

Drayton, having failed to win Fletchall over to his side, proceeded to march out in the following month at the head of about 400 mounted men and 800 foot to disarm the loyalists of Ninety-Six district, especially those in Fletchall's regiment. Colonel Fletchall met this threat by ordering out his regiment and marching to meet Drayton, who on the 11th. had written somewhat confidently to the Council of Safety that Colonel Fletchall, Colonel Thomas Brown, and Captain Robert Cunningham were still endeavoring to assemble men, but had no force embodied, and assuring the Council of the declining political influence of these three prominent loyalists and of the terrified state of their adherents, adding that they had no intention to fight in view of the expected help promised them by the governor (Drayton, *Memoirs*, Vol 1, p. 388) Drayton, however, in his letter of the 17 September, in a less confident tone, estimates Fletchall's force at over 1200, while his own barely reached 1000, which is 200 less than Fletchall's figure for Drayton's force. In this letter Drayton alleges that while his own men were anxious to fight, he wished to avoid bloodshed, insinuating that the loyalists would not hold long together because of their lack of discipline and of supplies. (*Ibid.*, p. 389.) A different version comes from a loyalist source, David Fanning, who maintains that the "rebels," finding themselves not strong enough for an attack, sent an express to

Fletchall, inviting him to treat with them. (Colonel David Fanning, "Narrative," ed by A. W. Savary, *Canadian Magazine*, 1908) This version is supported by Fletchall's unpublished memorial, in which he says that on advancing within six miles of Drayton's camp, determined to support Government, Drayton offered terms of accomodation (A O. 12/52, fos. 127-141.) A treaty was now made by which hostilities between the two parties should be avoided, Fletchall stating that each party agreed to return home and "remain peaceable." This treaty was signed, 16 September, 1775, by Drayton of the one part and by Fletchall, Captains John Ford, Evan McLaurin, Thomas Greer, and Benjamin Wofford of the other part. (Drayton, *Memoirs*, Vol. I , pp. 399-403; Force, *American Archives*, Series IV, Vol 3, pp. 720-1.)

Captain (afterwards Brigadier-General) Robert Cunningham declined in his letter of 6 October to Drayton, in the most vigorous terms to be bound by this treaty, which he characterized as false and disgraceful and as having been devised to take advantage of men "half scared out of their senses at the sight of liberty caps and sound of cannon" (Force, *American Archives*, Series IV, Vol 3, p. 755). Cunningham's repudiation of a treaty, made in his opinion without authority, and his determination not to disband his men, was supported by other stalwart loyalists. (McCrady, *The Hist. of South Carolina in the Revolution, 1775-1780*, pp 51-52.)

Colonel Thomas Fletchall carried out the terms of the treaty both in the letter and the spirit and forthwith disbanded his regiment, while Drayton and his followers tacitly ignored it. To Fletchall's chagrin, information reached him in November, within a few weeks of making the treaty, that the "rebels" had been re-armed. He instantly embodied his regiment on the 17th and ordered an attack to be made on the fort of Ninety-Six Meanwhile, Captain Robert Cunningham was arrested by a party disguised as Indians, under orders from Major Andrew Williamson upon an affidavit of Captain John Caldwell, charging him with sedition, and was committed to Charleston jail, 1 November As an uncompromising loyalist, Cunningham did not deny the use of the seditious words, but though he did not consider himself bound by the Fletchall-Drayton treaty, he had since behaved himself as peaceably as any man. He had, however, retained his political opinions, though he had not expressed them unless asked to do so. (McCrady, *ibid.*, p. 86).

Colonel Fletchall's militia force, numbering 2400, now besieged the fort, in accordance with orders mentioned above. The command of the loyalists had been given to Major Joseph Robinson by Fletchall, who was too heavy in weight for active service (Fanning, "Narrative"), while the defenders to the number of 562 were commanded by Majors Andrew Williamson and James Mayson. On the second day of the siege, which lasted from the 18th to the 21st. of November, the loyalists, represented by Majors Joseph Robinson and Evan McLaurin and Captain Patrick Cunningham, had a conference with Major Mayson and Captain Bowie regarding the loyalists' demand for the surrender of Williamson and his force. While Williamson was considering this demand, two of his men are said to have been seized and the attempt to rescue them brought about the first bloodshed of the revolutionary war On the 20th, however, the ammunition of both sides was almost exhausted and by agreement hostilities ceased for twenty days (Drayton, *Memoirs*, Vol II, pp. 117-122; Force, *American Archives*, Series IV, Vol. 3, p. 1606; Vol. 4, p. 216), while the messengers of each party were allowed to proceed to Charleston to inform the governor and the Council of Safety of the terms of the treaty. Major Robinson's loyalist force was allowed to return home. The signatories to this treaty were Majors Andrew Williamson, James Mayson, and Joseph Robinson, Captains Patrick Cunningham, Richard Pearis, Joseph Pickens, and John Bowie. (A. S Salley, Jr., *Hist. of Orangeburg County*, 1898, pp. 308-312.)

Thus ended the inglorious siege and conflict of Ninety-Six, a conflict largely brought on by the fear of the loyalists that the Indians were about to attack them at the instigation of the Americans. (McCrady, *The Hist. of South Carolina in the Revolution, 1775-1780*, pp 90-93.) The loyalists were without a capable leader. Robinson, the nominal commander, appears to have been ignored and the virtual command devolved upon Pearis, who declared his opposition to making the treaty, though it bears his signature.

For the second time the Revolutionary party violated a solemn treaty by the refusal of Colonel Richard Richardson and his army to be bound by it, despite the stipulation of Majors Williamson and Mayson that any reinforcements which might arrive should regard the treaty as binding equally upon them. Richardson, under the government presided over by Drayton, disregarded the treaty and marched upon the loyalists, who on the faith of this same solemn covenant had been disbanded. Colonel Fletchall, despite the suspicion of his secret encouragement of further military activity by the loyalists, was scrupuously observing the treaty, and to his astonishment and mortification, he was taken prisoner, 12 December, with other loyalists of the "first magnitude," including Captains Richard Pearis, Jacob Fry, and George Shuberg, who were sent to Charleston four days later. (McCrady, *ibid.*, pp. 89-96; Salley, *ibid.*, p. 323). Drayton, in commenting on the capture of these loyalists, avoids any reference to the violation of the treaty and stigmatizes Fletchall's capture as dishonorable to his military talents, concealing the fact that Fletchall had returned to his plantation and discharged his force, in agreement with the spirit of the treaty, while Colonel Richardson now had an army of about 3000 men (Drayton, *ibid.*, Vol. II, p 129) Colonel Thomas Fletchall's capture was accomplished at his own house, which was surrounded by 400 mounted men detached from Richardson's main body. He was sent as a prisoner to Charleston and there kept in close confinement until 10 July, 1776, when he appears to have set forth for his plantation which had in the meantime been plundered and ruined. Nothing more is recorded of any further military service by Colonel Fletchall. The corpulence for which he was conspicuous as well as his age, may have been a deterrent factor. In July, 1780, he was visited at his old home by the well-known loyalist, Lieutenant Anthony Allaire, who records in his Diary his interesting examination of the Fletchall mill, a curiosity such as he had never seen before. ("Diary," in Draper's *King's Mountain and its Heroes*). The worthy colonel was not allowed to remain at home in tranquility, for on 10 October in the same year he was obliged to escape, with his wife, Leah, and five children, from threatened violence and to seek sanctuary at Charleston, then in possession of the British. Here they remained until 1 December, when at the age of 62 he left South Carolina for ever, accompanied by his wife, two sons and two daughters, in the transport, *Milford* (John May, master), for the West Indies, where he settled on the land of Ralph Montagu in the parish of St. James in Cornwall county, Jamaica. Here also settled two other loyalist refugees from South Carolina, namely, Colonel Thomas Edghill and Lieutenant-Colonel James Vernon (see pages 78-9). Mrs. Fletchall's sister, Anne Brown, was the second wife of Colonel Ambrose Mills, of North Carolina (see page 72).

A long list of the debtors of Colonel Thomas Fletchall in South Carolina and a list of the grants of land made to him there are in the Public Record Office. (A. O. 13/128).

In July, 1787, Colonel Fletchall was proposing to make the voyage to England to prosecute his claim on the British Government for compensation for the loss of his property in South Carolina, but was prevented by illness from leaving Jamaica His claim of £2,181 was met by a grant of £1,400 (A O. 12/109). Colonel Fletchall died in 1789, apparently in Jamaica, leaving a widow Leah Joseph Fletchall, a planter, of St James's parish, Jamaica, who had lived from infancy in the district of Ninety-Six in South Carolina, was probably his son (A.O. 12/52, fos. 127-141; A O. 13/128; *South Carolina Hist and Gen Mag*, Vol XVIII, pp 44-51).

COLONEL AMBROSE MILLS

Born in England in 1722, Ambrose Mills was taken in childhood to Maryland There he married Mourning Stone, a spinster, and settled on James river in Virginia, afterwards removing to the frontiers of South Carolina, where his wife was killed by Indians in the Indian risings of 1755-61. Ambrose Mills married (II), Anne Brown, a sister of Leah Fletchall, wife of Colonel Thomas Fletchall (see page 71). In or about 1765 he settled on Green river, North Carolina The issue of his first marriage was a son, William, born 10 November, 1746, and by his second marriage, three sons and three daughters.

The military services of Ambrose Mills during the Revolutionary war include actions against the Cherokee Indians in 1776, in ignorance of the alleged alliance between the Cherokees and the British, an ignorance which was shared with the loyalists, Colonel John Phillips (see p 65) and Alexander Chesney. In 1778, Ambrose Mills and Colonel David Fanning raised a corps of 500 loyalists for the purpose of joining the royal standard at St Augustine in East Florida, but this scheme was frustrated by the treachery of a traitor in the camp betraying their plans to the enemy Colonel Mills and sixteen others were apprehended and taken to Salisbury jail. On the way thither, David Fanning with characteristic courage endeavored to rescue his brother loyalist, but his small force was too weak to break through the American guard

One of the first engagements of Colonel Ambrose Mills after his liberation was the action at Baylis Earle's ford on the North

Pacolet river, North Carolina, when he surprised and attacked the American camp of Colonel Charles McDowell on the night of 15 July, 1780. In this action the loyalists under Mills, and Major James Dunlap's party of seventy dragoons, killed Noah Hampton, son of Colonel Hampton, and wounded Colonel John Jones of Burke county, North Carolina—an attack which was revenged later by Captain Edward Hampton's exploit in overtaking Dunlap's party and inflicting defeat upon it. Draper, in his *King's Mountain and its Heroes*, is very severe in his condemnation of the killing of Noah Hampton by Dunlap while he was asleep, an act which he rightly regards as murder, though a precisely similar surprise, achieved by the deception of Colonel John Jones, is regarded as almost heroic. (*Op. cit*, p 79). Major Dunlap, who had been appointed an officer in the Queen's Rangers in 1776, and was one of the most adventurous spirits among the loyalists, neither giving nor expecting quarter, was killed on or about 25 March, 1781, by his guard after his surrender at Beattie's mill on Little river in South Carolina. General Pickens offered a "handsome reward for the murderers" (Draper, *op. cit*, pp 163-4). The feud between Colonel John Jones and the loyalists had become exceedingly bitter after his deception in palming himself off as a loyalist and thereby gaining entrance into a loyalist camp, with the object as he had averred of taking revenge on some "rebels" who had slain loyalists in a recent skirmish Arriving at the camp, which was in a state of self-security and the loyalists mostly asleep, Colonel Jones ordered an attack by his party and killed one and wounded three. (Draper, *op cit.*, p. 79).

Returning to the career of Colonel Ambrose Mills, he commanded the North Carolina loyal militia in the memorable battle of King's Mountain and was taken prisoner. The subsequent severity of his treatment as a prisoner and his execution has been the subject of hostile criticism (Draper, *op. cit.* p 82) Lord Cornwallis in his protest against his execution describes him as "always a fair and open enemy," a verdict which was endorsed by his opponents (*Correspondence of Lord Cornwallis*, Vol. I, p. 67). Early in the military life of Colonel Ambrose Mills, Lord Cornwallis had experienced some difficulty in restraining his ardor, and in complaining of his premature activities, desired him to act only on the defensive until ordered to act otherwise. (*Ibid., op. cit.*, p. 47.)

William Mills, his son, was very popular, and was engaged with his father in the campaign against the Cherokee Indians, and at King's Mountain, where he was severely wounded, he acted as major under his father. He died in North Carolina, 10 November, 1834, aged 88.

Colonel Ambrose Mills has been confused with Colonel William Henry Mills, an Irishman who had gone out to America as a surgeon's mate in the British army. Here he served until 1764, when he retired from his military duties and settled in South Carolina, marrying two years later an American lady at Georgetown in that Province. Early in the Revolutionary war, Colonel William Henry Mills served in the South Carolina Provincial Congress, but in June, 1778, he was appointed colonel of the Cheraws loyal militia. He died at Liverpool, England, 7 May, 1786, leaving a widow, Elizabeth, and one daughter. (A O. 12/52, fos. 45-46, 327-340; Stedman, *American War*, Vol. II, p. 223, Tarleton, *Hist of the Campaigns of 1780 and 1781*, p. 127; Draper, *King's Mountain and its Heroes*, p. 373; B. F. Stevens, *Clinton-Cornwallis Controversy*, Vol. II, pp. 236-7).

LIEUTENANT-COLONEL JOSEPH ROBINSON

Joseph Robinson, a Virginian by birth, was settled on a plantation on Broad river in South Carolina, where he was deputy surveyor.

In 1775 he was appointed major of militia and, 18 November of that year, he was in command of 2400 loyalists at Ninety-Six when he surrounded an American force under Majors Andrew Williamson and James Mayson. This inglorious affair ended by the offer by Robinson of a cessation of hostilities for twenty days—an offer which was joyfully accepted by Williamson and Mayson, whose force had nearly expended their ammunition. A party to this treaty was Lieutenant-Colonel Evan McLaurin (see pp 69, 102).

Colonel Robinson's men were afterwards allowed to return home, while he himself went among the friendly Cherokee Indians. In his absence his plantation was plundered, his house and buildings burnt, and his family driven from home by the Americans. Among his possessions destroyed was his valuable library, which included 60 books on law, the destruction being witnessed by Moses Whealley, a loyalist

In her petition of October 1, 1816, to Viscount Palmerston, secretary of state for war, his wife, Lilley Robinson (whom he had married in 1760 in Virginia) states that while a prisoner in the hands of the Americans in 1776, she was promised restoration to her husband on condition that he consented to be neutral in the war. Her answer is not recorded, but she was released in a few days. Lilley Robinson proceeded, not to join her husband, but to start on a painful journey of 300 miles, accompanied by her two small children, to her father's family in Virginia, traveling mostly by night to escape the vigilance of American scouting parties and enduring indescribable sufferings. (W. O. 42/R8).

In May, 1778, Colonel Robinson was appointed lieutenant-colonel of the South Carolina Royalists, and in July it was decided that this corps should consist of eight companies of 50 rank and file each. With this regiment he was present at the battle of Stono, 12 June, 1779.

Mrs. Lilley Robinson, who had returned to South Carolina from Virginia, accompanied her husband on the evacuation of Charleston by the British, to East Florida, where they intended to settle, only to find shortly after their arrival that the Colony had been ceded to Spain and that they would be included in the 10,000 loyalists in that Province who suffered privations in consequence of its cession. (Hist. MSS. Comm., *Report on the American MSS in the Royal Institution,* Vol IV, p. 348.) The harrassed Robinson family, in common with many others from the Southern Colonies, now sought refugee in the West Indies, but once again they were dogged by misfortune, their ship having been wrecked off the coast of Florida. Eventually, however, Colonel Joseph Robinson and his family reached Jamaica, but after a year's sojourn there, they were compelled by the unhealthiness of the climate to seek a home in a northern clime. With this object in view, they now set sail for that asylum of so many American loyalists, New Brunswick, where they lived for three years until 1789, when Colonel Robinson was invited to settle at Charlottetown in Prince Edward Island by his friend, Colonel Edmund Fanning, lieutenant-governor of that island and formerly commanding officer of the loyalist corps, the King's American regiment.

Meanwhile, Colonel Robinson had been put on the list of seconded Provincial officers and received the half-pay of a lieutenant-colonel. He was also relieved of anxiety by the grant of £521 from his claim of £1,618. 10s. for the loss of his property in South Carolina and by his appointment as surrogate and judge of probate at Charlottetown. This South Carolina loyalist died in that city, 24 August, 1807, leaving a will (dated 19 July, 1807, and proved 10 November,) by which he bequeathed property to his widow, Lilley, and his three daughters. Lilley Robinson, widow of Colonel Joseph Robinson, died at Charlottetown, 11 July, 1823. Elizabeth, the eldest daughter born in New Brunswick in 1788, died unmarried. One daughter, Rebecca, married Robert Hodgson, lieutenant in the Prince Edward Island Fencibles (reduced in 1802), member of the Legislature and speaker until his death, 5 January, 1811, when he left four sons and one daughter Rebecca Hodgson died, 12 May, 1825, aged 54. Robert Hodgson, the eldest son of Robert and Rebecca Hodgson, became judge of probate, chief justice, and lieutenant-governor of Prince Edward Island, and died a knight at the age of 82, 16 September, 1880 The names of the other children of Robert and Rebecca Hodgson were: Joseph, Daniel, Christopher, and Jane Deborah

Matilda, third daughter of Colonel and Lilley Robinson, married Ralph Brecken in Prince Edward Island. A daughter of Ralph and Matilda Brecken married Donald Macdonald, president of the Legislative Council of Prince Edward Island, and a son of this marriage was Sir William Christopher Macdonald of Montreal, whose munificent gifts to McGill University and Macdonald College remain as monuments to his memory (A O. 13/92, A O 13/138; A O 12/109; Ind 5605; Hist MSS. Comm, *Report on the American MSS. in the Royal Institution*, Vol. II, pp 274, 276, 371; *Second Report of the Bureau of Archives, Province of Ontario*, 1905, pp 791-801; *The Royal Commission on Loyalist Claims, 1783-1785*, ed. by H E Egerton, Roxburghe Club, 1915, pp 272-3; notes from Judge Æneas Macdonald of Charlottetown)

GENERAL ANDREW WILLIAMSON

Andrew Williamson, then a major in the American service, received the thanks of the Provincial Congress of South Carolina for his services in causing the well-known loyalist, Robert Cunningham, to be apprehended and sent to Charleston He with Major James Mayson was in command of the American force at Ninety-Six in the siege of 18-21 November, 1775 (see pp. 70, 80). In 1776

Major Williamson was in command of the expedition against the Cherokee Indians. (See p. 7, n. 47).

Promotion came to this officer in 1778 when he was appointed brigadier-general of the Upper brigade of South Carolina militia, formed in that year.

According to Sabine (*Loyalists of the American Revolution*), Williamson changed sides during the war and was active on the side of the crown after the fall of Charleston in May, 1780. There is not, however, any foundation for the allegation of his martial activity for the British. Believing the American cause to be lost, he took protection from his enemies to save his large landed estates, just as loyalists had done on the other side He regarded himself as a faithful American and supplied General Greene with information of military value while he was inside the British lines.

By more than one historian he is described by the opprobrious epithet of the "Arnold of Carolina" and the "Southern Arnold" (Stevens, *History of Georgia*, Vol. II, p. 345). The actual capitulation of Williamson occurred at Ninety-Six, and was regarded by the British as a good omen. (Hist. MSS. Comm., *Report on the Stop-ford-Sackville MSS.*, Vol. II, p. 169; Bancroft, *Hist. of the United States*, Vol. V, p. 378).

James Simpson, the attorney-general for South Carolina, advised the protection of his considerable estates in order to secure his influence. (Hist. MSS. Comm., *Report on the American MSS. in the Royal Inst* , Vol. II, p. 150). One of the acts of infamy alleged against him was his advice to his officers when encamped near Augusta to return to their homes and accept royal protection, an act of treachery for which he is said to have been rewarded by a colonel's commission in the British service. (C. C. Jones, *Hist. of Georgia*, II, p. 448). General Williamson's name is included with those of General Isaac Huger, Colonels Andrew Pickens, Peter Horry, James Mayson, LeRoy Hammond, John Thomas, Sr., and Isaac Hayne, and Majors John Postell and John Purvis, in a list of American officers who unresistingly gave up their arms and took royal protection when detachments of the conquering British troops were sent among them (Draper, *King's Mountain and its Heroes*, p 47).

It is evident that the Revolutionary party regarded Williamson as a deserter or a renegade from the event of 5 July, 1781, when Colonel Hayne and his party surrounded his house near Charleston, seized him, and carried him away. The British thereupon sent Major Thomas Fraser and 90 dragoons of the South Carolina Royalists next day to rescue him. On the 8th. Fraser surprised Hayne's camp at Horse Shoe and killed fourteen of the party and wounded several others. Colonel Hayne was taken prisoner shortly afterwards by Captain Archibald Campbell, of the South Carolina Royalists, known as "Mad Archy." (E. McCrady, *Hist of South Carolina in the Revolution, 1780-1783,* pp 319-321.)

Although the belief was general in the report of General Williamson's acceptance of a commission in the British service, the present writer has failed in a diligent search among the loyalist documents to find any evidence of the grant of such a commission or of any active military service by him on the British side.

Lieutenant-Colonel James Vernon

James Vernon emigrated from Scotland in 1760 to Pennsylvania, where he resided for four or five years until his removal to the district of Ninety-Six in South Carolina. Here he bought, in conjunction with one John Nicholls, 640 acres of land on Fair Forest creek in the present county of Craven. Part of this land was sold afterwards by the joint owners to James Martin, and subsequently John Nicholls disposed of the whole of his share to Aaron Harling. The original deed for the purchase of this tract of land is still preserved. (A O. 13/123.)

James Vernon was granted a commission as ensign, 2 February, 1774, in the militia regiment of his neighbor, Colonel Thomas Fletchall, the original commission being preserved with the deed just mentioned. Called up for active service at the commencement of the Revolutionary troubles in his own district, this prosperous Scotch settler lost all his farm stock in confiscation after the affair of Ninety-Six in November, 1775. (See pp 69, 70.)

Promoted later by Major Patrick Ferguson to the rank of captain in the South Carolina loyal militia, James Vernon received further promotion from Lieutenant-Colonel Nisbet Balfour, 2 December, 1780, to lieutenant-colonel, the original commission for which has survived with the deed and the ensign's commission, mentioned above. In this rank he would seem to have taken over the command of Colonel Daniel Plummer's regiment of loyal militia.

This loyalist officer suffered the ignominy of being taken prisoner twice during the war.

According to a letter of introduction from Major James Dunlap to Lieutenant-Colonel Nisbet Balfour, dated from Ninety-Six, 26 January, 1781, Vernon is described as having been driven from home by the "rebels" and as "one of the most deserving of our Militia Officers." The letter goes on to say that after "Ferguson's affair," (presumably his defeat at King's Mountain), Lieutenant-Colonel Vernon kept his company together and was of infinite service in protecting the neighborhood from plundering parties, as well as doing "very material service by killing the noted Ned Hampton." (A.O. 13/123.) Ned Hampton was probably Lieutenant-Colonel Edward Hampton (son of Anthony Hampton) who defeated Major James Dunlap. (See p. 73.) This American officer's name disappears from the pay lists in October, 1780, and therefore it is assumed that he was killed between July, 1780—the date of the Dunlap affair—and October.

At the end of the war, Lieutenant-Colonel James Vernon sought refuge with other loyalists in the West Indies, and found employment in a subordinate capacity on the estate of William Hall (a brother and partner of Thomas Hall of Englefield Green, Egham, in Surrey) in the parish of St. James, Jamaica, where also were his wife and four sons and two daughters, two of whom were being educated in 1790 by the Foundation of the parish of St. James. In 1790 he was in London, prosecuting his claim for compensation for the loss of his property in South Carolina

Alexander Vernon, a near kinsman of James Vernon, married Margaret Chesney, and resided about ten miles west of Spartanburg in South Carolina. (A.O. 12/46, fo. 147; A.O. 12/52, fos. 387-400; A.O. 12/75, fos. 145-147; and A.O. 13/128.) (Papers of Colonel Thomas Fletchall.)

COLONEL ZACHARIAS GIBBS

Born in Virginia in 1741, Zacharias Gibbs migrated to South Carolina in or about 1763. Here he was the owner of large plantations on the fork of Broad river and Saluda river in the district of Ninety-Six, as well as large tracts of land at Camden, bought in 1779 and 1780 from two loyalists, Drury Bishop and John Brown. A further addition was made to his property by the purchase in 1781 of 100 acres at Orangeburg from George Dykes, a loyalist. These purchases by Zacharias Gibbs during the war are an indication of his faith in the permanence of the subjugation of South Carolina in 1780 by the British.

Captain Zacharias Gibbs, to give him his exact military rank at this time, began his military services on the side of the crown at Ninety-Six in November, 1775, the engagement which caused the first bloodshed in South Carolina in the Revolutionary war, when he was present with his company in the attack by the loyalists commanded by Major Joseph Robinson, on the Americans under Major Andrew Williamson. (See page 74.) In his evidence before the commissioners of American Claims in London he asserted that his company took the fort.

After many adventures and temporary occupations of his plantations from time to time, he helped Colonel John Boyd to raise 600 men for the loyalist forces early in 1779, and marched with these men to Savannah, which they reached 350 strong in February, after fighting in two engagements on the way. Shortly afterwards he was captured at the battle of Kettle creek in Georgia on 14 February, 1779, and was marched in irons with other prisoners to Ninety-Six, a distance of nearly 400 miles. In this battle the loyalists under Colonel Bond were defeated, and Colonel Bond killed. Lieutenant-Colonel John Moore, of North Carolina, was second in command, and Major Spurgen third in command. (C. C. Jones, *History of Georgia*, 1883, pp. 339-342; W. B Stevens, *History of Georgia*, 1859, Vol. II. pp. 190-192.)

At Ninety-Six Captain Gibbs was put into prison for fifteen months and sentenced to death, but was reprieved. On this occasion twenty-two other loyalists were sentenced to share the death penalty with him. Five only of this number were executed, including his brother-in-law, the remainder having been reprieved on two conditions, namely, that they sign their own death warrants and that they make written declarations never to return to the district of Ninety-Six. During his imprisonment, the gallows and grave prepared for him were ever in sight. On his release on 3 April, 1780, Colonel Gibbs went to Camden, remaining there until the capture of Charleston by the British, when he emerged again into military activity, and was on 6 July, 1780, commissioned major and later was promoted to the command of his regiment.

The life of Colonel Zacharias Gibbs from the outbreak of hostilities in South Carolina until his final departure from the Province was full of adventure, as is proved by the loyalist documents. His military services were highly praised by Colonel John Harris Cruger, one of the most distinguished and successful military leaders on the loyalist side, in an original certificate which is still preserved.

Colonel Nisbet Balfour, sometime commandant at Charleston, testified in evidence in London to his excellent qualities as a man and as one of the truest of loyalists, though, with the traditional prejudice of the British regular officer against the Provincial or militia forces, qualified his praise by adding that Colonel Gibbs was not a very good soldier.

The good-natured Lord Cornwallis gave him a certificate of merit, as well as Colonels Balfour and Cruger, all of whose original certificates are in the Public Record Office. (A.O. 13/79.) A high opinion of the loyalty and meritorious conduct of Colonel Zacharias Gibbs was entertained by the commissioners of American Claims

Captain Alexander Chesney was one of his neighbors, their plantations being separated by only four miles.

The name of Colonel Zacharias Gibbs' first wife, who left at least two children, is not recorded. His second wife was Jane Downes, widow of Major William Downes, an Irish merchant, blacksmith, and turner, who settled in Camden district, South Carolina, after the peace of 1763, having served in the "Royal Irish Artillery" in the war in America against the French. He had by his industry and thrift acquired valuable plantations and lived in comfort. By Lord Rawdon, himself an Irishman, William Downes was appointed captain of militia His military career in the Revolutionary war was cut off prematurely by his death on 15 April, 1781, when, by an act of treachery, his house was attacked by a party of 164 Americans. William Downes ended his life in a gallant defence of his home, in which he was assisted by his overseer, who was also killed, and by his devoted wife and children in loading his fire-arms. This lady was a widow at the time of her marriage in 1773 to this Irish loyalist, her first husband having been one William Lindsay, the elder, whom she had accompanied in 1763 to South Carolina, where they settled near Georgetown William Lindsay died in 1772, leaving a son, Thomas, and two daughters.

For the loss of her property in South Carolina, derived from her husband William Downes, the sum of £2,143 was claimed by Jane Downes, and she was awarded £955, as well as a pension of

£40. She appears to have had seven children by her first and second marriages In September, 1785, she was living with her children at Springfield in county Down, Ireland, and was about to join her husband, Colonel Zacharias Gibbs, in Nova Scotia; but according to one document she was still at that Irish place in May, 1789.

Colonel Zacharias Gibbs settled in 1784 on his grant of 1000 acres of land in Rawdon in Nova Scotia, where also were settled fifty-five other loyalists from South Carolina. (See page 118) In his letter of 4 May, 1787, to Lewis Wolfe, a London agent for American loyalists, he gives a picture of his life in Nova Scotia, adding that he has the large and helpless family of Richard Fenton with a wife and four children employed on his wild uncultivated land at great expense to him. Fenton was a loyalist from South Carolina, though he and his wife were natives of Whitby in Yorkshire.

Among the other troubles and trials of Colonel Gibbs were the absence of his wife in Ireland and the anxiety for his two little children by a former wife, in South Carolina. He had made two unsuccessful attempts to obtain these children. One of the attempts was made through the agency of a loyalist who was going on a visit or returning to that State, but who, on his arrival there, was "maltreated and much abused" because of his loyalty. Letters to South Carolina were equally ineffectual in securing them.

A daughter of Colonel Gibbs by his first marriage, or of Mrs. Jane Downes his second wife, by a former marriage, was married to Robert Cooper or Cowper, a planter, of Georgetown, South Carolina. Colonel Zacharias Gibbs was awarded £1,200 on his claim of £2,384. 15s. for the loss of his property in South Carolina. (F.O.4/1; A O. 12/46, fos. 145-162, 240-252; A.O. 12/99, fos 26, 225; A.O. 12/109; A. O. 13/79; A. O. 13/129; *The Royal Commission on Loyalist Claims, 1783-1785*, ed. by H. E. Egerton; Roxburghe Club, 1915.)

MAJOR PATRICK FERGUSON

Patrick Ferguson was born in Scotland in 1744, and at the age of 15 a commission as cornet was bought for him in the British Army He served with conspicuous success in the 2nd. Dragoons in the wars in Flanders and Germany From this regiment he was transferred as captain to the 70th. Foot, with which he served in the American war of Independence until his appointment to the command of a body of riflemen, known as the "American Volunteers," composed mostly of native-born loyalists who were selected because of their intelligence and skilful marksmanship. The command of such a corps was especially congenial to Major Ferguson, the best rifle shot in the British Army, and the most versatile and brilliant leader in guerilla warfare on the British side, as well as the inventor of the first breech-loading rifle used in the British Army. The officers were chosen from several of the loyalist regiments, the officers in their turn selecting their own men. The original muster rolls have been preserved. (Jonas Howe's article in *Acadiensis*, Vol. VI. pp. 237-246 and Vol. VII. pp 30-41, 149-159.)

Major Patrick Ferguson was appointed, 22 May, 1780, inspector of militia and major-commandant of the first battalion of loyal militia raised in South Carolina. (Hist. MSS. Comm., *Report on the American MSS. in the Royal Inst.*, Vol. II., pp. 126, 129.) During the campaign in South Carolina, Ferguson, while yet a prisoner at Charleston, in the house at 5 Liberty Street, of a resourceful and resolute English woman, one Elizabeth Thompson, was enabled to view the works of the Americans outside, by a daring ruse of that loyalist Ferguson, disguised, was driven by Elizabeth Thompson in her own chaise from Charleston through the American lines and obtained information of military value. (A O. 12/46, fos 74-81; *The Royal Comm. on Loyalist Claims, 1783-1785*, ed. by H. E. Egerton, 1915; Roxburghe Club, pp. 30-31.)

The death of the gallant officer occurred in the battle of King's Mountain (see p. 86; *Scots Magazine*, Vol. 43, pp. 29-30) He is in the *Dictionary of National Biography*.

COLONEL ALEXANDER INNES

Alexander Innes had been secretary to Lord William Campbell, governor of South Carolina, before his appointment in January, 1777, as inspector-general of the Provincial forces in America. In 1779 he was given the command of the South Carolina Royalists. (Hist. MSS. Comm., *Report on the American MSS. in the Royal Inst.*, Vols. 1-4.)

Colonel Rudolphus Ritzema, a New York loyalist who had previously been in the American service, describes Colonel Innes as "a man, whose haughty and supercilious conduct has estranged more minds from His Majesty and the British Gov^t than perhaps all the other blunders in the conduct of the American war put together. This every American officer, not under a national bias, will avouch " (Ritzema's petition to Pitt, chancellor of the Exchequer: Chatham Papers, Bundle 220.)

The signature of Colonel Alexander Innes appears in a petition shortly after 1791 from officers of the late British-American regiments on half-pay, now in England, offering upon "the present prospect of war" with France their military services, which to their painful mortification could only be accepted if they joined the British Army as ensigns, whatever their rank may have been in the American war of Independence. (F O 4/1.)

CAPTAIN ABRAHAM DE PEYSTER

Captain Abraham De Peyster was born in New York in 1753, the son of James De Peyster and his wife, Sarah, daughter of Hon. Joseph Reade.

Joining the British forces, with other members of this well-known New York family, early in the Revolutionary war, he chose as his regiment the King's American regiment, composed of volunteers mostly from the Province of New York and formed in December, 1776, with Edmund Fanning as colonel. Abraham de Peyster was granted a commission as captain within two days of the formation of the regiment, namely, on 13 December

His brothers, Frederick and James, also joined loyalist corps, the former as captain in the "Nassau Blues," a New York corps which was raised 1 May, 1779, with William Axtell as colonel, and was disbanded in December following, when most of the officers and men joined the New York Volunteers. Frederick de Peyster became a captain-lieutenant in his brother's regiment, the King's American regiment

After serving in the Northern Colonies for some time, Captain Abraham de Peyster was moved to the South where he went through much of the hard fighting in South Carolina in the picked loyailst force commanded by Major Patrick Ferguson. (See pp 82, 83.)

A brave and enterprising officer, upon him fell the invidious duty at the age of 27 of taking over the command of the loyalist force at the death of Major Patrick Ferguson, the most brilliant leader in guerilla fighting on the British side, at the memorable battle of King's Mountain—a battle which was fraught with such dire consequences to the British in South Carolina. Captain De

Peyster's conduct in surrendering has been criticised. Tarleton, whose judgments of his brother officers and criticisms of operations must be received with caution, maintains that Captain De Peyster hoisted the white flag before the blood in Ferguson's body had become cold, but inasmuch as he was not present in the battle, his opinion is not helpful. (Tarleton, *History of the Campaigns of 1780 and 1781,* p 65) On the other hand such competent eye-witnesses as Captains Samuel Ryerson and John Taylor, both of the New Jersey Volunteers, and Lieutenant Anthony Allaire, of the Loyal American regiment, supported the decision of Captain de Peyster to surrender, acquitting him of the charge of timidity and declaring that his conduct was in all respects proper. (Mackenzie, *Strictures on Lieut.-Colonel Tarleton's History,* 1787, pp. 58-68). From a consideration of the evidence on both sides of the controversy, it would seem that a defeat for the hard pressed and much shaken loyalists, valiant as they were, was inevitable, and that he was not guilty of excessive caution in saving his force from further suffering. (Draper, *King's Mountain and its Heroes,* p. 479)

It is unfortunate that Alexander Chesney, a participant in the battle, has not offered a definite opinion on the alleged premature surrender of the loyalist commander. One important comment, however, amounts to a virtual acquittal of the odious charge, namely, that the Americans having resumed fire after Captain De Peyster had sent out a flag of truce, he ordered a resumption of the battle, in the belief—as subsequent events proved to be true—that no quarter would be given to the loyalists, when a "dreadful havoc" ensued until the flag was sent out a second time   (See p. 18.)

At the peace, Captain Abraham De Peyster found an asylum with his brother officers in New Brunswick, where he became a justice of the peace, treasurer of the Province, and colonel of militia. Here he died, 19 February, 1798, leaving a widow and five young children. After his death, his widow, a daughter of John Livingston of New York, returned to New York. (Lawrence and Stockton, *Judges of New Brunswick and Their Times,* p 274 ; J.W De Peyster, *Local Memorials relating to the De Peyster and Watts and affiliated families,* 1881, pp. 40-45 ; J. W. De Peyster, "The Affair at King's Mountain," in *The Magazine of American History,* Vol 5, pp. 401-404 ; Sabine, *Loyalists of the American Revolution.*)

The Battle of King's Mountain

The memorable battle of King's Mountain was fought October 7, 1780, between the Americans under the command of Colonels Campbell, Shelby, Cleveland, Sevier, and Williams, and the loyalists commanded by Major Patrick Ferguson, composed of detachments from the King's American regiment, the Queen's Rangers, the New Jersey Volunteers, and South Carolina loyal militia, and was one of the most desperately fought battles in the Southern Colonies.

It is not proposed to enter into the controversy regarding the numbers of the forces engaged Whatever the figures may have been, the combatants on both sides fought with unsurpassed courage and determination. The exploit of the Americans deserves all the praise bestowed upon it as one of the finest examples of the application of Washington's disregarded advice to Braddock to seek cover behind trees, and of the splendid marksmanship of the Americans.

The loyalists had fought with unwavering bravery until the fall of the intrepid Ferguson somewhat early in the battle, when their courage failed them for a moment until their rally by the new leader, Captain Abraham De Peyster. The criticisms of this officer's alleged premature surrender are considered under the notes on Captain De Peyster.

King's Mountain was the only important battle in the war in which the British force was composed entirely of loyalists, except Major Ferguson.

Just as the surrender of Burgoyne at Saratoga was a momentous event, not only in hastening the alliance of the Americans with France, but also as a great turning point in the war, so the battle of King's Mountain may be regarded as the turn of the tide in the South, leading to the heartening and the re-organization of the American forces in South Carolina for the final triumph in the war of Independence.

It is regrettable that the memory of this signal victory should be tarnished by the cruelties inflicted on the loyalists and by the execution of nine loyalist officers—Colonel Ambrose Mills, Captains James Chitwood, Wilson, Walker, Gilkey, and Grimes, and Lieutenants Lafferty, John McFall, John Bibby, and Augustine Hobbs. (Tarleton, *Hist of the Campaigns 1780 and 1781*, p 168, Moultrie, *Memoirs*, pp. 242-6; Stedman, *American War*, Vol. II, pp. 245-7;

Draper, *King's Mountain and its Heroes*, pp 332-7; Fortescue, *Hist. of the British Army*, Vol. III, pp. 323-4; E. McCrady, *The Hist. of S. Carolina in the Rev., 1775-1780*, p. 805; S. G. Fisher, *The Struggle for American Independence*, Vol. II, pp 349-366).

BRIGADIER-GENERAL ROBERT CUNNINGHAM

Robert Cunningham, born in 1741, was the son of John Cunningham, a member of a Scotch family which settled about 1681 in Virginia and removed early in 1769 to the district of Ninety-Six in South Carolina. (E. McCrady, *The History of South Carolina in the Revolution, 1775-1780*, p. 38.) Robert Cunningham acquired a plantation of his own at Island ford on the Saluda river and by energy and industry became a man of wealth and influence.

From the dawn of the Revolution Robert Cunningham displayed the most uncompromising spirit of loyalty. (Hist. MSS. Comm., *Report on the MSS. of the Earl of Dartmouth*, Vol. II, p. 355.) The treaty of neutrality made between that urbane and easygoing loyalist, Colonel Thomas Fletchall, and William Henry Drayton, September 16, 1776, provoked his bitter opposition and brought forth his refusal to be bound by it, in a letter to Drayton, dated October 6 following (see p. 69 and Drayton, *Memoirs of the Revolution*, Vol. I, p. 418). So dangerous a foe was not permitted to remain at large and on November 1, while holding the rank of captain in the loyal militia, Cunningham was committed to Charleston jail on a charge of committing high crimes and misdemeanors against the liberties of South Carolina, having, according to a letter written from Savannah on the 19th., been seized by a party disguised as Indians. He was detained a prisoner until February, 1776. (Force, *American Archives*, Series IV, Vol. 3, p. 1606; *ibid.*, Vol 4, p. 29; E. McCrady, *The Hist. of South Carolina in the Revolution, 1775-1780*, p. 86; A. S. Salley, Jr., *Hist. of Orangeburg County*, 1898, pp 304-7; Moultrie, *Memoirs*, Vol. I, p. 100.) His brother, Major Patrick Cunningham, with a party of loyalists made an unsuccessful attempt to rescue him from the hands of his captors. (See p. 104.)

The British Government awarded him compensation to the amount of £1,080 from his estimated loss of £1,355 for his South Carolina property confiscated by the State. (A.O. 12/109.)

Brigadier-General Cunningham at the conclusion of the war in his own Province set sail for the Bahamas with other compatriots and settled at Nassau in the island of New Providence, so aptly named as the harbor of refuge for the distressed loyalists. In this new home Robert Cunningham settled on the tracts of valuable land which had been granted to him for his services in the American Revolutionary war. Here he died, 9 February, 1813. On his tombstone in the western cemetery is inscribed " . . . exiled from his native Country in the American Revolution for his attachment to his King and the Laws of his Country." His wife, Margaret, survived him only a few weeks, having died 26 March at the age of 76.

Four children were left by Robert and Margaret Cunningham, namely, John, who married, 5 March, 1795, Ann Harrold; Charles; Margaret, who was married, 22 June 1790, to Richard Pearis, son of Colonel Richard Pearis, a loyalist from South Carolina (see p. 104) ; and Elizabeth, who married, 1 May, 1792, Robert Brownlee, a loyalist. In his will are mentioned, in addition to his wife and children, the following family connections: John, natural son of John Cunningham by a woman named Hannah Ridley; his sister, Margaret Cunningham, and her son, Robert Andrew Cunningham; his cousin, Jean, daughter of Thomas Edwards, his cousin, Robert Cunningham, son of David Cunningham, to whom was bequeathed 300 dollars for his education; and his two cousins, Margaret Fenny and Elizabeth Brown, daughters of Joseph Jefferson.

Patrick, David, and John Cunningham, three loyalist brothers of Brigadier Robert Cunningham, remained in South Carolina after the war (A.O. 12/3, fos. 8-10; A O 12/48, fo. 215; A.O. 12/92; A.O. 12/109; A.O. 13/97; A O. 13/127; Sabine, *Loyalists of the American Revolution,* Vol I, 346, 349; A T Bethell, *The Early Settlers of the Bahama Islands,* 1914, pp 21-23.) William Cunningham, known as "Bloody Bill," was a cousin of Brigadier-General Cunningham He was only nineteen at the beginning of the war, and was lively and jovial, open-hearted and generous, and a remarkable horseman. (E. McCrady, *The History of South Carolina in the Revolution, 1780-1783,* pp. 467-476.)

COLONEL DANIEL PLUMMER

Daniel Plummer, a planter in the district between Fair Forest and Tiger river in what is now Spartanburg county in South Carolina, derives his military title from his command of one of the loyal militia regiments, established by Lord Cornwallis in 1780. His regiment formed part of the brigade of militia in the district of Ninety-Six in South Carolina, commanded by Brigadier-General Robert Cunningham, the loyalist Among his officers was Alexander Chesney, who was appointed adjutant and captain in the autumn of 1780 (*Vide* his original certificate for pay due to Chesney in T. 50/2.)

At a period in the Revolutionary war when passions were furious on both sides, Colonel Plummer was regarded both by friend and foe as honest and generous As an example of his humanity, at a moment when severe measures towards enemies were demanded by the loyalists, he spared the life of young Jonathan Hampton, a prisoner in his hands in September, 1780, as well as giving security for his appearance at trial.

Colonel Plummer was present with his militia at the memorable battle of King's Mountain, the turning point in the war in the South, and is stated to have been killed there (E McCrady, *History of South Carolina in the Revolution, 1775-1780*, p. 798) , but there is evidence not only from Chesney (p. 20), but also from an official document in the Public Record Office (T. 50/2) that he was alive at Charleston on 11 April, 1782. He appears, however, to have been badly wounded and to have been incapacitated from active service sometime before the conclusion of the war.

A list of his officers and men who accompanied Lieutenant-Colonel John Harris Cruger, of De Lancey's brigade, to Orangeburg from June to December, 1780, is in T. 50/1.

Colonel Daniel Plummer would seem to have found a temporary home at Savannah in Georgia before the end of the war. (A O 13/ 100.) A daughter died at Charleston in December, 1781. (T. 50/5.)

It is assumed from the absence of his name from lists of claims and pensions that this worthy loyalist died before the end of the war.

(For other accounts of Colonel Plummer, see Draper, *King's Mountain and its Heroes,* pp. 142-4, 154-5, 483.)

LIEUTENANT-COLONEL JOHN HARRIS CRUGER

John Harris Cruger, of New York, was appointed September 6, 1776, lieutenant-colonel of the 1st battalion of De Lancey's brigade of loyalists, raised by his father-in-law, Oliver De Lancey, of New York. In 1778 he sailed with the British force under Colonel Archibald Campbell for Georgia and was present in several actions in

South Carolina. His defence of Ninety-Six was one of the immortal episodes of the Revolutionary war. Shut up with a small force of about 300 loyalists of his own regiment and of the New Jersey Volunteers, under the command of Lieutenant-Colonel Isaac Allen, and 150 loyal militia of South Carolina under Lieutenant-Colonel Richard King, a total of about 450 against General Greene's besieging army of over 4,000 and a train of artillery, (which was flushed with the conquest of five successive posts), Cruger held on with indomitable courage and resource for 28 days, from May 22, 1781, until June 19, when he was relieved by Lord Rawdon. His merits as a leader of irregular troops and his natural abilities have not received adequate appreciation. (Cruger's original memorial is in the Public Record Office, A.O. 13/54.)

THE BRITISH LEGION

The regiment of the British Legion was raised in America by Lord Cathcart in 1778 and was at first composed of six troops of cavalry and six companies of infantry, Banistre Tarleton being appointed lieutenant-colonel commandant, August 1 in the same year at the age of 24 (Ind: 5604) A detachment of its cavalry served under Banistre Tarleton in his destruction of Colonel Buford's force at the Waxhaws in June, 1780. (Hist. MSS. Comm., *Report on the American MSS. in the Royal Institution,* Vol. II, p 143.) Lord Rawdon, in recognition of the gallantry of the mounted infantry of the Legion at the battle of Hanging Rock (when by a ruse of forty of their number spreading themselves out and creating the illusion of being a formidable force, they deceived Sumter) offered colors to the corps and medals to the officers, an offer which was declined by Tarleton (Carleton Correspondence in the Public Record Office) Captain Kenneth McCulloch, of the British Legion, was distinguished for his bravery in this action, where he received such wounds as caused his death shortly afterwards. (Hist. MSS. Comm , *Report on the MSS of Mrs. Stopford-Sackville,* Vol II, p. 178.) Major John Carden, of the Prince of Wales's American Volunteers, who was in command of a loyalist force in this action at Hanging Rock, was disgraced by resigning the command to Captain John Rousselet, of the British Legion, in the heat of action. (Stedman, *American War,* Vol. II, pp. 224-5)

The employment of prisoners of war as combatants was a common practice on both sides in the war For example, some of the prisoners captured by the British at the fall of Charleston, 12 May, 1780, and in the defeat of Gates at Camden, 16 August, 1780, were drafted in February following into the Duke of Cumberland's regiment (Loyal American Rangers), commanded by Lord Charles Greville Montagu, formerly governor of South Carolina, who endeavored to fill it with South Carolinians as officers. These men joined the regiment in the West Indies. In a roster, preserved in the Public Record Office, these prisoners' names, ages, heights, and country of origin, are given. Of a total of 187, the greatest number hailed from Virginia, namely, 54 North Carolina contributed 32, and England and Ireland 26 each, while 7 came each from South Carolina and Pennsylvania Six were Scotch and three each were French and German. Four were from Maryland and the remainder were from other American Colonies and from the West Indies and Bermuda. (State Papers Domestic, Military, 29.)

JOHN CRUDEN

John Cruden, the younger, was the son of the Rev William Cruden (1725-85), and his wife, Clementina, and was born in 1754. His father, a member of a well-known Aberdeenshire family, took the degree of M.A. at the University of Aberdeen in 1743 and, after acting as a minister in Scotland for thirty years, was appointed minister in 1773 of the old Scotch Presbyterian church, in Crown Court, Covent Garden, London, which was founded in 1718 This Scottish minister was in frequent correspondence with his son, John, during the American war of Independence, on the British side. He died in London, 5 November, 1785, and was buried in the well-known Puritan burial ground in Bunhill fields. (*Dictionary of National Biography.*)

The subject of this notice became a partner in the house of John Cruden and Company, merchants, of Wilmington and other places in North Carolina, which consisted of his uncle, John Cruden, and his younger brother, James, who was taken into partnership in 1770. His uncle had amassed a considerable fortune in trade in the West Indies and afterwards settled among his Scottish compatriots in North Carolina, as a merchant and planter

In a letter to his father, dated 28 January, 1778, from New York, John Cruden expresses his views on affairs in America, advocating stronger measures in the restriction of trade among the Americans, and condemning the laxity of Lord Howe, commander-in-chief of the British Navy on the North American station. In another letter he refers to his visit with a flag of truce to his uncle, John Cruden, then a prisoner "among the rebels."

From the outbreak of the Revolution young Cruden was an active loyalist, and during the war received a commission as lieutenant-colonel of a regiment of volunteers. Lord Cornwallis, discerning his merits, offered him a commission as commissioner "for the seizure, superintendence, custody and management of captured property" in South Carolina, the commission (still preserved) being dated 16 September, 1780. (Hist. MSS. Comm., *Report on the American MSS. in the Royal Inst.*, Vol. II, p. 183.) An example of the receipts issued by Cruden for the rents of the sequestered property is to be found in the original receipt for the estate of Henry Laurens, then a prisoner in the Tower of London. (With the papers of Robert Frogg in A O. 13/128)

John Cruden published in London, as "President of the Assembly of the United Loyalists," a pamphlet entitled, *An Address to the Loyal Part of the British Empire, and friends of Monarchy throughout the Globe.* (*Report on the Management of the Estates Sequestered in South Carolina, by Order of Lord Cornwallis, in 1780-1782, by John Cruden.* Edited by Paul Leicester Ford, 1890.)

This Scotch-American loyalist was the writer of an interesting letter to Lord Dartmouth, dated 28 October, 1784, from St. Mary's river, East Florida, wherein he refers to his plan for the restoration of America to England "America," he says, "shall yet be ours, but the House of Brunswick do not deserve the sovereignty of it."

In another letter from John Cruden, dated 12 December, 1784, from the same place, he pictures his great distress, having twice sacrificed his fortune, and recounts his services in the cause of the crown. He had been paymaster to the North Carolina Provincials and had refused the offers pressingly made by the enemies of Great Britain to join them. An address from the loyalists of East Florida to the governor, Patrick Tonyn, testified to John Cruden's great services and applauded the governor's choice of Cruden, who by his influence, zeal, and spirit had prevented the Province from being overrun by a band of desperate men His precise duties are not, however, stated in this address. (Treas. 1/622.)

During his duties in East Florida, Cruden had occasion to disapprove strongly of the actions of one William Brown, commissioner for the evacuation of St. Augustine, whom he alleges had aided and abetted one Dobbins, master of a transport, in shipping a cargo of mahogany, etc. to Charleston, by which means Dobbins had so enriched himself as to be able to buy a vessel. (Treas. 1/622.)

John Cruden was a facile writer. In a letter to the lords commissioners of the Treasury, dated 10 February, 1786, he alludes to criticism, apparently made in England, of his former endeavors to make Florida "a gathering spot to shake in due time the baseless fabric of American Independence," and combats the doctrine that England was better off without the American or any other Colonies, claiming that perhaps he knows more of North and South America than any man attached to Great Britain. This letter also contains an eloquent plea for the promotion of trade between the Bahamas, Bermuda, and Great Britain. A second letter from the same facile pen, dated 7 May, 1786, from Nassau in the island of Providence in the Bahamas, mentions his lottery scheme for the benefit of the distressed American loyalists there

John Cruden made the voyage to Nova Scotia later in the year, with the object of presenting his claim for compensation for the loss of his American property, to the commissioner, Colonel Dundas, to whom he mentions in a letter written from Halifax, 30 October, 1786, his "unfortunate and ill-fated kinsman, D. Forrester of Donavon"

Returning to the Bahamas, John Cruden, the younger, died there in the following year, on 18 September, at the age of 33, unmarried Here also died his uncle, John Cruden, the elder, in the island of Exuma in 1786, leaving a widow and an infant son, also named John.

James Cruden, the younger brother and former partner in the business in North Carolina, made a claim on the British Government, as sole surviving partner of John Cruden and Company, for the sum of £9,621 and was awarded £2,400 (A.O. 12/109.) He was in London in 1789 (A O. 12/37, fos 9-29; A O. 12/73, fos 117-120; A O. 13/28; A.O. 13/97; Hist. Miss Comm., *Report on the Mss. of the Earl of Dartmouth*, Vol. II. pp. 413, 447, 448, 458, 460, 469, 480, 481.)

COLONEL ROBERT BALLINGALL

Robert Ballingall was a prosperous planter in St. Bartholomew's parish, South Carolina, as is indicated by the inventory of his personal estate—furniture, plate, jewels, and 300 volumes of books. His wife, whose name is not recorded in the documents, bequeathed to him for his use during his life a plantation in that parish, and a large pew in the chapel there, as well as a pew at St. Edmundsbury's. All this property was to pass at Robert Ballingall's death to her daughter, who was born in 1775   (A.O. 13/125.)

Robert Ballingall was appointed by Lord Cornwallis to the command of the Colleton county loyal militia, with the rank of colonel, in 1780. (See p 113.)

As chairman of a body of South Carolina loyalists, he signed the original address (undated) to Lieutenant-General Alexander Leslie, relying upon Leslie's willingness to adopt such measures as would effectually prevent the execution of the laws passed by the "usurped" Legislature of South Carolina, confiscating the estates of the loyalists, and for the accomplishment of these measures tendering their services at the risk of their lives and fortunes. (Hist. MSS. Comm , *Report on the American MSS. in the Royal Institution,* Vol. II, p. 436) Colonel Ballingall as secretary of the committee of the South Carolina loyalists signed the report, dated July 8, 1784, regarding their losses sustained by the payment of debts due to them in the depreciated paper currency of South Carolina instead of in the lawful money of the State. The other signatories to this report were: John Rose, Robert Williams, Dr. Alexander Garden, John Hopton, William Ancrum, Robert Williams Powell, Charles Ogilvie, and Gideon Dupont. (A.O. 12/48; A.O. 12/99; A O. 12/101.)

Colonel Robert Ballingall was awarded £2,070 as compensation by the British Government for the loss of his property in South Carolina, from his claim £3,974 (A.O 12/109.) In the year 1788 he was living at Montrose in Scotland.

COLONEL ISAAC HAYNE

Isaac Hayne was senior captain of the Round O company in the Colleton county regiment when it surrendered to the British at the capitulation of Charleston in May, 1780.

His execution at Charleston, August 4, 1781, excited great resentment among the Americans One of many charges made in justification of his execution was that Hayne, although he had renewed his oath of allegiance to the king, had been found in arms against the British and therefore deserved death. To General Greene's threat of reprisals for his death, Colonel Nisbet Balfour replied that at the moment when three loyalist officers suffered death (Lieutenant Fulkes, publicly executed at Motte's house; Colonel James Grierson, murdered after his surrender at Augusta; and Major James Dunlap, put to death by his guard;) he had in his hands the lives of several American officers whom he had spared. (Hist. MSS. Comm, *Report of the American MSS. in the Royal Institution,* Vol. II, p. 327.)

Colonel Isaac Hayne's execution was the subject of a motion for information by the duke of Richmond in the House of Lords on 4 February, 1782, a motion which was negatived Lord Rawdon, considering that a serious imputation had been made on his humanity, demanded and ultimately received a public apology from the duke. *(Parl. Hist , Vol XXII., pp. 966-970, n.)*

(See Sabine, *Loyalists of the American Revolution;* Thomas Jones, *Hist. of New York,* Vol. II, pp. 213-220, 473; E. McCrady, *Hist. of South Carolina in the Revolution, 1780-1783,* pp. 382-398; S. G. Fisher, *The Struggle for American Independence,* 1908, Vol. II. pp. 333, 432; Roderick Mackenzie, *Strictures on Lieut -Col. Tarleton's History of the Campaigns of 1780 and 1781 in the Southern Provinces of North America,* 1787, p. 140; Moultrie's *Memoirs,* Vol. II, pp. 241-2; *Scots Magazine,* Vol. 43, pp. 702-5).

MAJOR JOHN ROBINSON

John Robinson, an active loyalist, was a carpenter and journeyman who emigrated from Ireland in 1771 and settled on a plantation in the Waxhaws in South Carolina. In casting lots for serving in the American militia early in the Revolutionary war, the lot fell upon John Robinson and he served for two months. In his memorial he claims to have joined the loyalist corps in June, 1780, under Colonel Rugeley, presumably Colonel Rowland Rugeley of Clermont, or Rugeley's Mills, in Kershaw county. It is not clear whether Robinson was present on 1 December, 1780, when Colonel William Washington with some light cavalry reconnoitered this home of Colonel Rugeley, which was occupied by about 100 loyalists. Observing that the log barn by which the place was protected could only be successfully attacked by artillery, Colonel Washington ingeniously deceived Colonel Rugeley by having the trunk of a tree formed in the shape of a field piece, and placing it in a menacing position in front of the loyalists, whose surrender was thereupon formally demanded Colonel Rugeley, fearing that his defences would be powerless against the dummy field piece, surrendered with his whole party without firing a shot, to the mortification of the loyalists and to the indignation of Lord Cornwallis, who had apparently contemplated promoting him to the rank of brigadier-general (B. E. Stevens, *Clinton-Cornwallis Controversy*, Vol. I, pp. 205, 239, 251, 308; S. G. Fisher, *The Struggle for American Independence*, 1908, Vol. II, p. 373)

He served at several actions, including the battle of Camden, where he was a captain, and was afterwards promoted major of the First regiment of Camden militia, commanded by Colonel Robert English. In April, 1781, he was wounded in a skirmish at Beaver creek, about twenty miles from Camden. A loyalist brother of Major John Robinson was killed in action. According to his memorial, he was one of the organizers of a race meeting held for the purpose of collecting together the loyalists of the district of Great Lynch creek with the object of taking the American magazine at Camden, but this ruse to disarm suspicion failed and the party, to the number of about seventy, was dispersed and he was taken prisoner.

The loyalist, Colonel William Fortune, says that Major Robinson was "the most beloved by his men of any captain except Mr. McCulloch" (probably James McCulloch).

The pay list of his company of Camden militia is in the Public Record Office in London.

Major John Robinson claimed £751 for the loss of his real property in South Carolina and was awarded £240.

He returned to his native Ulster at the end of the war and received the appointment of tide waiter at Larne.

(Public Record Office: A O. 12/46, fos 262-269; A.O. 12/99, fo. 228; A.O. 12/109. *The Royal Commission on Loyalist Claims, 1783-1785*, Roxburghe Club, 1915, pp. 55-56.)

MAJOR MICHAEL EGAN

Michael Egan was one of many Irish emigrants from the Province of Ulster to South Carolina, where he had settled in 1771 within nine miles of Camden in partnership with one Inglis in a plantation, having saved £500 by industry and frugality between that date and 1775.

Early in the Revolutionary war, Michael Egan bore arms for the Americans against the loyalist, Brigadier-General Robert Cunningham, and soon afterwards sold his share in the plantation for £500 and settled as a storekeeper at Charleston   At the capitulation of that city to the British in 1780 Egan joined the loyalists and was subsequently given a commission as major in the First Camden militia under Colonel Robert English.

At the end of the war Major Michael Egan returned with his wife to Ireland.

The commissioners of American Claims expressed their dissatisfaction with his conduct in bearing arms for the Americans, but in view of the strong certificates to his merits from Lord Cornwallis, Lord Rawdon, and General Alexander Leslie, he was allowed a bounty of £30 a year and granted compensation for £110, from his estimated loss of £272 for property in South Carolina.

Major Michael Egan probably died in 1831, the date of the cessation of his pension   (T 50/8; T. 50/28; A.O. 12/99, fo. 341; A.O 12/109.)

JAMES BARBER

James Barber emigrated from Ireland to America in 1776, at the age of 16, first to Pennsylvania, where he worked as a laborer. Rather than take the oath of allegiance to the Americans he betook himself to South Carolina, where he appears to have become the owner of a small plantation   After the capitulation of Charleston in May, 1780, this young Irishman joined a corps of loyal militia under Colonel Rowland Rugeley, with whom he was taken prisoner when this officer surrendered without firing a shot, and thus lost his chance of promotion to the rank of brigadier-general (see p 96) James Barber served in more than one action in South Carolina and rose in rank from private to quartermaster. He returned to his native land and received as compensation for the loss of his little property the sum of £42. (T. 50/1; A.O. 12/46, fos. 82-85; A.O. 12/109)

PHILIP HENRY

This loyalist was born in London in 1749 and emigrated at the age of 19 to South Carolina. For many months he was in the employ of one Michie, a Charleston merchant. After the death of

Michie, whose partner he would have become, he started business
on his own account as a factor and quickly achieved prosperity, his
income varying from £400 to £800 a year.   He was the owner of
large tracts of land in South Carolina and was the agent for the
estates of one Bruton; Dr. James Clitherall, surgeon to the South
Carolina Royalists, a loyalist regiment; Dr. John Farquharson, a
loyalist; and others.

Philip Henry in the early days of the Revolutionary war, confident of success of British arms, embarked on extensive specula-
tions in land.

As a loyalist who declined to take the oath of allegiance to the
Americans, (passed by act of 28 March, 1778,) he was banished
from South Carolina and was obliged to embark with other loyalists
on board the *Providence* (Captain Richard Stevens), bound for Rotterdam.   Among the fellow exiles of Philip Henry on board were his
friends and part owners of this vessel, Robert Rowand, Daniel Manson, and James Weir.   The warrant, authorizing the master to take
Philip Henry on board, was signed by Rawlins Lowndes and dated
22 June, 1778   The *Providence* was captured off the American coast
by the British frigate *Rose* (Captain James Reed) and taken to
New York, where she was libelled in the Vice-Admiralty Court and
the crew pressed into the British navy.   Both the vessel and the
cargo were, however, ordered to be returned to the owners by the
decision of the judge, Robert Bayard.

Philip Henry advertised in the *South Carolina and American
General Gazette* for June 25, 1778, requesting all his debtors to discharge their debts and all his creditors to call for payment before
the date fixed by the General Assembly for his banishment   His
furniture and silver, which are further proof of his prosperity, had
been advertised in the same paper for sale on 3 June

Accompanying this loyalist on his voyage to Europe on board
the *Sally* from New York were his wife, S. M. Henry, and Miss
Thorney.   Soon after landing in England he was appointed to a post
in the Irish board of Customs   In a letter written from Dublin, 18
February, 1786, Philip Henry complains bitterly of his reverse of
fortune by the war and gives a long account of the capture of the
Providence

Philip Henry before his death had become a clerk of the Sta-
tionary at Dublin, as well as an officer in the Customs.

He was awarded £2,723. 16s. as compensation for the loss of his property in South Carolina, from his claim of £16,351 and a pension of £100 a year. (A O 12/46; fos. 122-143; A.O 12/99, fo 2; A.O. 12/109; A.O.13/79; A.O. 13/129; *The Royal Comm. on Loyalist Claims, 1783-1785*, ed. by H. E. Egerton; Roxburghe Club, 1915, p. 44.)

JAMES SIMPSON

James Simpson was the son of William Simpson, chief justice of Georgia, who died in 1768, and was admitted clerk of the Council in South Carolina in 1764 and five years later received the appointment of judge of the Admiralty. In 1774 James Simpson was appointed attorney-general for South Carolina. During the Revolutionary war he took an active but judicious part on the British side and was regarded by political opponents with respect, being described by one of these as a "humane and just man." (Alexander Garden, *Anecdotes of the American Revolution*, 1828, p. 112.)

As a member of the committee of the South Carolina loyalists for investigating the value of their property, he made a report to the commissioners of American Claims in which he says: ". . . many well disposed people [loyalists] were obliged to go down the stream who anxiously desired to be rescued from a situation from which they could not extricate themselves . . . ," in consequence of the lack of energetic measures taken by the governor, Lord William Campbell, and of the "sudden and violent introduction of the system adopted by the Americans" (A O 12/107, fos 5-13, 39-40). His observations on the condition of South Carolina in July, 1780, when he wrote as follows to Sir Henry Clinton, are of interest: " . . . Nothing but the evidence of my senses would have convinced me that one half of the distress I am a witness to could have been produced in so short a time in so rich and flourishing a country as Carolina was when I left it. Numbers of families, who, four years ago, abounded in every convenience and luxury of life, are without food to live on, clothes to cover them, or the means to purchase either. It hath appeared to me the more extraordinary, because until 12 months ago it had not been exposed to any other devastation of war except the captures made at sea . . " (Hist. MSS Comm., *Report on the American MSS. in the Royal Inst.* Vol. II, 149-150.)

James Simpson was admitted a member of the Honorable Society of the Middle Temple, 14 November, 1777, while occupying the

dignity of attorney-general of South Carolina—an historic inn
which includes on its roll of membership five signatories to the
Declaration of American Independence: Edward Rutledge, Thomas
Lynch, Thomas Heyward, Arthur Middleton, and Thomas McKean,
as well as Peyton Randolph, president of the Continental Congress.
His eldest son, William, was admitted to the same Inn, 13 May,
1775.

Such was James Simpson's prosperity in South Carolina that
of his claim of £20,608 for the loss of his property there he was
awarded by the British Government the sum of £8,077   In addition
he received £3,518 for the loss of his professional income *per annum*, and was also granted a pension of £860 a year. (A.O. 12/109.)

Barbara Simpson, wife of James Simpson, died March 2, 1795,
and was buried in Westminster Abbey, near Poet's Corner. Her
husband died November 30, 1815, aged 78, and was buried in the
Temple Church.

Mentioned in his wills and codicil, dated June 9, 1809, and
April 26, 1815, and proved December 22, 1815, are his three daughters, Elizabeth Loftus, Margaret Roadington (who predeceased
him), and Anne, wife of Henry Trail, his executor, and his son,
George Augustus, who died between June 9, 1809, and December
22, 1815, leaving two children, Henry George and Dorothea.

Captain James Miller

James Miller was an Irish emigrant who settled in February,
1775, at Jackson's creek in Camden district, South Carolina, where
he bought 200 acres of land from one James Phillips for £2 an acre.
In his petition he states that in the spring of 1775, a Mr. Tanner,
(probably the Rev. William Tennent) and one Richardson brought
to his district an association against Great Britain for signature. In-
cited by this minister in a sermon to sign this association, half the
congregation signed it, but James Miller and other loyalists refused.
In this same petition, Miller maintains that the Revolutionary party
in the spring of 1776 issued a proclamation, promising that all
loyalists who returned at once to their plantations would not be
molested   This promise was not fulfilled, however, the planters
having been seized.   After suffering imprisonment for over nineteen weeks, James Miller appears to have joined a loyalist force
under Captain James Phillips, which had been engaged in the siege
of Ninety-Six in November, 1775, and was a member of the party

of loyalists piloted up to Palocet by Alexander Chesney (see page 6). His steadfast loyalty was rewarded in August, 1780, by his appointment as captain in the Jackson's creek loyal militia, commanded by his friend and neighbor, Colonel John Phillips, who had known him from infancy. With this corps, or a detachment of it, Captain Miller served under Lieutenant-Colonel George Turnbull, of the New York Volunteers, some time during the war. In 1778 he was induced to buy 150 acres of land on Great Beaver creek from George Ray for £300, because the settlers in his own district had become "so disaffected to the King that he could not live peacably among them." Captain James Miller was not, however, destined to live on his new plantation, which was bought or sequestered by Captain Hugh Millen, an American officer. He left South Carolina before the end of the war and received an appointment as Customs officer in Ireland, and a pension of £30 a year. The sum of £370 was awarded to him as compensation by the British Government for the loss of his property in South Carolina. His wife died at Charleston in August, 1782. (T. 50/5; A.O. 12/109; A.O. 12/46, fos. 202-210; A O 13/79; A O. 13/133; *The Royal Comm. on Loyalists Claims, 1783-1785,* ed. by H. E Egerton; Roxburghe Club, 1915, pp. 51-2.)

Captain James Miller was an executor of Colonel John Phillips (see page 62).

LIEUTENANT-COLONEL EVAN MCLAURIN

Evan McLaurin. a Scotsman, had settled in the Dutch fork, at a place called Spring Hill, 15 miles from the Saluda river on the road from thence to Kennedy's ford on the Enoree river, by the Long lane, commonly called the Charleston road, on the west side of Broad river and 3 miles distant from that river. It was at this spot that Drayton held a public meeting early in the Revolution, with the object of persuading the inhabitants of the district to sign the association of support for the American cause. Ten had already signed, when McLaurin appeared on the scene and by his influence prevented the addition of another signature. Drayton, chagrined at the Scotsman's opposition, forthwith recommended the Council of Safety at Charleston to stop all goods destined for McLaurin's store at Dutch fork, a method of coercion by which it was hoped to undermine McLaurin's influence among his neighbors. (Drayton *Memoirs,* Vol. I, pp. 363-4, 369-370).

Lieutenant Colonel Evan McLaurin was one of the signatories to the treaty of neutrality of September 16, 1775, as well as to the later treaty in November following. (See Colonel Thomas Fletchall, Additional Notes, p. 69).

In December, 1779, his name appears as lieutenant-colonel in the muster roll of the South Carolina Royalists, a rank which he shared with Joseph Robinson.

Lieutenant-Colonel McLaurin died at Charleston in June, 1782, leaving a widow, Isabella, and two children. (A.O 12/109; T. 50/8; T. 50/27.)

COLONEL RICHARD PEARIS

Richard Pearis was born in Ireland and settled in Frederick county, Virginia, before 1750 At the outbreak of the Revolutionary war he was a successful planter and Indian trader on the Enoree river in South Carolina.

An orator of rude, savage eloquence and power, he commended himself to Governor Dinwiddie by his loyalty and efficiency He became lieutenant in the Virginia Provincial regiment in 1755 and was commissioned captain in 1756 to command a company of Cherokees and Catawbas in an expedition against the Shawnee towns west of the Ohio, under Major Andrew Lewis. Pearis served under Generals Forbes, Stanwix, Monckton, and Bouquet He was the first to enter Fort Duquesne. His military ability was apparent in his services on the borders of Maryland, Pennsylvania, and Virginia, with headquarters at Fort Pitt.

Having married a Cherokee wife, Captain Pearis acquired great influence among the Indians, and was consequently ordered south. In 1768 he was settled at the Big Canebrake, on the Reedy river, South Carolina.

Every effort was made by the Whigs in 1775 to induce this powerful man and the Indians to join them, or at least to secure their neutrality However, Pearis took part in the siege of Ninety-Six on the British side (see page 71) and many other actions.

In July, 1776, he was one of a party of 260 loyal militia and Indians which unsuccessfully attacked 450 "rebels" in a wooden fort (Colonel David Fanning's "Narrative," edited by A. W. Savary, *Canadian Magazine*, 1908)

According to his own narrative, his services to the crown in the same year include the dispersal of 700 "rebels" in the district of Ninety-Six (A O 13/93). By the turn of fortune he was captured and consigned to Charleston jail, where he was a prisoner in irons for nine months. On his release, Pearis wended his way on foot, traversing 700 miles, to West Florida, through the settlements of the Indians, who supplied him with food. Arriving at Pensacola, he was on 13 December, 1777, commissioned captain in the West Florida loyalist refugees, by Colonel John Stuart, superintendent of Indians in the Southern Colonies, who ordered him to capture Manshac on the Mississippi river, a task which he accomplished. This corps was also engaged in the suppression of the rum trade at Mobile Bay with the northern Creek Indians. (W. H. Siebert, "The Loyalists in West Florida and the Natchez District," in the *Mississippi Valley Historical Review*, Vol. II, 1916, p. 467) Pearis was present at the capture of Sunbury in Georgia.

The romantic tale of his exploits includes the raising of 5000 to 6000 loyalists and the disarming of all rebels from the Savannah river to Broad river, near the borders of North Carolina, as well as destroying their forts and capturing men, arms and ammunition. To his mortification, this series of successes was no sooner accomplished than Colonels Innes and Balfour ordered the arms and ammunition to be returned to the "rebels" and their leaders released. Incensed by this treatment, he returned to Georgia and settled his family near Augusta.

While Pearis was a prisoner at Charleston, his wife, two daughters, and a son were surprised at home by Colonel John Thomas and 400 followers, who subjected them to abuse and punishment, as well as carrying away their portable property and burning the rest. Not content, Colonel Thomas forced the family to march on foot 25 miles a day, without food and without protection for their heads from the sun. They were also confined for three days without food, and were afterwards sent off in an open wagon a ditsance of 100 miles, to shift for themselves among "a parcel of rebels," without money or provisions. For three years Captain Pearis was separated from his family, who were in daily fear of massacre by their enemies.

A son of Captain Pearis was an ensign in the West Florida Rangers.

For the loss of his real estate in South Carolina, Colonel Richard Pearis claimed £15,576. 18s. and was awarded £5,624. An account of his property has been published. (*S. C. Hist. and Gen. Mag.*, Vol. XVIII, pp. 97-9; *Sec. Rep. Bur. of Archives, Ontario*,

1904, pp. 190-4.) The name appears also as Paris, whence Paris Mountain, near Greenville in South Carolina.

After the war he settled in Abaco in the Bahamas, where he had a grant of 140 acres of land, and where Margaret Pearis, presumably his wife, received a grant of 40 acres. Colonel Pearis received a military allowance of £70 a year from 1783 to 1804, when he probably died. It was perhaps his son, Richard, who married Margaret, daughter of General Robert Cunningham, the South Carolina loyalist, in Abaco, 22 June, 1790 (see page 88). (Public Record Office: A.O. 12/109; A. T. Bethell, *Early Settlers of the Bahama Islands*, 1914, pp. 21-22; Public Record Office· Ind. 5606.)

MAJOR PATRICK CUNNINGHAM

This officer, a brother of Brigadier-General Robert Cunningham. was an active loyalist from the outset of the Revolutionary war As a participant in the siege of Ninety-Six he was one of the signatories to the treaty of neutrality of 22 November, 1775 (see p. 70) Major Patrick Cunningham and his party of loyalists attempted to rescue his brother, Robert, from his captors while being taken to Charleston as a prisoner, but failed in the attempt (see p. 87). He was, however, compensated for this failure by his capture of the ammunition sent as a gift by the Americans for the Cherokee Indians (see p 64). A member of this party was William Gist, who took up arms "to protect some loyalists who had taken a magazine of powder which was sent by the rebels to the Indians." (*The Royal Commission on Loyalist Claims, 1783-1785*, ed. by H. E. Egerton; Roxburghe Club, 1915, p 56; Moultrie, *Memoirs*, Vol. I. pp 96-100.)

Patrick Cunningham was appointed in 1780 to the command of a corps of loyal militia, consisting of 24 officers and 155 men, forming a part of the brigade of militia in the district of Ninety-Six, commanded by his brother, Robert.

Great was the joy of the Americans at the capture of so dangerous a loyalist as Patrick Cunningham, who was condemned to a term of imprisonment in Charleston jail Shortly after his release he offered his services to Major Andrew Williamson for his expedition against the Cherokee Indians in July, 1776, an expedition which was accompanied by Alexander Chesney and other loyalists, though the Cherokees at this time were supposed to be allies of the British Williamson, however, refused the offer of Cunningham's services, as he did that of Richard Pearis on the same occasion (Drayton, *Memoirs,* Vol II, pp 343-4). (See pp 65.)

Major Patrick Cunningham in or about 1785 returned to South Carolina and was elected a member of the Legislature, dying in 1794 (Sabine, *Loyalists of the American Revolution,* Vol I, p. 348).

CAPTAIN MOSES KIRKLAND

Moses Kirkland was a prosperous planter in the fertile district of Ninety-Six in South Carolina. In 1774 he was chosen a member of the Provincial Congress, and was regarded as a warm supporter of the American cause (see p 67) According to his memorial, however, he maintains that he spoke strongly in the House of Assembly at Charleston in January, 1775, against the proceedings of the Continental Congress at Philadelphia, but that his side was defeated by vote, and after protesting he returned home.

In June following, he was appointed by the Assembly to command a company of rangers, and his commission was sent to him in a letter which he refused to accept. (A.O. 12/52, fos. 209-233.)

Kirkland's next step was to assemble the inhabitants of his district and by his influence, combined with the assistance of Colonels Thomas Fletchall and Thomas Brown, he opposed Congress so effectually that he had raised over 5,000 signatures to a resolution to support the king's Government. In consultation with some of his leading neighbors it was now decided that, in view of the improbability of immediate military support from the governor and from the want of arms and ammunition, he should leave the Province and join the British army at Boston. In this scheme Kirkland was supported by his friends and he forthwith left his home in disguise, accompanied by his only son, a boy of twelve summers, and eventually reached the house of Governor Lord William Campbell, at Charleston, thence going on board H M S *Tamar.* From Charleston he proceeded to St. Augustine in East Florida, armed with letters of recommendation from Lord William Campbell to Governor Tonyn and others, and after a brief stay departed for Boston, where he arrived in September, 1775. Kirkland's sojourn at Boston was of brief duration, for he is next seen in Virginia, serving under the governor, Lord Dunmore. Returning again to Boston, his ship was captured, 10 December, near that port by the American schooner, *Lee,* commanded by Captain Manly who was probably the American officer of that name who was in command of the American privateer, *Hancock*, described by Sir George Collier as the second officer of rank in the American navy, "a man of talent and intrepidity" and more capable of doing mischief than General Lee," whom it was "a piece of good fortune" to have captured in June, 1777, with the *Hancock*. (Hist. MSS. Comm., *Report on the Mss. of Mrs Stopford-Sackville*, Vol. II, pp. 69-70)

Kirkland was sent to Washington's headquarters at Cambridge, where he was detained for 22 days, and then removed to Philadelphia. Here he was a prisoner until June, 1776, when he escaped, and by traveling in disguise succeeded in getting to Lord Dunmore's vessels in Chesapeake Bay at the end of July. Kirkland afterwards joined General Sir William Howe on Staten Island, and was present at the capture of Long Island, New York, White Plains, and Fort Washington. At the end of March, 1777, Howe requested Kirkland to carry despatches to East and West Florida, and he accomplished his mission without mishap, arriving, 1 May, at St. Augustine. Proceeding overland, he reached Pensacola, a journey of twenty days, and delivered the despatches to Governor Chester and to General John Stuart, superintendent of the Indians, who appointed him deputy superintendent of Indians, by command of General Howe, 22 May, 1777. He remained in West Florida until January, 1778, when he went among the Indian tribes, distributing presents and endeavoring to persuade them to be loyal and to act in concert with the British. Returning to St. Augustine on 1 March, Kirkland prepared a plan for an expedition composed of loyalist refugees and Indians, against Georgia, which he submitted for the approval of the governor and the general, presumably Prevost. The consent of the commander-in-chief was, however, necessary before the scheme could be put into force, and with this object in view, the indefatigable Kirkland set sail for Philadelphia, which he reached in May, only to find that Howe had resigned and was about to return to England. He succeeded, however, in submitting his plan to Howe and Sir Henry Clinton, both of whom approved of it Kirkland remained at Philadelphia until the evacuation of the city by the British in June, when he accompanied Clinton to New York. Here he was on duty until requested in October by Clinton to accompany Colonel Archibald Campbell's expedition to Georgia, and there to render every assistance in his power. His first taste of war here was at the capture of Savannah by the British. At the action of Brier creek, 60 miles from Savannah, Kirkland commanded part of the Georgia militia and a party of loyalist refugees. Later he accompanied Prevost on the expedition to Charleston

Kirkland appears to have returned to Georgia, for on 9 October, 1779, he was captured with about 100 other loyalists under Captain French at Ogeechie, 15 miles from Savannah, and he and his son, were bound in irons and put on board a galley Happily, this vessel was captured by the British, and he re-joined the British forces at Savannah.

Lord Cornwallis, it will be remembered, appointed Robert Cunningham to command a brigade of loyal militia in the district of Ninety-Six in 1780. One of the regiments was allotted to Moses Kirkland, the date of his commission being 6 July. He continued on active service in his own district until he joined Colonel John Harris Cruger on the expedition for the relief of the gallant Colonel Thomas Brown and his force at Augusta in the middle of September.

Major Kirkland's memorial adds but few details of his subsequent career, beyond mentioning that he was put in command of the garrison at Augusta after the relief of Brown, and that he would seem later to have settled near Savannah.

After the evacuation of South Carolina by the British, Moses Kirkland sought refuge in Jamaica, where he settled in St. George's parish and married Catherine Bruce. His life was ended by drowning while on a voyage from the West Indies to England in December, 1787. Richard Bruce Kirkland, his only son, was born in 1786 and became a planter in Jamaica. (A.O. 12/52, fos. 209-233)

Drayton gives a different version of the reasons for Kirkland's departure from South Carolina, alleging that after his (Drayton's) manifesto of 30 August, 1775, warning all persons who should without lawful authority assemble in arms with, or by the instigation of Kirkland, that they would be regarded as public enemies, to be suppressed by the sword, and that Kirkland was confounded and his exertions paralyzed. Offering to surrender on a promise of pardon, Drayton demanded his surrender at discretion, but Kirkland fled in disguise, with two trusty friends (Drayton, *Memoirs*, Vol. I, p. 382.)

Kirkland conceals one important event in his career, namely, that he was concerned with Major James Mayson and Captain John Caldwell in the seizure of Fort Charlotte and its stores of ammunition, which was the first overt act in the Revolutionary war in South Carolina. It was after the re-capture of the fort by the loyalists that Kirkland turned over to the other side (see p. 67).

˙Iajor Moses Kirkland's prosperous position as a planter may be gauged from the extent of his award of £4,000 from his claim of £12,160 for the loss of his property in South Carolina (A.O. 12/109). This property was sold by the State of South Carolina and realized £1,972. 2s. (A.O. 13/36, A O. 12/92, *S C. Hist. and Gen. Mag.*, Vol. XVIII, pp. 69-71.)

LIEUTENANT-COLONEL JOHN FANNING

John Fanning was a South Carolinian by birth and lived on his own property in Camden district. In addition to this property he was the owner of 250 acres of land on Broad river, received by deed of gift from his eldest brother after his father's death, and of other property in South Carolina. *(Second Report of the Bureau of Archives, Province of Ontario, 1904, pp. 717-719)* John Fanning first joined the loyalist militia of South Carolina in March, 1779, receiving a commission as captain, and later as lieutenant-colonel. All his brothers were also loyalists

In an engagement at Parker's ferry he commanded a troop of horse under Major Thomas Fraser, of the South Carolina Royalists.

Alexander Chesney was appointed a lieutenant in John Fanning's Independent company of Scouts, 20 April, 1781.

At the end of the war, Lieutenant-Colonel John Fanning would seem to have settled in Nova Scotia. For his property confiscated at Camden he was awarded £440 as compensation by the British Government, from his claim of £1,103   (A.O. 12/109)

This loyalist officer must not be confused with Colonel David Fanning (author of the well-known "Narrative," or with Colonel Edmund Fanning, of the King's American regiment, who was appointed lieutenant-governor of Prince Edward Island as a recompense for his services in the Revolutionary war (A O 12/49; A.O. 12/68; A O 12/92, A O. 13/138.)

CAPTAIN JOHN SAUNDERS

John Saunders was born, 1 June, 1753, in Princess Anne county, Virginia, and was the only son of Jonathan and Elizabeth Saunders, grandson of Captain John Saunders of that county and great-grandson of the Rev. Jonathan Saunders, of Lynnhaven parish in the same county, the date of his birth being recorded in a family Bible which in 1834 was in the possession of his brother-in-law, Colonel Jacob Ellegood in New Brunswick, Canada.

According to Sabine *(Loyalists of the American Revolution)*, this young Virginian was descended from an English royalist family which had emigrated to Virginia and there acquired large estates. An ardent anti-Whig in his youth, his was the only voice raised in opposition to the sending of delegates to attend a Whig convention at Williamsburg, at a meeting organized in his own county in July, 1774. John Saunders abandoned his academical studies and accepted, against the entreaties of his friends and neighbors, a commission as captain in the Queen's Own Loyal Virginian regiment, from the governor, Lord Dunmore, 16 November, 1775. This regiment, the only loyalist corps raised in Virginia, was commanded by his brother-in-law, Colonel Jacob Ellegood, of Rosehall on Lynnhaven river, who had been in charge of the estate of John Saunders during the last six years of his minority. (A.O. 13/33)

The studied contempt of this youthful loyalist for the Revolutionary party in his county aroused much ill-feeling, with the result that he and two other loyalists, Benjamin Dingley Gray and Captain Mitchell Phillips, were not only regarded as inimical to the liberties of America, but their neighbors were recommended to cease commercial intercourse with them, an act which virtually endeavored to stop their supplies of all kinds, including food (Force, *American Archives,* Series IV, Vol. 2, pp. 76-77.)

The Queen's Own Loyal Virginian regiment was incorporated, some time after its defeat at Great Bridge, with the First American regiment, better known as the Queen's Rangers. In the dragoons of this loyalist corps, John Saunders received a commission as captain on 25 November, 1776 From that time until the end of the year 1780, Captain Saunders served in every action of that regiment, and was severely wounded at the battle of the Brandywine, where his brother-in-law, Major John McKay of the same regiment, was also wounded. Colonel John Graves Simcoe, commanding officer of the Queen's Rangers, treated Captain Saunders as his confidential friend and described him as an officer of "great address and determination" and as one who had performed gallant and active services in the war (Simcoe, *Military Journal*). An original certificate of Simcoe states that from a sense of the merit and eminent services of Captain John Saunders, he did his utmost to procure him the rank of major (A.O. 13/133). These compliments of Colonel Simcoe were reciprocated by Captain

Saunders in later years by the bestowal of the name of Simcoe on his only son, John Simcoe Saunders.

Captain Saunders accompanied General Leslie on the expedition to Virginia in October, 1780, when he commanded the cavalry detachment of his regiment. From Virginia he was removed with the Queen's American Rangers to South Caloina, where he was on duty until April, 1782, when he sailed for New York and there took command of the remnant of his regiment saved from the surrender at Yorktown. (A.O 13/79.) This regiment was placed on the British establishment, 25 December, 1782, and at the peace Captain John Saunders was granted half-pay.

The Saunders estate on Lynnhaven river, near Kempe's landing place (Kempsville) in Princess Anne county, was confiscated and sold by order of the court of that county in March, 1780. The considerable sum of £4,850 was granted to Captain John Saunders as compensation for the loss of this estate, by the British Government after the war. This sum was only £238 below the estimated value put upon it by him or his advisers. Captain Saunders, having studied law in his youth in Virginia, returned at the end of the war to the land of his English ancestors and entered the Middle Temple, being called to the bar in 1787 Three years later he married Ariana Margaretta Jekyll Chalmers, daughter of Colonel James Chalmers, of the Maryland Loyalists, also an American refugee in England, and his wife, Arianna Margaretta, daughter of John Jekyll, the younger, sometime collector of the Customs at Boston, Massachusetts, and his wife, Margaret Shippen, of Philadelphia, the marriage having taken place at St. Luke's Church, Chelsea, February 16, 1790. (W.O. 42/S4.) Immediately after his marriage Captain Saunders proceeded to New Brunswick, where he had earlier in the same year been appointed fourth puisne judge in the Province, through the influence of Colonel John Graves Simcoe. In 1822 he was raised to the dignity of chief justice, as well as that of president of the Legislative Council of New Brunswick. Colonel Jacob Ellegood and Major John McKay, brothers-in-law of Captain John Saunders, settled in York county, New Brunswick, on half-pay.

Ever ready to defend his adopted country against threats of invasion, by the French in 1798 and by the Americans in 1808, he took an active part in the latter year in calling out the militia as a defensive measure, and from his long and arduous experience in the American war of Independence he was chosen commanding officer of one of the two battalions. The fear of invasion having passed away, the battalions were disbanded in three months by Judge Edward Winslow, who did not share in the feelings of alarm of his predecessor, Gabriel G. Ludlow, president and commander-in-chief of the Province.

John Simcoe Saunders, the only son of Captain Saunders, was sent to England for his education and matriculated at Worcester College, Oxford, in 1810, taking the degree of B.A. in 1815. Following in his father's footsteps, he was called to the bar, by Lincoln's Inn, having previously read in the chambers of a well known lawyer, Joseph Chitty. John Simcoe Saunders became an eminent lawyer in New Brunswick, and during his life held the offices of advocate-general, surveyor-general, and lieutenant-governor of the Province, as well as president of the Legislative Council. As author of *The Law of Pleading and Evidence in Civil Actions*, his name is remembered in legal circles

The arms of Captain John Saunders and his son are illustrated in an article on book plates by D. R. Jack in *Acadiensis*, Vol. II, pp. 189-197.

Chief Justice Saunders died, 24 May, 1834, at Fredericton, New Brunswick, where also his wife died in 1845, at the age of 77. (F.O. 4/1; Lawrence and Stockton, *The Judges of New Brunswick and Their Times*, pp. 100-1, 111, 116, 141, 274-5, 352, 423-4, 440, 509; notes from Mr Charles McIntosh; Ind. 5604.)

MAJOR THOMAS FRASER

This officer's name appears more than once in the course of the preparation of the above Additional Notes. He was appointed major of the South Carolina Royalists, 10 August, 1780, at the age of 25 and was present in many of the sanguinary actions in South Carolina, having served throughout the war in the Provincial forces.

At about the time that the British were preparing for their final evacuation of South Carolina, Major Fraser was married on 7 November, 1782, to Anne Loughton Smith at Charleston by Rev. Edward Jenkins, chaplain to the South Carolina Royalists. His wife was the daughter of Thomas Loughton Smith, a prominent Charleston merchant and a member of the Commons House of Assembly, and his wife, Elizabeth, daughter of George Inglis, merchant, of Charleston Thomas Loughton Smith died, 16 April,

1773, and his widow married in 1775 Dr. James Clitherall, surgeon to the South Carolina Royalists.

Major Thomas Fraser died, 31 May, 1820, at Philadelphia and was buried there in Christ Church burying ground. His wife died, 6 August, 1835, at the house of her son-in-law, Prince Lucien Murat, at Bordentown, New Jersey. (W.O. 42/F13; Ind. 5604-5-6.)

LIEUTENANT-GOVERNOR WILLIAM BULL

William Bull, a South Carolinian by birth and one of the most beloved of men, served his native Province in public offices for thirty-five years, acting as governor at various intervals for nine years.

Attempts were made in his behalf by influential friends at Charleston to secure his valuable estate from confiscation by the State To this end his estate was conveyed temporarily to his nephew Stephen Bull, who, as will be shown later, retained possession of it by fraudulent means, in spite of the determination of the commissioners, appointed to sell confiscated estates, to contest the validity of the conveyance. Stephen Bull, by his undoubted political and social influence at Charleston, prevented a suit against him for the recovery of the property by the State by representing his devoted attachment to the American cause, and by alleging great depredations committed by the British troops on his own property.

Lieutenant-Governor Bull was prevented by the confiscation law of South Carolina from bringing a suit against Stephen Bull for the recovery of his property, but the Legislative Council went so far as to offer him the rights of citizenship upon the express condition that he would return to South Carolina and take the oaths of allegiance and fidelity to the State. His nephew, fearing that his uncle might agree to these conditions, and thus jeopardize his possession of his uncle's property, had exerted his influence with the Legislative Council to prevent the offer of these terms, but without success. The deep conscientiousness of William Bull and his high-minded character, however, were insuperable barriers to his renunciation of his oaths of loyalty to the British, deeply as he loved South Carolina.

The 134 prime slaves of Lieutenant-Governor Bull had been distributed among American soldiers as bribes to induce them to re-inlist in the American forces.

His first four attorneys in South Carolina—Manigault, Russell, Stephen Bull (his nephew), and Robert Williams—conveyed the estate of William Bull to Pringle, speaker of the House of Assembly, who conveyed it to Stephen Bull. These attorneys had agreed that the conveyance should be in trust and that Stephen Bull's bond was to be taken with it. Such was the treachery of Stephen Bull that he did not throw off the mask until an offer of 4,000 guineas was made to Lieutenant-Governor Bull for a piece of land, when Stephen Bull refused the conveyance.

William Bull died in 1791 in London, an exile from his native land, and was buried at St. Andrew's Church, Holborn. (Public Record Office: A.O. 12/52, fos. 85-118.)

THE LOYAL MILITIA OF SOUTH CAROLINA

Lord Cornwallis in a despatch to Sir Henry Clinton, dated 30 June, 1780, says that (1) as the different districts submitted he formed the inhabitants into militia and appointed the officers according to the old divisions of the Province; (2) that he had invested these field officers with civil as well as military power; (3) that he had divided the militia into two classes, the first to consist of men above the age of 40 and of certain property, family, or service, to keep order in their respective districts and to do patrol duty, but never to be called out for active service, except in case of an insurrection or an actual invasion of the Province. The second class to be composed of the younger men, who would assist in the home duties and would be liable to serve in either of the Carolinas or Georgia for six months of every year. This class, however, would be called upon in such proportions as to cause the least distress possible to the country; and (4) that temporary commissions had been given these militia regiments. (Hist. MSS. Comm., *Report on the MSS. of Mrs. Stopford-Sackville*, Vol. II., p. 169.)

Robert Cunningham, a well-known and active loyalist (see page 87) was appointed brigadier-general of the brigade of militia of the district of Ninety-Six, the most populous and powerful district in the Province. From June to December, 1780, this brigade consisted of six regiments commanded by the following officers:

Colonel Daniel Clary, with 6 officers and 45 men.

Major Daniel Plummer, with 4 officers and 62 men.

Major Patrick Cunningham, with 24 officers and 155 men.

Colonel John Cotton, with 26 officers and 141 men.

Colonel Richard King, with 12 officers and 11 men.   Colonel King died, 10 July, 1786.

Major Zacharias Gibbs, with 13 officers and 50 men.

The loyal militia in South Carolina from November, 1781, to July, 1782, included:

Jackson's creek regiment, commanded by Colonel John Phillips (see p. 101), and divided into two companies under Captains John Huey and James Sharp, one of the officers being Lieutenant William Sharp.

Stevenson's creek regiment under the command of Colonel John Cotton.

First Camden regiment, commanded by Colonel Robert English.

Second Camden regiment, commanded by Colonel William Ballentine.

These two Camden regiments would seem to have been formed into ten companies, commanded by Captains Adam Thompson, Joshua English, Hugh Smith, Michael Egan, Joseph Holt, John Robinson, Jasper Rogers, James McCulloch, George Platt, and Abraham Cook.

The Orangeburg militia at this date consisted of eight companies under the command of Colonel John Fisher, with the following captains:

Christian House, Henry Giesondanner, Joseph Noble, Samuel Rowe, Thomas Pledger, Daniel Kelly, L Stromer, and Elias Buckingham.   Captain L. Stromer afterwards deserted to the Americans.   Under Colonel Fisher's command was also Captain John Sally's company from the Fork of Edisto and Orangeburg.

Two companies of militia from the Dutch fork of Ninety-six, under Colonel Daniel Clary, were commanded by Captains George Stroup and James Wright, while Captain George Long was in command of a company in Colonel Richard King's regiment.

Lieutenant-Colonel William Young commanded the Little river militia at this period.

Among other loyal militia regiments included in the lists for the year 1782 are the following:

Colleton county, commanded by Colonel Robert Ballingall.

Ninety-Six, commanded by Colonel Thomas Pearson.

Dragoons, commanded by Major William Young.

Mounted militia, commanded by Major William Cunningham.

Cheraws, commanded by Colonel Robert Gray.

Georgetown, commanded by Lieutenant-Colonel James Gordon.

1st Regiment Camden, commanded by Colonel James Carey.

Santee, commanded by Colonel Samuel Tynes.

Rocky Mount, commanded by Colonel William Vernon Turner, a surgeon at Camden, who at the evacuation of South Carolina by the British went to Jamaica, West Indies, with his wife and six children. (A.O. 13/96.)

Colonel Hezekiah Williams was in command of a regiment of loyal militia in South Carolina in 1782.

The following officers' names have been taken from various lists:

Lieutenant James Johnstone in Colonel Robert English's Camden militia.

Captains Alexander Harvey, Andrew Cunningham, and John Barton, and Lieutenant Benjamin Smith Legge in the Colleton county militia.

Lieutenant James Clatworthy in the Camden militia.

James Alexander, of St. George's parish, Berkeley county, was selected, 27 May, 1780, as captain of the Indian Field company of foot in that parish, with James Shepperd as lieutenant and Silas Canadais as ensign. It was Captain Alexander who with several other loyalists deemed it their duty to capture Captain John Felder, a magistrate of Orangeburg district, because of his cruel oppression of the loyalists. The party in due course assembled at Captain Felder's house and demanded his surrender. Anticipating no quarter, Captain Felder and his companison, John Fry, defended themselves to the bitter end, and killed the first loyalist who knocked at the door. Such was Captain Felder's determination that the loyalists, finding it impossible to force him out of his house by any other means, set fire to it, and in attempting to escape, both Captain Felder and John Fry were shot dead. (A O 13/125.)

Colonel William Mills is noticed on page 74.

The pay of the loyal militia in 1780 was as follows:

> Colonel, 10s. a day.
> Lieut.-Colonel, 7s. 6d. a day.
> Major, 7s. 6d. a day.
> Captain, 4s. 8d. a day.
> Lieutenant, 2s. 4d. a day.
> Cornet and Ensign, 2s. 4d. a day.
> Adjutant, 3s. a day.
> Quartermaster, 3s. a day.

Sergeant, 1s. a day.

Corporal, 6d. a day.

Private, 6d. a day.

Many muster rolls of officers and men of the South Carolina loyal militia, with memorials of widows of officers and men who lost their lives in the war, and other details, are preserved in the Public Record Office. (T. 50/1, T. 50/2, T. 50/3, T. 50/4.)

A list of loyalists in South Carolina who held royal commissions during the Revolutionary war is published as an appendix to *The Journal and Letters of Samuel Curwen,* 4th. edition, 1864, pp. 494-5.

Lieutenant William Elliott, of Captain Elisha Robinson's company of lower Ninety-Six regiment of militia, fought at King's Mountain and was probably killed there. Here also fought Lieutenant Thomas Cunningham, of Major Patrick Cunningham's company, and was wounded and taken prisoner. The memorial of Sergeant James White of Cotton's Ninety Six militia is in T. 50/2.

LOYALISTS' WARRANT

Attached to the papers of Charles Ogilvie, Sr., is the original warrant, dated August 13, 1782, authorizing him and Gideon Dupont, Jr., to proceed to New York on behalf of the loyalists of South Carolina for the purpose of making representations to the commander-in-chief of the British army of the true state of that Province and the distress of mind of the inhabitants at the prospect of its evacuation by the British troops there. (A.O. 13/133.) These two men were urged to make every endeavor to secure such guarantees as would make an evacuation as little injurious as possible to the loyalists, and, in the event of an evacuation, to obtain leave for the loyalists to indemnify themselves from the sequestered estates within the British lines in South Carolina.

The warrant is signed by the following committee of loyalists:

Robert William Powell, chairman

John Champneys	James Gordon
Colonel John Phillips	Colonel Gabriel Capers
William Greenwood	Robert Johnston
John Hamilton	Thomas Inglis
Alexander Baron	Colonel Zacharias Gibbs
Colonel Robert Ballingall	Colonel David Fanning
Colonel William Fortune	Colonel Thomas Edghill

Charles Ogilvie was an Englishman or Scotsman who journeyed backwards and forwards between America and London on business.

Gideon Dupont, Jr., was probably the son of Gideon Dupont who was a member of the South Carolina Provincial Congress for the parish of St. Peter's, Purrysburg, in January, 1775.

South Carolina Loyalists in Nova Scotia and Elsewhere

Reference has been made elsewhere (p 75) to the large numbers of loyalists banished from the Southern Colonies who sought refuge first in Florida and afterwards in the West Indies. A memorial dated 9 February, 1785, from seventy-two loyalist officers from North Carolina was presented to Lord Sydney, stating that they had forfeited their estates and regretting that their most gracious sovereign had been compelled by the rigors of necessity to cede to his late refractory subjects all that happy, temperate, and Southern climate in America, to which the memorialists and their numerous adherents had been accustomed. Many had gone to Nova Scotia, but were unable in their present state of finances to clear the ground and raise the necessaries of life in a climate to Southern constitutions inhospitable and severe. The memorial suggests the Bahamas as the only place in the British dominions suitable for these loyalists and strongly recommends Colonel John Hamilton, late of the Royal North Carolina regiment, as governor of the islands, when that dignified office should become vacant. John Hamilton, a Scotsman and member of the large firm of Archibald Hamilton and Company, merchants and importers in North Carolina and Virginia, was one of the most interesting figures on the loyalist side in the Revolutionary war. An active partisan, he had raised 1200 men during the war and had seen much fighting in the South. At the battle of Camden he fought with great spirit until put out of action by wounds. Dr. David Oliphant, surgeon in the American forces, was a debtor to the house of Hamilton and Company for the amount of about £15,000, for which he was imprisoned at Charleston until released by Lieutenant-Colonel Nisbet Balfour in the belief that he would be of service in arranging the exchange of prisoners of war. (A.O. 13/95.) In 1794 John Hamilton was British consul-general at Norfolk, Virginia, having been selected for that appointment because of his popularity, and while in discharge of his duties there, his loyalty again manifested itself by his offer of active service in war against the French.

It is estimated that about 500 souls had sailed from South Carolina for Nova Scotia at the evacuation of Charleston by the British. Of this number 300 were at Halifax in that Province in February, 1783, when an appeal was made to the British Government for further allowances of provisions, clothing, and farming utensils, which in their extreme poverty they were unable to procure. (Hist. MSS. Comm., *Report on the American MSS. in the Royal Inst.* Vol. III, p. 361.)

In 1784 grants of land were made at Rawdon, Halifax county, Nova Scotia, to the following fifty-six South Carolina loyalists; Colonel Zacharias Gibbs, Captain John Bond, and Captain William Meek, who received 1000 acres each; Captain George Bond, James Nichols, Adam Fralick, John Saunderson, William Bowman, John McGuire, Henry Martindale, Reuben Lively, William Wallace, John Murphy, Henry Green, John McCullum, William Bryson, Samuel Covell, Samuel Meek, John Meek, Richard Attwood, James Fitzsimmonds, William Wier, Eli Hoyt, John Lewis, John Withrow, William Cunningham, Colonel Thomas Pearson, Shubal Dimock, Benjamin Wier, and Robert Alexander, who were severally granted 500 acres; John Bryson, Samuel McAllister, Richard McMullen, Thomas Thornton, Samuel Procter, Joseph or Jacob Ellis, Jacob Withrow, David Withrow, William Bryson, Jr., Jeremiah Crossian or McCrossian, Henry Martindale, Jr., George Snell, Peter Ryland, Robert Costley, John Landerkin, Daniel Snell, David Snell, John Bond, Joseph Simpson, Eli Thornton, Abraham Thornton, Moses Bruce, Philip Murphy, Roger Wilson, Thomas Williams, and Robert Scott, each of whom received 250 acres in this tract of 23,000 acres of land.

IMPORTANT CLAIMS AND AWARDS OF SOME SOUTH CAROLINA LOYALISTS

A list of the more important claims of South Carolina loyalists, and the amounts awarded as compensation by the British Government follows:

Colonel Elias Ball, Sr.	£23,573	£12,700
Major James Ballmer	£16,000	£400
Thomas Boone (claims for the Colleton family)	£41,207.4s	£22,533.8s

Robert Brailsford's children	£15,568	£500
James Brisbane	£20,049	£2,274
Lieutenant-Governor William Bull	£40,086	£6,400
James Burns	£12,350	£5,000
John Champneys	£20,212	£5,204
Hugh and Daniel Campbell	£11,350	
Thomas Fenwick	£14,627	£5,000
William Greenwood	£49,604	
Captain Richard Graves and his wife	£16,852	
Philip Henry	£16,351	£2,723.16s.
Zephaniah Kingsley	£16,691 12s	£785
Moses Kirkland	£12,160	£4,000
Lord Charles Greville Montagu, formerly governor of the Province	£36,830	
Captain John Orde	£10,705.10s.	£1,208.14s.
Gideon Dupont	£14,131	£2,387.4s.
R. W. Powell and John Hopton	£22,644	£1,518
Colonel Richard Pearis	£15,576.18s.	£5,624
John Rose	£40,084 10s.	£16,526.16s.
James Simpson	£20,608	£8,077
Robert Williams	£22,692	£1,705
Alexander Wright	£12,916	£8,121

The three claims of Lord Charles Greville Montagu, Captain Richard Graves and his wife, and of William Greenwood were disallowed because those claimants failed to produce documentary or other satisfactory proof of the definite loss of their property by confiscation or other means.

According to the report (A.O. 13/85) of the committee of South Carolina loyalists, dated May 24, 1783, the estimated values of the property lost by the loyalists of that Province were as follows:

Real estate.............	£569,631.
Slaves	£206,324.
Debts..	£389,968.
Losses by depreciation..	£155,688.
Contingent losses	£ 82,240.
Removable property....	£ 22,699.
Total..............	£1,426,550. sterling

Official salaries and incomes from professions, *per annum*, were estimated at £28,280, and the total amount of the award was £17,400.

The committee, having found that in many cases the values were over-estimated, deducted the sum of £165,314 from the aggregate amount.

The value of land was based in most cases on the personal knowledge of members of the committee, but where such knowledge did not exist, it was valued at six shillings sterling per acre.

Slaves were valued at an average of £60 sterling each, which was the price realized for them at public auction before the war.

The report of the committee of the South Carolina loyalists bears the autograph signatures of Thomas Irving, James Simpson, Henry Peronneau, William Ancrum, Robert Williams, John Hopton, and James Johnston. (A.O. 13/85.)

The amount awarded by the British Government on the claims for compensation was £257,000. In addition, pensions exceeding £6,600 *per annum* were granted to the South Carolina loyalists. (A.O. 12/109.)

Compensation for debts (£389,968) was refused on the ground that by the fourth, fifth, and sixth articles of the peace treaty, no impediments were to be put in the way of the recovery of debts by the colonists. But the States by ignoring these articles (J. B. McMaster, *Hist. of the People of the U. S.*, Vol. I, p 107; *Cambridge Modern History*, Vol. VII, 1903, p. 307.) and the Congress by its helplessness to enforce the stipulations of its treaties, brought America at once into conflict with Great Britain. Many loyalists, who had returned to their former homes in America in expectation of receiving payment of at least a part of their just debts, and in many cases with the intention of remaining there, were not only refused payment but were subjected to such abuse and ill treatment as to compel them to quit the country forthwith.

Evidence of the refusal of debtors in South Carolina to pay their just debts to loyalists is obtained from, among other sources, a letter written from Charleston, 4 April, 1785, to Colonel John Hamilton. In this letter the writer states that several loyalists who had come there in consequence of the peace were ordered to depart th country in 60 days, while others had only 30 days to remain. The writer, in picturing the lawlessness of the State, mentions the case of a loyalist who was hanged, after his acquittal by the circuit judge. (A.O. 13/85.)

A senator of South Carolina refused payment of a note, dated 1773, due to Paul Hamilton, a loyalist planter there. (From a letter from Alexander Chisholm, dated 14 February, 1787, from Charleston: A.O. 13/129.)

APPENDIXES
FROM ORIGINAL AND UNPUBLISHED
MATERIAL IN THE PUBLIC RECORD
OFFICE, LONDON, ENGLAND

APPENDIX I

MINUTES OF THE EXAMINATION OF ALEXANDER CHESNEY BY THE
COMMISSIONERS OF AMERICAN CLAIMS, IN LONDON.[1]

6th. May 1783.

Resided on broad River in the district of Ninety six—lived
with his Father but had Plantations of his own—he married a Wife
& had 200 Acres with her—he had 700 Acres besides—he went there
from Ireland in 1772—He values the whole 900 Acres (70 of which
are cultivated) above 1000 at £1516 Sterling—the Value is certified
by Col°. Philips [2] & likewise by Lord Cornwallis & Col°. Balfour—
his Personal Estate amounted to £480.—he first joined the Kings
Troops after Charles Town was taken in 1780—Has a Wife & one
Child in Belfast [3]—he came home in April 1782—he married in
America—he has no Property of his own in Ireland but he is supported by his Friends who advance him Money when he wants it—
He has some little Support Lord Rawdon gave him a Supernumary
Tidewaiters Place which is worth about £20 a year—he does not
wish to continue in it—he came over from Ireland in Order to at-
tend here which will be an Expence to him of £20.

Certificate very sufficient & no further Attendance require

Decision   £50 p Ann from 5th. January 1783.

This Person had very singular Merit in South Carolina—his
property was worth £2000. Sterling & we think it would be proper
to pay him after the Rate of £50. p Ann. from the 5 January 1783.

---

[1] These minutes are in A O 12/99, fo 219.

[2] Colonel John Phillips (see p 60)

[3] Alexander Chesney was married for the second time, March 1, 1783 The child here
mentioned was his son, William, by his first wife He was in South Carolina at that time, not
at Belfast. It was Alexander Chesney's wife who was at Belfast

APPENDIX II.

Docket: N° 193

Alexander Chesney
his Memorial

rceeived 21ˢᵗ November 1783

To the Honourable the Commissioners appointed by Act of Parliament for enquiring into the Losses and services of the American Loyalists.

The Memorial of Capᵗ Alexander Chesney
Late of the Province of South Carolina

Sheweth

That your memorialist for several years prior to the Late unhappy Rebellion in america resided on Pacolet River in Ninety six district in the Province of South Carolina aforesaid

That at the commencement of the Rebellion in that Province, your memorialist took an active part in favour of the British Government and rendered the Loyal subjects in that country as well as his Majesties army essential services as appear by the certifycates hereunto annexed.

That soon after the reduction of Charles Town by Sir Henry Clinton your memorialist was appointed a Captain of a company of militia, and Adjutant of the different batalions of militia under the late Major Ferguson of the 71ˢᵗ Regiment in which capacity he acted untill the defeat of that officer on Kings Mountain where your memorialist was wounded and taken prisoner.

That your memorialist after he obtained his Liberty, again acted in his military capacities untill the out posts were drove into the garison of Charles Town

That your memorialist has Lost all his Lands and other property, in consequence of his Loyalty, and attachment to the British Government; the same being long since seized and confiscated by the rebels.

Your memorialist therefore prays that his case may be taken into your consideration, in order that your memorialist may be enabled under [your] Report, to receive such aid or relief, as his Losses and services may be found to deserve.

And your memorialist as in duty bound will ever pray

London 20th Novr 1783   Alex^r Chesney.

at 31 Brownlow Street

Long acre, London.

Witnesses names	Places of Residence of the witnesses
Colonel John Phillips	N°. 31 Brownlow Street Long Acre, London
Col. Zacharias Gibbs	N°. 32 Charles Street Westminster.
Captn James Miller	N°. 18 Drury Lane London.

APPENDIX III

AN ESTIMATE OF ALEXANDER CHESNEY'S PROPERTY

An estimate of the Lands, and other property, of Cap^{tn} Alexander Chesney, Late of Pacolet River, in the Province of South Carolina, Lost by his Loyalty and attachment to Great Britain.

DESCRIPTION OF THE LANDS	Sterling value pr. acre	
80 Acres situate on the north bank of Pacolet River, being part of a tract of 300 acres granted by Gov. Tryon Late Govr. of North Carolina, and purchased by me from Peter Howard, as will appear by conveyances now in my possession. on said tract was about 40 acres cleared and well fenced in convenient fields, with good houses and other improvements, and a valuable fishery together with a commodious seat for a saw and flower mill, greatest part of the irons and other materials for said works I had provided before I was obliged to abandon said Lands, the *improvements were made by me,*	40s	160
150 acres adjoining the above tract, being part of a tract of 400 acres, Granted by Lord Charles Grenville Montague,[1] Late Govr. of		

[1] See Additional Notes, p. 59.

DESCRIPTION OF THE LANDS	Sterling value pr. acre	
South Carolina, to Robert Chesney my father, from whom I received the same under deed of gift A. D. 1778 which conveyance was Lost or destroyed at the time the Rebel Gen[1]. Morgan [2] took possession of my plantation before Col Tarletons Defeat at the Cowpens which happened on the 17th Jany 1781.	25s	187.10
200 acres situate on williams creek the waters of Pacolet River granted by the Gov[r]. of North Carolina to James Cook, from him conveyed to William Hodge, from whom I received it by a contract of marriage with his daughter, in the year 1780. On said tract was good houses and 30 acres or upward cleared Land, under good fences which improvements was rented out at the time I was oblidged to leave that place, for one third of its produce. the conveyance of this was also Lost or destroyed by Morgans army when they encamped at my plantation	40s	400
200 Acres situate on the waters of Williams Creek and joining one square of the aforesaid tract, surveyed for, and granted to me. the grant of this is in the public office in Charlestown, there is a valuable vein of copper ore runs through this tract	30s	300
100 Acres situate on Bush River,[3] granted to me on a bounty warrant during the Government of Lord Charles Granvile Montague the grant of this is also in the Public office in Cha[s] Town		
Amount of my Lands	£	1122.10

[2] General Daniel Morgan.
[3] Bush river is in Newberry county, South Carolina.

DESCRIPTION OF THE LANDS	Sterling value pr. acre	
OTHER PROPERTY		
One Negro woman named Moll, taken away by the Rebel Captn Vardrey Magbee[4]	60	
Three horses taken away by D° same time	40	
One Waggon and team with gears &c &c.	100	
Six Cows taken by Morgans army 40ˢ each	12	
Three hogsheads of Tobaco or thereabouts, with about five hundred bushels of Indian corn, in store, a quantity of oats and other crop taken by the aforesaid Morgans army	120	
The Schooner Dolphin which I left in America when I came to Europe for the recovery of my health, which same schooner cost me Seventy Guineas but just She is by the most authentic accounts since taken by the Rebels.	70	
Cash and Goods on board said Schooner	40	442.0
	£	1564.10

Alex:ʳ Chesney

London 20ᵗʰ Novʳ. 1783.[5]

I certify that Mʳ Alexander Chesney was employed by me in the Barrack department as Inspector of Wood Cutters from the 18ᵗʰ November 1790 to the 31ˢᵗ December following and that during that time he behaved himself with the greatest Fidelity & Industry in the discharge of the Trust reposed in him & was afterwards employed by my Successor in Office whom he was obliged to leave from his Ill state of Health

Given under my hand at Charles Town South Carolina the 30ᵗʰ day of March 1782 —

James Fraser.[6]

[4] Vadry McBee was a captain in Colonel Benjamin Roebuck's regiment of South Carolina militia. The name is pronounced in South Carolina to this day as if spelled Magbee.

[5] A.O. 13/126. A copy of the above claim is in A.O. 12/146, pp. 186-189.

[6] Dr. James Fraser (see p. 26, n. 185).

London Aug: 11

I certify that Alexander Chesney was of use to the Kings Troops under my command acting between the Broad River & the Mountains S° Carolina—in the beginning of the year 81

Ban: Tarleton[7]

Lt Col: Com^t B. L.

I Certify that the Bearer Mr Alx^r. Chesney commanded a Company of the Royal Militia in South Carolina; with which He acquitted himself as a faithful, zealous, and active officer, & by his attachment to the cause of Great Britain He lost a very good property.

J Doyle   Major 105th Reg^t [8]

APPENDIX IV

EVIDENCE ON ALEXANDER CHESNEY'S MEMORIAL [1]

Alexander Chesney the Claim^t Sworn.

Says he went from Ireland to America in 1772—the latter end of the Year—Settled on the Pacolet River in the district of Ninety-six in South Carolina in 1773.

Says at the time the Rebellion broke out he lived with his Father—Says in the Summer of 1775—he was pressed to enter into the Associat^n against Great Britain which he refused to do—He then went to join the Loyalists who were collected under Captain Phillips—brother to Col. Phillips and guided them up to Pacolet to his Fathers This was in the Winter the latter End of 1775—or beginning of 1776

The Body staid about a fortnight when they divided—He was soon afterwards made a prisoner for having lent his Assistance to these Loyalists—He was taken off from his Father's by a party of Rebels under Col: Steen he remained Prisoner 50 days[2] when he was bailed out—He soon after went home—In the summer foll^g in June he was again taken into Custody on the same Account and carried part of the way to Charles Town. He had the option of going to Goal or joining the party of Rebels and take Arms with them. He consented to the latter as his Father's Family wo^d other-

---

[7] Banistre Tarleton, lieutenant-colonel commandment of the British Legion, (see p 90)

[8] Major John Doyle (see p 25, n 180)

[1] Compare with his evidence published in *The Royal Commission on American Loyalists Claims* Roxburghe Club, 1915, pp 49-50

[2] He was kept in prison for about ten days *Ibid*, p 49

wise have been certainly ruined. He continued with the Rebels in Charles Town till the 16th of August following. In the course of a few days after he got to Charles Town he made an attempt in company of two others Ch⁵ and Chʳ Brandon to join Sir Henry Clinton who was then upon Long Island. Being discovered upon the River they were obliged to desist from their purpose and return. He was obliged to continue serving occasionally with the Rebels till June 1777—at wch time the Regᵗ was discharged & he returned home. In the summer of 1778 the State Oath became Genˡ and Claimant with a party consisting altogether of 30 resolved to go to Florida to avoid taking the Oath they accordingly joined Genˡ Williamson ³ who was marching into Florida intending to quit him upon the first favorable Opportunity and sent off one of their party to find the way for them but this Man (whose name was David Bayley) never returned. And therefore finding themselves unable to accomplish it They returned home at the end of the expedition & Claimant remained at home till after Charles Town was taken. He says the Oath was never tendered to him during the time he remained at home—and he took no part ⁴ till after Charles Town was taken.

When that Event took place the Loyalists embodyed themselves on Sugar Creek in Ninety six District and Claimant among the rest. The number was about 200—They dispersed again and afterwards in June 1780 embodied at Bullocks Creek upon hearing that a Body of Rebels was coming against them. Claimant was chosen by this Body to command them and an Action took place wherein the Rebels were beaten, and they soon afterwards joined Col: Balfour at Fair Forrest

He was afterwards put under the command of Major Ferguson who was Inspector Genˡ of the Militia and continued serving under him till his defeat at Kings Mountain on the 7th of Oct. 1780 He was durᵍ this time entrusted by Major Ferguson with private Instructions to a Capt. Moore who commanded a Post in Thicketty. He delivered the Instrˢ according to his orders.

He was afterwards employed to procure Intelligence of the numbers and motions of a large party of the Rebels then encamped on Cherokee Ford on Broad River He got undiscovered into their Camp, and discovered that 500 Men were detached to Nicholas's

---

³ See p 7, n 48
⁴ That is, no active military part on the loyalist side

Fort. He gave information of this to Major Ferguson in consequence of wch he intercepted and defeated the party at the Iron
Works above the Fort He undertook this Service in consequence
of a paper shewn him bv Col. Bibbes wherein a reward of 50 Gu'as
was offered to any Body who should perform this Service—Claimant tho he undertook it, yet refused the reward, and says he did it
meiely from a wish to serve the Kings Troops If he had been
taken on this Service he should have been hanged as a Spy—Major
Ferguson talkcd to him about payment after his return but he per-
sisted in his refusal to take anv thing. He was afterwards appointed adiutant of the different of Militia. He reced pay for his Service.
He was frequently employed by Major Ferguson many hazardous
Services for procuring Intelligence, and he had the command of
various parties committed to his charge against the Enemy in wch
he was always fortunate enough to conduct himself to the Major's
satisfaction When Major Ferguson was defeated at Kings Mountain, Claimant was with him and was taken prisoner and carried
to Moravian Town in North Carolina, where he was offered to be
restored to all his Rights & properties if he wo^d serve with the
Rebels only for one Month, & threatened him with death in case of
refusal. He did refuse, and was marched almost naked with other
prisoners in Moravian Town on the Gadkin River, in a course of
150 Miles. He made his escape from hence & returned home, where
in the begin^g of Decr 1780 he raised a Company of Militia and joined
Col. Tarleton.

Produces a Commⁿ of Capt in Col: Plummers Reg^t of foot
under the Hand of Col. Balfour dated 1st Decr 1780.

Says he continued with Col. Tarleton sometime & when the Col
Tarleton marched against Genl Morgan Claimant was with him in
the Action, of the 17th Janry 1781—at the Cow-pens on Thickctty
wherein Col· Tarleton was defeated—Claimant then retreated towards Charles Town, and in his way endeavoured to persuade Genl
Cunningham to embody the Militia but not succeeding in his appl'on
he went to Charles Town. He continued on different Military services till the Evac'n of Charles Town

Produces certificates of Loyalty and Credibility under the
Hands of Lord Cornwallis, Lord Rawdon, Col Balfour, Colonel
Tarleton, Major Doyle, Col. Cruden ⁵ & others.

---

⁵ John Cruden had a lieutenant-colonel''s commission (See Additional Notes, p 92)

Produces t'ndre dated 24 July 1777—being a Lease for a Year of 80 Acres of Land on the North Side of the Pacolet River being part of a Tract of 300— Says he has the Release at home in Ireland.

Says he purchased this Tract in the beginning of 1776 and paid part of the Con's'on then, but did not pay the rest till the date of the Conveyance— He gave 60^l Sterl in Money and Goods for these 80 Acres. When he bought them about 3 Acres were cleared. It was part of a large Plantation whereof 100 Acres were under Cultivation Says he erected a good dwelling house Stable and Corn House— He cleared as much as to make up 40 Acres They were on four Fields well fenced. Part of the Goods he paid for this Land were Horses, Salt &c. He paid £150 Currency in Money— Says when he bought this Land he imagined the British Cause would prevail, and that it was safer to invest his property in Land than any thing else.

He gave as much for it as he sho'd have given for it, two years before— Lands were rising in value every day— at the same time he thinks he got a good bargain of it, and he co'd have got more for it a short time afterwards as he was offered more within a month than he had given for it.

Says that £60 Sterling wo^d not have defrayed the expence of the Improvement, besides the Iron Work and Timber for the Mill. The Iron work was worth £8 Ster. Says he values it upon his Oath at 40/ Sterling an Acre.

Says his Father Robert Chesney conveyed to him by Deed of Gift 150 Acres adjoining to the above in 1778. It was granted to his Father in 1773— He has not the Deed in his poss'ion. It was taken away with other Papers from his House by the Rebels Says there was little or no Cultivation upon it. He considered this and the 80 Acres as one Tract, and was not at any expence on this part'lar part: No Cultivat^n had been made by him or his Father. Thinks it was worth 25^s per Acre to him, as it lay contiguous to his other property but wo^d not have been so to any body who had not posse'd the Tract of 80 Acres.

Says the 200 Acres sit. on Williams Creek he rec'd as a portion with his Wife from her Father William Hodge in the year 1780 But he paid Hodge £25 Sterling on this occasion. It was conveyed to Claimant in fee

Says there were good Houses, and upwards of 30 Acres of cleared Land upon this Tract, when it was conveyed to him and he rented it out for one third of its produce.

Says his Father in Law always took part with the Rebels,[6] but bel⁹ he is not in poss'ion of it at present. Claimant never rec'd but one Years rent for it, and does not think he got above £6 Sterling for his Share of the produce.

Says he was promised £100 as a portion with his wife & he looked upon this Land as a compensation for the £100

Says he thinks it would really have sold at that time that he left it for 35⁹ an Acre in Cash.

Says in the year 1773—he bought a Warrant for 200 Acres adjoining to this Land and applied for the Grant   He paid the Fees and understood the Grant was passed but he never had it.   There was no improvement upon this Land, and he never derived any advantage from it.   He gave £6 for the Warrant, and the Fees were about £4 more Sterling, and a small sum for Taxes.

Says he values this Land and thinks it wo'ᵈ have sold for 30/ an Acre

Says he bought a Warrant for 100 Acres on Bush River   he never had the Grant   He was at no other expence but £6 currency for the Survey   He values it at 15ˢ an Acre, but can't speak positively to the value.

Says he was poss'ed of a Negro Woman who was taken away from his House by a Rebel Capt[7] in the year 1780.   She was a valuable Slave both within and without Doors—And thinks she was worth more than £60.

The same Man at the same time took away three Horses   one was a fine riding Horse wch he thinks was worth 20¹—   the other two work Horses wch he values at £10 each

Says just before the taking of Charles Town a Waggon & Team of 4 Horses were taken from him   The Waggon was 3 year old, and he values it at £30.   The four Horses were worth 70¹ [8]

Says his Wife told him Morgans Army had killed 6 head of his Cattle—he values them at Forty Shillings a Head.

---

[6] See p 9, n 64
[7] See p 129, n 4
[8] The wagon and horses were impressed into the American service while Alexander Chesney himself was in that service   See p 9, n 62)

At the same time (as he was told) were taken away 3 H'h'ds of Tobacco w'ch were each 1000 lb weight. He values it at 20ˢ an Cwt w'ch it had cost him, and had paid for it.

Says at the same time were taken 500 Bushels of Indian Corn to the best of his belief—he had the Account from his Wife, he values yᵉ Corn at 10ˢ Currency per Bushel—Oats and Rye worth £5 Sterling.

Says he meant to include in this Article of his Memor¹ his Plantation tools and Household Furniture wch he values at £10 Ster.

Says he bought a Schooner in the year 1781 for wch he paid 70 G'as. He sent her with Cash and Goods on board to the Value of £40 to St. Johns in Florida and to bring back a Cargo— He has since been informed She was taken by the Rebels.

Col John Phillips—Sworn

Says he has known Claimant since he was a year old. He first came to America in 1772—or 1773—They lived near Witness at first, and then went to settle on Pacolet

Says the first Action of Claimant's Loyalty was after the Battle of Ninetysix,[9] when Claimant took sev¹ Loyalists from Jackson's Creek to his Fathers at Pacolet & saved them from being taken prisoners. This was in the latter end of 1775. He was then a slip of a Boy about 18—among these Loyalists were two Brothers of Witness [10]—Thinks his motives were his attachment to Britain.

Says that he firmly bel³ Claimant in his mind a determined Loyalist from the beginning tho' he was obliged to carry Arms for the Rebels. Says that during the time he (Witness) was prisoner in Gen¹ Williamsons Army Claimaᵗ took every opportunity in his power to converse with Wit and communicated to him his intentions to make his Escape from that Army— Says he has known many Loyalists forced against their Wills to serve as Soldiers in the Rebel Army

From the time of the Reduction of Charles Town he was always most zealous and active Partizan in favor of Govᵗ. Major Ferguson has told Wit that he never knew such a little Boy as Claimant. He was particularly Serviceable both to Col. Tarleton and Major Ferguson and ran risques w'ch nothing would have tempted Wit. to

---

⁹ The siege of the fort of Ninety-Six, held by Major Andrew Williamson and Major James Mayson by the loyalists under Majors Joseph Robinson and Evan McLauren, from November 18 to 21, 1775. (See pp 69, 70.)

¹⁰ See Colonel John Phillips, p 60

have done. He does not know nor believe that he ever rec'ed any reward for these except a trifle from Col. Balfour in Charles Town.

Says he does not know enough of his Lands to speak to their Value   He heard of his having purchased Lands on Pacolet River, and that his Father had given him some more.   He had likewise been upon Land w'ch he was told had been given Claimant by his Father in Law.

Knew besides he had bounty Warrant, but knows nothing of the part'lars.

Knew Claimant had a Waggon wch he heard & bel^s was taken from him by the Rebels

Says he knew Claimant had a Schooner wch he purchas^d (he bel^s) for £70 Ster. in 1781   Wit lent him £60 of the M^s to pay for her.   Says he bel^s She was taken by the Rebels, for the Master returned to Charles Town and informed him she had been taken   Witness suspected the Master of her had behaved treacherously as he appeared in Charles Town in a more genteel manner afterw^ds tho he pretended the Schooner had been taken   Knows Claimant had £40 on board—part in Cash and part in Good.

He has heard and believes he had a Negro and is satisfied that he lost her.

Col. Zach^s Gibbes [11] Sworn.

Says he has known Claimant many Years.   He was a Friend to Gov^t he and all his Fathers Family from the commencement of the Troubles   Knows he concealed the Loyalists at his Father's—among others Col. Phillip's Brothers   When Wit. returned home after being exiled he went to the House of Claimant's Father to conceal himself knowing no body whom he co^d so securely trust, as he knew he had concealed some Loyalists.   Wit: lay concealed there but two days, & found Claimant a sensible Youth and attached to Gov^t.

Says that Claimant had been before forced into the Rebel Service—that he was then a Youth and held it was contrary to his Inclinat^n.

Says that they had not a more active Officer or Man in Major Fergusons Army during that Campaign.   Says that Major Ferguson sent to Wit and desired he woul^d point out to him a faithful Man who wo^d go into the Enemy's Camp then at Cherokee Ford &

---

[11] Colonel Zacharias Gibbs (see pp 79-82)

count the number of their Men and bring Intelligence of their Movements Wit. pointed out claimant, who went and brought the desired Intellig[cc] He did not get a Farthing reward for this Service. Wit. afterwards wrote to Col. Balfour [12] who gave him 5 G'as— Says he does not think he would have gone without the reward as it was a very dangerous Service.

Says that Claim[t] did propose to Wit. in 1776 for the Loyalists in general to sign a Paper testifying their abhorence of the Rebellion & their resolution to support the British Government.

Reads the paper produced by Claimant & bel[s] it was to the effect expressed in that paper.[13]

Says he bel[s] that Claimant entred into an Agreement with other Loyalists to escape to Florida from Gen[l] Williamson's Army.

Knows many instances of the Active Services of Claimant both in Action and by procuring Intelligence & had great Trust reposed in him.

He was taken in the Battle of Kings Mountain where he behaved bravely. He knows no Man of whom he can speak more highly.

Knows Claimant poss'ed 80 Acres on Pacolet River—w'ch he values at 30/ an Acre at least.

Knows he purchased and paid for it, and that he was offered 30/ an Acre for it. As to the offer he knows it only by hearing.

Says he heard he was poss'ed of a Tract of Land w'ch had been part of his Father's w'ch he bel[s] was 150 Acres. He values it at 20/ an Acre.

Says he knows he had Lands on W[ms] Creek w'ch had been W[m] Hodges. Does not know part'ly the number of Acres. He values it at 20/ an Acre.

Says he knew the Land adjoining but not the Title to them w'ch he values at 15/ an Acre.

Does not know the Land on Bush River.

Knew Claimant had a Negro which he values at £60.

Knew he had a Waggon and Team, he supposes it might be worth £70.

Knows he purchased a good deal of Tobacco—but does not know the part'lars of it.

---

[12] See p 132
[13] The Resolution of the loyalists is printed on p 144

Capt. James Miller   Sworn

Knows Claimant—confirms his account of conducting the Loyalists to his Father's in 1776—w'ch he did from Motives of Loyalty —He s^d so at the time   He was always looked upon as a Man in whom they might perfectly rely.

Cannot speak positively as to his property but heard he had a Tract of Land from Hodge his Father in Law.[14]

APPENDIX V

A. ALEXANDER CHESNEY'S ORDERS FOR WOOD CUTTING

Capt Alexander Chesney is employed to Superintend the Refugees cutting wood for the Barrack Department.   No wood Cutt by any person will be paid for unless the Cutter produces a receipt sign'd by Capt Chesney—he will also take care that the wood is cutt as near as possible to the best Landing & that the Cords are full measure so that when they come to Charlestown they may hold out measure in Case of any disputes arrizing between him & the Proprietors of the Lands on the Neck   he will apply to M^r. Hodge who will take the proper measures for settling them

By Order of the Barrack Master

A Montell*

B. COPY OF ALEXANDER CHESNEY'S COMMISSION AS CAPTAIN

South Carolina

By Lieutenant Colonel Nesbit Balfour   Commandant

at Charles Town &c &c &c

To Alexander Chesney

By virtue of the Power & authority in me vested, I do hereby constitute & appoint you to be Capt. in Col Plummer's Regiment of Foot [1]—You are to take into your Care & Charge, and duly to Exercise as well the Officers as Soldiers thereof in Arms, & to use your best Endeavors to keep them in good Order Discipline; & I do hereby command them to obey you as their Captain respectively.   And you are to observe and follow such orders & Directions from time to Time as you shall receive from the General or Commander in Chief of His Majesty's Forces in North America, now & for the

---

[14] The above evidence on Alexander Chesney's Memorial is in A O 12/46 fos 190-200

[1] Colonel Daniel Plummer (see p 88)

* Two loyalists of this name, probably father and son, sailed from Charleston and settled in the Bahamas (A O 13/70)

Time being, your Colonel or any other your Superior officer, according to the Rules & Discipline of war, in Pursuance of the Trust hereby resposed [*sic*] in you.

Given under my Hand & Seal at ————————
the 1st Day of December 1780, and in the 20th year
of the Reign of Our Sovereign Lord George the 3d
by the Grace of God, of Great Britain, France & Ireland,
King, Defender of the Faith &c.

(Signed) N Balfour

C. Alexander Chesney's Commission as Lieutenant of Independent Scouts

To Mr. Alexr. Chesney

Reposing especial trust & confidence in your Loyalty and Abilities, I do hereby empower you to act as Lieutenant of Independent Scouts in Capt John Fanning's[2] Company—And all persons whatever are hereby required and directed to obey you as Lieutenant of that Company.

Given under my hand at Charles Town
20th April 1781

(L. S.)   N Balfour
Commandant

We do hereby certify, that the above is a true copy compared with the original this 7th day of Octor. 1782

J. Mackintosh
Lew: Wolfe [3]

D. Testimonial to Alexander Chesney's Services in Connection with Sequestered Estates

I hereby Certify that Mr Alexander Chesney was Employed by me as an overseer of the Sequestered Estate of Thos Ferguson Esqr. and withal Capacity he behaved himself to my Sattisfaction—He was also Employed by me as a Lieutenant in a Corps embodied for the Defence of the Sequestered Estates. and during the time he was so Employed. In justice to him I can not but acknowledge that he gave proof of Zeal & Spirit as well as activity & Enterprise, which

---

[2] Lieutenant-Colonel John Fanning (see p 108)
[3] Lewis Wolfe (see p 31, n 207)   The above documents are in A O 13/126

I hope will recommend him to the Notice of all those attachd to His Majestys Government

Cha⁹ Town 8th Febry 1782   J. Cruden ⁴
                                        Commr. Loyᵗˢ. Estates

E. OTHER TESTIMONIALS TO THE SERVICES OF ALEXANDER CHESNEY

Cherlestown, April 1ˢᵗ 1782

Captain Alexʳ Chesney having an inclination to return to England on account of his Health—

I know him to be a very determin'd Loyalist, & that he has render'd many Services to His Majesty's Government ever since the present Rebellion—That he always has done his Duty as an Officer, & has ever faithfully accomplished every matter that has been entrusted to him

Given under my Hand at Charlestown this 1ˢᵗ April 1782
N Balfour.

Culford Augˢᵗ: 14ᵗʰ 1782

I believe the contents of the Memorial of Mʳ. Alexʳ. Chesney to be perfectly just and recommend him as a proper object of the consideration of Government   Cornwallis

To The Lords Commissioners
of His Majesty's Treasury

The Bearer Mʳ. Alexander Chesney, having requested me to give him some testimonial of his good conduct in America, I have much pleasure in certifying, that in the Command of a Company of Royal Militia he behaved with exemplary zeal & fidelity. Given under my hand this 18ᵗʰ of August 1782   Rawdon

Mansfield Street, Nov. 20ᵗʰ 1783

I know Mʳ. Alexander Chesney to have been a deserving Man, and an active and zealous Loyalist, and I have every reason to believe that his estimate of his Losses is perfectly just.⁴
                                        Cornwallis

F. LETTER TO THE COMMISSIONERS FROM COLONEL JOHN PHILLIPS.⁵

Ballymena 12ᵗʰ. Decʳ. 1785

Capt: Chesney showed me your letter of the 28: Novbr: and Requests me to write to the Commisʳˢ. Respecting his property—

---
⁴ A O 13/126
⁵ Ibid

I know that I was informed that after Capt Chesney's wife and family was Drove of from his house & Lands that the Rebell Coll. Branon [6] took poseson of said house and Lands and put a rebell family in possion of it and I am perfectly Convinced it is Conficated and I am shure it is irecoverably Lost to him from the many services both publick and secret he rendered Goverm^t.

indeed all who bore Commisons in the British army were included in the Confication act and as he was one of the most active one I am convinced he has as littell Chance to Injoy any part of his property in Caralenia as any Loyalist. I know also that Capt James Miller Lands [7] is sold and a rebell Capt Hugh Millen [8] is living on them and their is two Loyalists heare can and will take their oath that they were on the spot in 1784 and saw Millen in possion of the same

G. Major Doyle's Certificate to Alexander Chesney.[9]

Montalto—Ballynahinch Decr. 14th. 1785

I Certify that Captain Alexander Chesney late of the Carolina Militia was a very active zealous officer in support of his Majesty Goverment during the late War: & by that means is (I am convinced) totally & for ever, deprived of his property in America, although He may not have been mentioned in a Confiscation List; which however must affect him as having held a Commission in the British Service

J: Doyle Major
late 105th Reg-^t

H. Colonel Zacharias Gibbs' Certificate.[10]

On an application made to me by Captain Alexander Chesney late of Ninety-six in his Majesty's Province, now the State of S° Carolina In Justice to his Charector, and Merit I think it my Duty to Certify that at the Commencement of the unhappy war, he took an Early part for and in Behalf of his Majesty's Government· and

---

[6] Colonel Thomas Brandon

[7] Captain James Miller (see p 100)

[8] Hugh Milling, of that part of South Carolina now embraced in Fairfield county, enlisted in Captain Charles Cotesworth Pinckney's company of the 1st South Carolina regiment, June 16, 1775, and was immediately appointed a sergeant He was subsequently promoted captain in the 6th Regiment, South Carolina line, and in February, 1780, was transferred to the 3rd Regiment, South Carolina line, with which he served until the fall of Charleston in May following, when he was taken prisoner In 1781 he was exchanged. Captain Hugh Milling died in July, 1837

[9] A O 13/126

[10] Ibid

Rendered many essential Services to Government. More especially at the Return of the Royal Government in the year 1780, he joined the Royal army and from his Zeal and activity was Appointed Adj^t. of a Royal Reg^t of Militia, and Captain of a Company— And to my knowledge remained Singularly active Dureing the British Troops Remaining in that Country which was near two years— And I must further say I know no man of Captain Chesney's Rank that Rendered more Services Dureing that time, and to my knowledge, and By my Direction he Rendered many both Publick and Secret Services, such as Rideing with Hazardous Expresses &c and in Particular to Major Patrick Ferguson, of the 71st. Reg^t. Lord Rawdon, and Col. Balfour; and was taken at the memorable Battle at King's Mountain the 8th Octr. 1780, when Major Ferguson was killed, and was taken some Hundred Miles Prisoner into North Carolina, in Close Confinement, and Treated with the Utmost Severity. At length made his Escape back and Raised another Company of Militia, and Cooperated with the British Troops—In Consequence of which I believe and know from Circumstances that his property both Real and personal are Irrecoverably lost, as the americans Immediately Seized on his Property, having Drove his wife and Child off and Into the British lines; and I think his Chance Equally as Dangerous to return as mine or any other Loyalist.

Given under my hand at Springfield, County Down Ireland this 15th day of Decr. 1785

Zach^s. Gibbs
late a Col^l. Royal Militia
South Carolina Ninety-Six District-

I. LETTER TO THE COMMISSIONERS FROM ALEXANDER CHESNEY.[11]

Bangor Decr. 16th 1785

It gave me infinite pain, to find by Mr Forsters Letter, that there remained a doubt with you, of the confiscation, and irrecoverable loss of my Property in America   I was in hopes that it had already been made appear to your satisfaction, by the very respectable Witnesses examined on my case, that as early as Jan^y, 81 the Rebel Col. Brandon,[12] seized all my Lands, and other Property under the Confiscation Act, and drove off my family into the British Lines, not allowing my Wife so much as a Blanket to protect her

[11] A O 13/126
[12] Colonel Thomas Brandon

Child of 3 Months old, from the inclemency of the weather. And that he (Brandon) immediately apply'd all my Personal Property to his own, and the use of Genl. Morgans [13] army their encamped on the spot.

I also flattered myself with the hopes that, from my uncommon exertions in the *field as an officer*, and from the many very essential *secret services* I rendered Gov^t. during the late War, and from the certifycates in my favour, from Lord Cornwallis; Lord Rawdon; Col. Balfour, Col Tarleton and other Officers, under whom I srved in America, to be classed with the most meritorious, and deserving men And to have received some compensation with them, to enable me to support my family. And as I have ever placed an unlimited confidence on the faith of Goverm^t. and sacrificed my *all* for its support, I hope you will see that my Property is confiscated, & for ever gone from me, and include me in your next Report And be ashured Gentlemen, that I am one of the last men, that would be admited back to Carolina. Shou'd I be abandoned by Gov^t. and left in poverty, and despair, a prey to the Rebelion, yet in that case I cou'd not even think for a moment, of soliciting any favours from the late Rebellious States.

If it will give you any further satisfaction, I will make Oath before Lord Moira,[14] or a Justice of Peace, that, all the Lands, and other Property, for which I gave you in Claims, are to the best of my information, and belief, confiscated And that I have not the most distant expectation of ever receiving any part of it except from Gov^t., And that I never intend to return to any part of the United States unless they are again under a British Gov^t

I have called on Col Phillips, and Col Gibbs and got them to certify what they know of the matter, and would be glad you wou'd enquire the oppinion of my Lord Cornwallis, Lord Rawdon, Col. Balfour, Col Tarleton, or Major Saunders [15] of the Queen's Rangers, and from any of those Gentlemen, you will learn that from my services, it is impossible I shou'd ever enjoy or recover any part of my confiscated Property. And as my situation is singularly distressing, having been oblig'd to borrow Money to defray the expences of three different Journeys to London, on this business already. I hope your hon^{rs} will see the merit of my conduct, and the

---

[13] General Daniel Morgan
[14] Lord Moira, the father of Lord Rawdon
[15] Captain John Saunders (see Additional Notes, pp 108-111)

distresses of my situation, and grant me, and my family some relief as soon as in your Power.

J. LETTER TO THE COMMISSIONERS FROM LEWIS WOLFE.[16]

College Street
22ᵈ. Dec 1785

The enclosed letter & Certificates I received by the Post this Day from Mʳ. Chesney, who resides at Bangor in Ireland, in answer to your Letter to him for further Proofs in support of his Claim; with a desire fro him to lay them before the Commissioners for their Information; & to request the favor of being informed whether they are satisfactory or not; as Mʳ. Chesney lives at a great Distance, the expence of coming to Town would be attended by much Inconvenience to him.

K   LETTER TO THE COMMISSIONERS FROM LORD CORNWALLIS.[17]

Culford Dec: 26ᵗʰ. 1785

Having received a letter from Mʳ. Alexʳ. Chesney, informing me that the Commissioners were of opinion that he had not produced satisfactory evidence of the confiscation and sale or irrecoverable loss of his property; I think it my duty, in justice to that very deserving Man, to assure the Commissioners, that I am perfectly convinced, from the active and very material services which Mʳ. Chesney rendered to the British Troops, and from the violence with which He and his family were persecuted, that his return to Carolina is impossible, and that the loss of his property is irrecoverable.

APPENDIX VI

RESOLUTION OF THE LOYALISTS ON PACOLET RIVER,[1]
SOUTH CAROLINA. [1775]

We the principle inhabitants of the neighbourhood of pacolet River, beholding with the utmost abhorrence and detestation, the dareing proceedings of those infatuated people, who call themselvs committee men, or Liberty boys, feloniously breaking open the houses of his Majesties subjects, and thence carrying away Arms,

---

[16] A O 13/126
[17] Ibid
[1] A O 13/126

Ammunition, and other warlike stores; as well as putting their persons in confinement, which proceedings must terminate in the ruin and misery, of the poor deluded people themselvs

In order therefore to shew our attachment to our King and country, we promise goverment and each other, that we will embody ourselves at the shortest notice, to support the rights of the crown, as soon as called by any Legal Authority from thence—

APPENDIX VII.

PARTY DIVISIONS IN SOUTH CAROLINA FAMILIES

Family divisions in the war were many in South Carolina. Such well-known families as Bull, Moultrie, Lowndes, Pinckney, Drayton, Garden, Manigault, Heyward, Huger, and Horry were represented on both sides of the conflict, as were many less conspicuous families in South Carolina.

Draper mentions the brothers Goforth fighting as enemies at the battle of King's Mountain, where also fought the four brothers Logan—William and Joseph on the Whig side and John and Thomas on the loyal side. (Draper, *King's Mountain and its Heroes*, pp. 314-5.)

APPENDIX VIII.

JUSTIFICATION OF THE TAKING OF THE OATH TO THE STATE BY THE COMMITTEE OF THE SOUTH CAROLINA LOYALISTS IN LONDON.[2]

At
A Meeting of the General Committee of the South Carolina Loyalists
Present
Thomas Irving—Chairman

John Rose	Robert Williams
Charles Ogilvie	Gideon Dupont
James Simpson	Robt Wm Powell

John Hopton

The Committee having agreed to the following Report, M^r. Powell and M^r. Dupont are requested to wait on the Honourable William Bull and Thomas Boone [2] Esquires; their Agents, and to beg the favor of them to deliver the same as soon as possible to the Honourable the Commissioners appointed by Act of Parlia-

---

[1] A O 13/85
[2] These gentlemen were former governors of South Carolina

ment for enquiring into the Losses and Services of the American Loyalists.

The Committee of South Carolina Loyalists being informed that the taking of the Oath to the State is construed to their prejudice, on the investigation of their Claims for Compensation of their Losses and Services under the late Act of Parliament, think it their indispensable duty to offer the following Observations to the consideration of the Honourable Board of Commissioners, in justification of their Conduct, through the intervention of their Agents

It is a clear proposition that the King's Subjects born in *any part* of his Dominions owe him a *Natural Allegiance*, which cannot be cancelled by any change of time, place, or circumstance, without the concurrence of the Legislature   This Allegiance is founded on principles of Universal Law, which the Wisdom of the Nation has incorporated into its Jurisprudence: And although the Subject takes an Oath of Allegiance to any foreign Power, that allegiance is only *local and temporary*   And his Majesty hath an indubitable right to require such Subjects to return to his *Natural Allegiance*, under severe penalties.

Natural Allegiance always *pre-supposes Protection*, which are *reciprocal* duties; but the Governor and other Officers of the Crown in South Carolina, having been early forced to relinquish the Exercise of their respective Offices, and afterwards sent off the Province, the loyal Inhabitants were totally destitute of Protection, and exposed to every insult and indignity.   In this situation many of them would have come away with their Families and what little property they could have collected. by the Sale of their Estates for a depreciated paper-Currency, there being no Gold or Silver then in circulation; but the prohibitory Act passed here, put a stop to all Commercial intercourse between the two Countries, and declared such *property subject to Capture;* so that the loyal Inhabitants being obliged to take a circuitous voyage, expected they and their Families would be utterly ruined in that event, and reduced to a state of poverty and wretchedness, in partts of the world where they had neither Money, Credit, nor Connexions.   Human Nature revolts at the idea of those scenes of misery and distress to which they would have been liable   and if the Officers of the Crown ran that hazard, in case of disappointment, they had a prospect of availing themselves of the patronage and influence of those, by whose Interest they had obtained their Offices: and the restitution of their captured property was owing to a *liberal construction* of the Act of Parliament in their favor, *contrary to the express words,* which could not be preseen. But others of unquestionable Loyalty in private Stations, who destitute of that prospect, were induced to remain in the Country to take care of their helpless Families, and be ready on every occasion to promote the King's Service, when he could give them protection, endured the *severest persecution,* some by painful Imprisonments, others by being dragged in chains to work on the Fortifications, and several of them were *condemned and executed* for their Attachment to the British Government.

Hence it is obvious that the loyal Inhabitants were compelled to take the Oath to the State, by the highest *legal* necessity, a fear of injury to their lives or Persons; to which the people of the Kingdom in its Civil Wars have submitted by taking an Oath of Allegiance to Usurpers, until the rightful Heir to the Crown asserted his Title, rather than leave their Country, Families and Fortunes. Besides it is declared to be Law, that in time of War or Rebellion, "a man may be justified in doing *many treasonable Acts by compulsion of the Enemy, or Rebels,*" which would admit of no excuse in time of Peace"; And "that if a person be under circumstances of *actual Force and constraint,* through *a well-grounded apprehension of injury to his life or person,* this fear or compulsion will excuse his even *joining with either Rebels or Enemies* in the Kingdom, provided he leaves them whenever he hath a safe opportunity": And Obedience to the Government de facto, is so strongly inculcated by the Laws, that *Attempts against an Esurper,* unless in defence or aid of the rightful King, have been Capitally punished, after the true Prince regains the Sovereignty; because of the breach of that *temporary Allegiance,* which was due to the Usurper as King de facto, to whom even the power of pardoning Offences belongs, and not to the King de jure.

But even supposing the conduct of the loyal Inhabitants of Carolina, in taking the Oath to the State, under such circumstances was criminal, of which they are not conscious, the Right of the King *to require them to return to their Natural Allegiance,* in this instance as well as that where a Subject takes an Oath of Allegiance to a foreign Power, is equally clear, with his right of pardoning both by the Constitution. And his Majesty having in pursuance of an Act of Parliament, issued a Commission for that purpose under the great Seal, to certain Persons, who by their several Proclamations, bearing date the third day of March, the twenty-second day of May, and first day of June in the year of our Lord 1780, not only required all his Subjects in his American Colonies, under the *severest Penalties*, to return to their *Natural Allegiance*, but in the most solemn manner, explicitly promised *pardon, forgiveness,* and *Oblivion* for all past Offences, and effectual Countenance, protection and support to such as should do so and persevere in their Loyalty   With a few Exceptions, it is humbly conceived, that all those not included in the exceptions, who, relying on the public Faith of those Proclamations, did return to their *Natural* Allegiance, and with integrity discharge their duty to their King and Country, (wherein they were afterwards encouraged to persist, from time to time, by other Proclamations of the Commanders of his Forces, and his gracious assurances to maintain his and their Constitutional Rights, signified by the Secretary of State to the Lieutenant-Governor, and communicated by the King's Order to the loyal Inhabitants;) by all Laws, divine and human, are unquestionably entitled to the benefit of those Proclamations, and the Act of Parliament "appointing Commissioners to enquire into the Losses and Services of all such persons who have suffered in their Rights, properties and professions, during the late unhappy dissentions in America, in consequence of their Loyalty to his Majesty and Attachment to the British Government," in which act those Proclamations are expressly recited: especially as the Commanders of the King's Forces advised the loyal Inhabitants of the Colonies from time to time, to submit to the Government de facto, until he could give them such effectual countenance, protection and support

   Some of the Persons who were compelled to take the Oath to the State, for want of protection from their Government, and when that protection was tendered to them, cheerfully returned to their Natural Allegiance, pursuant to those Proclamations, *died Martyrs* to their Loyalty in the Field of Battle · Some have manifested it by their *wounds* and loss of Limbs; and others have demonstrated it by the *faithful discharge* of the most important Trusts reposed in them, as well as by the most *essential Services;* for which they have been subjected to Banishment and Confiscation of Estate, and even submitted to the Sacrifice of almost *every thing that is dear to Mankind*: So that they have *nothing they can call their own* but their Families and their Sufferings.   The Act of Attainder against them is likewise an unequivocal proof of their zealous Attachment to the British Government, which can be corroborated by the most ample testimonials of many of the King's Officers Civil and

Military; and by their Memorial to Sir Guy Carleton, previous to the Evacuation: wherein, urged by a sense of loyalty to their King and love of their Country, they expressed their earnest desire of defending their Religious, political and private Rights, with all the Ardor which a violation of them could inspire: And therefore they trust that their taking of the Oath to the State, and temporary submission to the Government by the Usurpers, being legally justifiable by the cruel necessity to which they were reduced without any misbehaviour on their parts, cannot militate to their prejudice on the investigation of their Claims for compensation of their losses and Services under the late Act of Parliament: and that in any construction of their conduct the Public Faith, Justice and honour of the Nation, which have invariably been held sacred with her Enemies, will not be violated with those who, actuated by principles of the purest loyalty and encouraged by the above proclamations and Royal Assurances, have given such indubitable proofs of their Zealous Attachment to their Sovereign and the British Government, whereof they are the Natural born Subjects, which always was, and ever will be their greatest Felicity.

(Signed)   Thomas Irving

London, Feb. 21st: 1785

INDEX

ABACO, see Bahama Islands

Abduction, family of Col Richard Pearis, 103

Abuse of returned loyalist in South Carolina, 82, of Col Richard Pearis's family, 103

Address, loyalists (E Fla), to Governor Patrick Tonyn, 92, loyalists (S C), to Lieut.-Gen Alexander Leslie, 94

Address to the Loyal Part of the British Empire, by John Cruden, 92

Alexander, James, loyalist (S C), captain Indian Field company 115

Alexander, Robert, loyalist (S C), land grant in Nova Scotia, 118

Allaire, Lieut. Anthony, loyalist, *Diary*, xi, 13, n 92, n 94; 14, n 104, 71, 85

Allen, Lieut.-Col Isaac, loyalist (N J), 21, n 145, at defense of Ninety-Six (S C), 90

Ancrum, William, loyalist (S C), 94, member, committee to estimate losses of South Carolina loyalists, 120

Anderson's Fort (S C), see Forts

Arnold, Gen Benedict, loyalist (Conn), 32

Association, American Loyalists, in London, v 32, n 216, United Loyalists, 92 (See also Tory association, Whig association)

Atkinson, John, 40

Atwood, Richard, loyalist (S C), land grant in Nova Scotia, 118

Augusta (Ga), see Georgia

Axtell, Col William, loyalist (N Y), forms Nassau Blues, May 1, 1779, 84

BAHAMA Islands, Brig.-Gen Robert Cunningham, loyalist (S C), and others settle in, 87, 88, trade with, advocated, 93, John Cruden, the younger, dies in, 93, Col and Mrs Richard Pearis, loyalists (S C), receive land grants in Abaco island, 104, suggested for settlement of Southern loyalists, 117

Balfour, Col Nisbet, commandant at Charleston, 10, n 69, orders Alexander Chesney to raise troop of horse, iv 23, 24, orders "rebels" released, 103 certificate to Col John Philipps, 62, appoints James Vernon lieutenant-colonel, 78, letter to, 79, testifies for Col Zacharies Gibbs, 81, replies to Gen Greene, 95 certifies to value of Alexander Chesney's estate 125, joined by loyalists (S C), 131, mentioned, 132, rewards Alexander Chesney, 136, 137, issues captain's commission to Chesney, 138, 139, Chesney carries expresses to, 142, testimonials to Chesney, 140, 143

Ball, Col Elias, Jr, loyalist (S C), claim and award, 118

Ballingall, Col Robert, 94, in command of Colleton county (S C) loyal militia, 114, member, South Carolina loyalists' committee, 116

Ballmer, Maj George, loyalist (S C), claim and award, 118

Banishment, from South Carolina, Robert Phillips, loyalist, 61 Philip Henry and other loyalists, 98, Southern loyalists, 117, Solomon Smythe, 28, n 197

Barber, Lieut. James, loyalist (S C), goes to Ireland, 28, 97

Barclay, Thomas, loyalist (N Y), *Correspondence of*, xi

Baron, Alexander, member, South Carolina loyalists' committee, 116

Barrett, Ensign Robert, 60

Barton, Capt Robert, Colleton county (S C), loyal militia, 115

Battles Baylis Earle's ford, 72, 73, Beaver Creek (S C), 96, Blackstocks Hill (S C), 20, n 138, Bullock's creek (S C), 131, Camden (S C), 91, 96, Col John Hamilton, loyalist (N C), in, 117, Cedar Springs (S C), 12, n 83, Cowpens (S C), Jan 17, 1781, 11, n 79, 22, 60, Col Banistre Tarleton defeated, 128, 132, Great Bridge (Va), 109, Hanging Rock (S C), 90, Kettle creek (Ga), Feb 14, 1779, 80, King's Mountain, Oct 7, 1780, 17, 18, 19, n 129, 23, 31, 65, 73, 79, 83, 84, 85 89, 126, 131, 132, Alexander Chesney taken prisoner, 137, 142, Musgrove's Mills, 13, n 96, Fort Ninety-Six (S C), siege of, Nov 18-21, 1775, 65, 100, 135, n 9, Col Thomas Fletchall's attack on Ninety-Six, 69, 70, Lieut.-Col J H Cruger's defense of Ninety-Six, May 22-June 19, 1781, 90, Stono Ferry (S C), June 12, 1779, 75, Waxhaws (S C), June, 1780, 90

Bayley, David, loyalist (S C), 131

Beattie's Mill (S C), 73

Beechey, Sir William, 49, n 333

Beers, William 49, n 330

Bell, George W, 55, n 357

Bell, John, schoolmaster, 62

Benson, Capt George 10, n 69

Bermuda, Solomon Smyth, loyalist (S C), takes refuge in, 28, n 197, prisoners from, join Duke of Cumberland's regiment, 91, trade with, advocated, 93

Bernard, Scrope, loyalist (Mass), 35, n 246, 36

Bibby, Lieut John, loyalist, executed, 86

Bibliography, xiii, xiv

Big Canebrake (S C), 102

Bishop Drury, loyalist (S C), 79

Blackstocks Fort (S C), see Forts

Blackstocks Hill (S C), battle, see Battles

Bobo, Capt Lewis, 11

Boehman, Jacob, loyalist, killed, 64

Bond, Col ...... , loyalist, killed, 80

Bond, Capt George, loyalist (S C), land grant in Nova Scotia, 118

Bond, John, loyalist (S C), land grant in Nova Scotia, 118

Boone, Thomas, former governor of South Carolina, 118, 145

Boston (Mass), see Massachusetts

Bouquet, Gen Henry, 102

Bowie, Capt John, 70

Bowman, William, loyalist (S C), land grant in Nova Scotia, 118

Boyd, Col John, loyalist (S C), helps raise 600 loyalists in 1779, 80

Brailsford, Robert, loyalist (S C), claim and award for children of, 119

Brandon Charles loyalist (S C), 4 6 20 23 131

Brandon, Christian, loyalist (S C), 131

Brandon ('Brannon') Col Thomas 9, n 64 14, n 98, 141, n 6, takes Alexander Chesney's property, 142

Brecken, Ralph, 76

Brereton, Capt William, 25, n 182, 26

Bricer creek (Ga), see Creeks

Brisbane, James, loyalist (S C), claim and award 119

British Legion see Tory corps

British troops, at Long Island, S C, 7, at Stono 9 take Charleston, 10, 71, at Camden, 13 restricted in South Carolina, 27, n 190, Maj Patrick Ferguson best rifleshot and inventor of first breech-loading rifle in use by, 83 all loyalists in battle of King's Mountain 86 at Savannah, Ga, 107

Broad river (S C) see Rivers

Brown, Anne, 71, 72

Brown, Elizabeth 88

Brown, Hugh, loyalist (S C), 64

Brown, John, loyalist (S C), 79

Brown, Lieut -Col Thomas, loyalist (Ga), 65 68, helps form Tory association in Ninety-Six district 105, needs relief expedition at Augusta, Ga, mid-Sept 1780, 107

Brownlee, Robert, loyalist (S C), 88

Brucee, Catherine, marries Capt Moses Kirkland, Jamaica, W I, 107

Bryson, John William, and William Jr, loyalists (S C), land grants in Nova Scotia, 118

Buckingham, Capt Elias, of Orangeburg (S C) loyal militia, 114

Bull, Stephen, gets property of Governor William Bull by fraud, 112, 113

Bull, William, lieutanant-governor of South Carolina, 32, n 218, 112, 113, claim and award, 119

Bullock, Capt Zachariah, 8, n 56, 9, n 62

Bullock's creek (S C), see Creeks

Burgoyne, Gen John, vi, 34, 86

Burns, James, loyalist (S C), claim and award, 119

Bush river (S C), see Rivers

CALDWELL, Capt John 66, 69, seizure of Fort Charlotte, S C, 107

Caldwell, Thomas, 60

Cambridge (Mass), see Massachusetts

Camden, (S C), 13, 14, 60, Col Zacharias Gibbs goes to, 80 defeat of Gen Horatio Gates at, Aug 16, 1780 91, battle of, 96, Col James Carey in command of 1st regiment, loyal militia, 114, Col John Hamilton, loyalist (N C), in battle of, 117

Cameron Alexander, loyalist (Ga), deputy-superintendent of Indians, 63

Campbell, Capt   , 47

Campbell, Col Archibald and British force sail for Georgia, 1778, 89

Campbell Charles Philip, loyalist (S C), 28, n 196, 30, 35

Campbell Daniel and Hugh, loyalists (S C), claim and award, 119

Campbell, Gen William, 17

Campbell, Lord William, last royal governor of South Carolina, 5, 63, 66, 67, 83, 99, Capt Moses Kirkland visits, 105

Canadais Silas, loyalist (S C), ensign in Indian Field company, 115

Carden Maj John, loyalist, in battle of Hanging Rock, S C, 90

Carey, Col James, in command of 1st regiment, Camden loyal militia, 115

Carleton Francis, 49, n 330

Carlisle (Pa), 2, n 10

Carr, James, 48

Castlereagh, Lord, viii, 47, n 325, 53, 54

Catawba Indians, see Indians

Cathcart, Lord raises British Legion (Tory corps) in 1778, 90

Cedar Springs (S C), battle, see Battles

Chalmers, Ariana M J, marries Capt John Saunders, loyalist (Va), 110

Chalmers, Col James, in command of Maryland Loyalists (Tory corps) 110

Champneys, John member, South Carolina loyalists' committee, 116, claim and award, 119

Charleston (S C), 3, 4, 5, 7, 13, 24, 26, Capt Moses Kirkland visits Governor Lord William Campbell in, 105 loyalist prisoners sent to, 71 Maj Patrick Ferguson, prisoner at, 83, Capt Robert Cunningham prisoner in, 87, Maj Patrick Cunningham prisoner in, 104, Col Richard Pearis, prisoner in, 103 Dr David Oliphant, prisoner in, 117, taken by British, 15, 91, 94, 97, 135, Alexander Chesney goes to, 22, 125, loyalist refugees in, 27, 61, garrison, 31, confiscation act published in 39, refuge of Col John Phillips' family 61 Sir Henry Clinton in, 61, hospital for refugees in, 61, Col Thomas Fletchall and family take refuge in, 71, Col Zacharias Gibbs goes to, 80 Maj Michael Egan joins loyalists in, 97 daughter of Col Daniel Plummer dies in, Dec, 1781, 89, Col Daniel Plummer in, Apr, 1782, 89, Lieut-Col Evan McLaurin dies in, June, 1872, 102, wife of Capt James Miller dies in, Aug, 1782 101, Col Nisbet Balfour commandant in, 10, n 69, 81, Maj Thomas Fraser married in 111 British outposts driven in, v 126, loyal refugees employed in wood-cutting, 129 138 Alexander Chesney in, 130, 131, commissioner of sequestered estates in, 139, distress of South Carolina loyalists over evacuation, 116, evacuation by British, 75 expulsion of returned loyalist, 120

Charleston Neck (S C), 27

Charlotte, Fort (S C) see Forts

Chatham, Lord, 49, n 331

Cheraws (S C), loyal militia regiment commanded by Col Robert Gray, 114

Cherokee ford (Broad river, S C), 11 17, 131 133, 135

Cherokee Indians, see Indians

Chesney, Alexander, loyalist (S C), birth, 1, family connections, 1, 2 3 arrival in South Carolina, 3 settles on Pacolet river, 3, 4, 5 opposes Congress party, 5, pilots company of loyalists 6 130 135, 136, taken prisoner, 6, fails to reach Sir Henry Clinton's army, 7, with "rebel" army, 111, 6, 7, 8, 9 in campaign against Indians, 111 7, 8, 65, 72, 104 trades with Whigs in Charleston, 111, 8 9, marries Margaret Hodge, 9, goes within British lines and enlists, 111, 10, 11, in various actions, 12, 13 14 in operations in North Carolina, 14 15, 16, taken prisoner, 16, in battle of King's Mountain, 16, 17, 18, 85, 111, reports wounding of Col Daniel Plummer at King's Mountain, 89 is marched prisoner to Gilbert's Town, N C, 18, escapes home and hides out 19, 20, raises company and joins Brig-Gen Robert Cunningham, 14, 20 captured and exchanged 21, at Ninety-Six 21, joins Lieut-Col Banistre Tarleton 21, in defeat at Cowpens, Jan 17, 1781, 22, brings off family, iv 22, removes family to sequestered plantation, 23 raises troop of horse, iv, 24, moves family to Dorchester, iv, 24 wounded,

iv, 24, military activities, 24, 25, 26, 27, lieutenant in Lieut-Col John Fanning's scouts, 108, commissioned captain, 138, 139 commissioned lieutenant in Independent Scouts 139, helps defend sequestered estates, 14, 139, 140, experience on Cooper river, 27 superintends wood-cutters, v, 27, 138, death of first wife, 27, returns to Ireland, v, 28, presents memorial and meets Philip Henry, loyalist (S C) v, 28, visits relatives, 29, gives family history 29, 30, pushes claims for losses, v, vi, vii, 30, 31, 33, 34, 37, 38, 39, memorial, 126, 127, 130 evidence on memorial, 130-138, examined by commissioners on American Claims, 125 estimate of property, 127-130, testimonials, 140 Col John Phillips' letter, 141, certificates, 141, 142, letter to the commissioners, 142-144 Lewis Wolfe's letter, 144 claims settled 40 n 285 11 appointed member loyalists' committee, v, 33, employed in Irish Customs, v, vi, vii, 36, 39, 40, 50 53, 55 marries Jane Wilson, 36, births of children 30, 41, 44, 48, 51, combats smuggling, vii, x, 41, 42, 52 53, 55, 56, active against rebellion in Ireland vii, 45, 46, 47, appointed justice of peace, viii, 46, family matters, viii, ix x, xi, 40, 45, 48, 49, 50, 51, 52, 53, 54, 55, 56, seeks superannuation, 48 burial place of, 43, n 299

Chesney Alexander, Jr, ix, 48, 52

Chesney, Charles Cornwallis, ix, x, 42, n 296, 48, 49, 50, 51 54, 55

Chesney, Charlotte, ix, x, 54, 55, n 357

Chesney, Eliza, viii, ix 39, n 272, 44, 48, 51

Chesney, Francis Rawdon viii, 41, n 290, 43, 44, 48, n 327 49, 50, 51, 52, 55

Chesney, Jane, ix 41, n 286, 54

Chesney, Marianne ix x, 44, n 301, 54

Chesney, Matilda, ix, 47, 53

Chesney, Robert, ix, 29, gives land to son, Alexander, 133

Chesney, Thomas Crafer, ix, 51, n, 339

Chesney, Sophia, 55

Chesney William, ix, x, 20, 43 54, n 356, 56

Chester, Governor Peter (W Fla), visited by Capt Moses Kirkland, 106

Chitty, John, lawyer, London, Eng

Chitwood Capt James, loyalist executed, 86

Claims and awards, of loyalists Col Robert Ballingall, 94, Alexander Chesney, v, vi vii, 40 n 285, 125, 129, John Cruden and Co, 93 Brig-Gen Robert Cunningham, 87, Maj Michael Egan, 97 Lieut-Col John Fanning, 108 Col Thomas Fletchall 72 Col Zacharias Gibbs, 82, Mrs Zacharias Gibbs (nee Jane Downes), 81, 82, Philip Henry, 99 Capt Moses Kirkland, 108, fourth duke of Manchester, 59 Capt James Miller, 101, Col Richard Pearis, 103, Col John Phillips, 63, Maj John Robinson, 75, 76 Capt John

Saunders, 110, James Simpson, 100, South Carolina loyalists, 118-121

Clarke, Col Elijah, 11, n 76, 16, n 109

Clarke, Capt John, 21

Clary, Col Daniel, in command regiment loyal militia (S C), 113, in command two companies loyal militia of Dutch Fork of Ninety-Six, 114

Clatworthy, Lieut James, of Camden (S C) loyal militia, 115

Clavering, Col Henry M, 46, n 318

Clerk, Capt John, see Clarke, Capt. John

Cleveland, Col Benjamin, 17, 19

Clinton, Gen Sir Henry, called on by Alexander Chesney, v, 33, at Long Island, S C, 7, 131, takes Charleston, 126, at Charleston, 10, 30, 61, handbill, 14, 15, n 100, 33, letter from Lord Conrwallis to, 65, accompanied by Capt Moses Kirkland on evacuation of Philadelphia, 106

Clitherall, Dr James, surgeon, South Carolina Royalists, 98, 112

Coates, Col James, 26, n 183

Cobbett, William, celebrated politician, 25, n 181

Cochrane, Sir Alexander F I, 28, n 192

Coke, Daniel Parker, commissioner of American Claims, 37, n 258

Colden, Alice, 49, n 334

Colleton county (S C) loyal militia commanded by Col Robert Ballingall 114, Colleton family, loyalists (S C), claim and award, 118

Collier, Sir George, 105

Commissioner of loyalists' (or sequestered) estates, Col John Cruden, 139

Commissioners of American (or loyalist) Claims, 37, n 258, 38 39, 41, 48, 59, 62, 93, 97, 99 examine Alexander Chesney, vi, vii, 125 memorial of Alexander Chesney to, 126, 127, letters to, 140 142 144, report of committee of South Carolina loyalists to, 145

Committee of South Carolina loyalists, in London, justify taking State oath, 145-148

Commons House of Assembly (S C), 111, 113

Concealment of loyalists by Alexander Chesney, 136

Confiscation of loyalist estates 26 n 185, act mentioned, 39, n 274 lists published, 39, n 274, protests against South Carolina laws for, 94, of estate of Capt John Saunders, 110, of Lieut -Governor William Bull's estate thwarted, 112, 113 extent of act (S C) 141 of lands of Capt James Miller, 141 of property of Alexander Chesney, 31, 142 143, of propert yof Lieut -Col James Vernon, 78

Congress Colonial (S C), and Indians, 63, Provincial (S C), resolves to sieze leading

loyalists, 64, Continental, 68, 100, Provincial (S C), 74

Connelly, Col John, loyalist (Pa), Narrative of, xi

Cook, Capt Abraham, loyalist (S C), of Camden loyal militia, 114

Cook, Hugh, loyalist (S C), 4, 20

Cooper, Robert, 82

Cornwallis, Lord, v, 13, 32, 35, 39, 41, 44, 48, loyalist refugees in British Isles helped by, 31, n 210 inauguratees loyal militia in South Carolina, 60, 88, 113, supports claim of Col John Phillips, 62, letter to Sir Henry Clinton, 65, protests against execution of Col Ambrose Mills, 73, certificate to Col Zacharias Gibbs, 81, appoints Robert Ballingall colonel, 94, indignant at surrender of Col Rowland Rugeley and loyalists, 96, certificate to Maj Michael Egan, 97, certifies to value of Alexander Chesney's property, 125, certificate to Alexander Chesney, 132, 140, 143

Corry, Isaac, 47, n 320

Costley, Robert, loyalist (S C), land grant in Nova Scotia, 118

Cotton, Col John, in command of regiment of (S C) loyal militia, 113, 114, 116

Council of Safety (S C), 63, 68, asked to boycott Lieut -Col Evan McLaurin, 101

Covell, Samuel, loyalist (S C), land grant in Nova Scotia, 118

Cowpens, battle of, 11, n 79, 21, n 147, 22, n 148, 60, defeat of Col Banistre Tarleton, Jan 17, 1781, iv, 22, 60, 128, 132

Crafer, Thomas, xi, 31, n 208, 44, n 392, 49, 50, 51

Crampton, Maj John, 55, n 360

Creek Indians, see Indians

Creeks Beaver (S C), 96, Brandywine (Pa and Del), 109, Brier (Ga), 106, Brown's (S C), 12, Bullock's (S C), 131, Cane (N C), 14, Crocky (S C), 61, Fair Forest (S C), 10, 14, 22, 78, 88, 131, Fishing (S C), 14, n 97, Great Beaver (S C), 101, Great Lynch (S C), 96, Jackson's (S C), 3, 4, 6, 60, 100, 101, 114, 135, Kettle (Ga), 80, Long Cane (S C), iv, 24, n 177 Silver (N C), 14, Sugar (S C), 10, 131, Stevenson's (S C), 114, Thicketty (S C), 11, n 76, 22, 132, Town (S C), 3, Turkey (S C), 3, Waxhaw (S C), 90, White Oak (N C), 16, n 110, Williams (S C), 128, 133, 137

Crossian, Jeremiah, loyalist (S C), land grant in Nova Scotia, 118

Crown and Anchor tavern (London, Eng), see England

Cruden, James, loyalist (S C), 93

Cruden, Col John loyalist (S C), iv, v, 23, 27, career, 91-93 Address to the Loyal Part *of the British Empire*, 92, certificate to Alexander Chesney, 132, testimonial to same, 139

Cruden, John, the elder, loyalist (S C), prisoner, 92

Cruger, Lieut.-Col John Harris, loyalist (N Y), 16, n 109, 21, 81, 89-91, accompanied to Orangeburg by Col Daniel Plummer's men, 89, Capt Moses Kirkland accompanies expedition to Augusta, Ga, 107

Cunningham, Capt Andrew, of Colleton county (S C) loyal militia, 60, 115

Cunningham, David, loyalist, remains in South Carolina after the Revolution, 88

Cunningham, John, loyalist, remains in South Carolina after the Revolution, 88

Cunningham Margaret widow of Brig.-Gen Robert Cunningham, dies in Bahama Islands, 88

Cunningham, Maj Patrick, loyalist (S C), 20, 22, 64, 67, 68, 69, 87-89, 97 Richard Pearis, Jr, marries daughter, 104 not rescued from Charleston 104, commands brigade of loyal militia, 104, 113

Cunningham, Robert Andrew, 88

Cunningham, Lieut Thomas, loyalist (S C), in battle of King's Mountain, 116

Cunningham, Maj William, loyalist (S C), 88, in command of loyal mounted militia, 114, land grant in Nova Scotia, 118

Curwen, Judge Samuel, loyalist (Mass), *Journal and Letters*, xi, 116

Cuthbert,   , surveyor-general, 44

DARTMOUTH, Lord, 92

Davis, Maj   , 14, n 97

De Lancey, Oliver, loyalist (N Y), raises De Lancey's brigade, see Tory corps

De Peyster, Frederick, loyalist (N Y), joins Nassau Blues (Tory corps), 84, joins King's American regiment (Tory corps), 84

De Peyster, James, Sr, 84

De Peyster, James, Jr, loyalist (N Y), 84

Dimock, Shubal, loyalist (S C), land grant in Nova Scotia, 118

Dinwiddie Robert, governor of Virginia, 1752-7, 102

Dombrain, Lieut James, 56

Dorchester (S C), iv, v, 24, 26

Downes, Jane, second wife of Col Zacharias Gibbs, 81

Downes Maj William, loyalist (S C), 81

Doyle, Capt Sir Bentinck C, 35, n 240

Doyle, Lieut.-Gen Charles W, 35, n 240

Doyle, Col John, 25, n 180, 35, n 240, 43, 53, n 348, certificate regarding Alexander Chesney, 130, 132, 141

Doyle, William, 35, n 240

Drayton, William Henry 63 64, 65 66, 68, 69, 70 71, 87, version of Capt Moses Kirkland's departure from South Carolina, 107

Drury, Capt   , , 48

Dublin (Ireland), see Ireland

Duet's Corner (S C), 8

Duke of Cumberland's regiment (or Loyal American Rangers), see Tory corps

Duke of Richmond, offers motion in House of Lords, 95

Dundas, Col Thomas, commissioner of American Claims, 93

Dunlap, Maj James, loyalist, 12, n 83, 73, 79, executed, 95

Dunmore, Lord John Murray, last royal governor of Virginia, Capt Kirkland serves under, 105, Capt Kirkland returns to Dunmore's ships, 106, commissions John Saunders captain, 109

Dupont, Gideon, loyalist (S C), 94, claim and award, 119, member, committee of South Carolina loyalists in London, 145

Dupont, Gideon, Jr, loyalist (S C), agent, South Carolina loyalists, 116, 117

Dutch Fork, of Ninety-Six (S C), 101, loyal militia from, 114

Dykes, George, loyalist (S C), 79

EAST FLORIDA, company of loyalists on way to St Augustine, 6, mentioned, 8, Patrick Tonyn, governor of, 61, 105, Robert Phillips takes refuge in, 61, John Cruden, the younger, in, 92, 93, address of loyalists to Governor Patrick Tonyn, 92, Cols Ambrose Mills and David Fanning try to lead 500 loyalists to, 72, St Mary's river, 92, Capt Moses Kirkland visits, 105, 10,000 loyalists suffer by cession to Spain, 75, Lieut.-Col Joseph Robinson and wife take refuge in, 75, East Florida Rangers, see Tory corps

Edghill, Col Thomas, member, South Carolina loyalists' committee, 116

Edisto river (S C), see Rivers

Egan, Maj Michael, loyalist (S C) goes to Ireland, 28, career, 96-97, in Camden loyal militia, 114

Ellegood, Col Jacob, loyalist (Va), commands Queen's Own Loyal Virginian regiment, 109, in New Brunswick, 108 110

Ellis, Joseph (or Jacob), loyalist (S C), land grant in Nova Scotia, 118

Elliott, Lieut William, of lower Ninety-Six loyal militia, 116

Enoree river (S C), see Rivers

England, Dr Frazier (James Fraser), loyalist (S C), goes to, 26, n 185, loyalist refugees meet in London, v, 32, n 216, commissioners of American Claims in London, vi, vii, 37, n 253, 38, 39, 41, 48, 59, 62, 93, 97, 99, 125, 126, 127, 130-138, 140, 142, 144, 145, Lieut-Col James Vernon in, 79, Philip Henry and other loyalists go to, 98, Capt Moses Kirkland drowns on way to, 107, Capt. John Saunders goes to, 110,

John Simcoe Saunders in, 111, Col James Chalmers and family in, 110, Alexander Chesney in, v, vi vii, 30, 31, 33, 34, 37, 38, 39, 125, 130-138, report of committee of South Carolina loyalists in London, 145-149

English, Capt Joshua of Camden loyal militia, 114

English Col Robert of Camden loyal militia, 96, 97, 115

Ennis, Col Alexander, see Innes

Estimate, of Alexander Chesney's property, 127-130

Eustace, Col Charles, 34, n 236, 35

Evidence on Alexander Chesney's memorial, 130-138

Evacuation, of Charleston (S C), distress of loyalists over, 116

Execution, of loyalists, 17, n 120, 25, n 182, 18 n 129, 86, 95, of American officer, Col Isaac Hayne, 94, 95

FAIR FOREST (S C), location, 10, n 68, Alexander Chesney at, 22, n 152, loyalists join Col Nisbet Balfour at 131

Fair Forest creek (S C) see Creeks

Fanning, Col David, loyalist (N C), Narrative, xi, helps raise corps of 500 loyalists, 72, 108, in command of King's American regiment, Dec, 1776, 84 member, South Carolina loyalists' committee, 116

Fanning, Col Edmund, loyalist (N C), in command of King's American regiment, Dec, 1776, 84 lieutenant-governor, Prince Edward Island, 108 career 108-111

Fanning, Capt John, loyalist Alexander Chesney in company of, 139

Farquharson, Dr John loyalist (S C), 98

Felder, Capt John oppressor of loyalists, killed, 115

Fenny, Margaret, 88

Fenton, Richard, loyalist (S C), and family in Nova Scotia, 82

Fenwick, Thomas loyalist (S C), claim and award, 119

Ferguson, Maj Patrick iii, 10, 14 n 99, 15, 17, 18, n 124 19 23, 31, 78 career, 83-93, loyal militia under command of, 126, inspector-general of loyal militia, 131 Alexander Chesney serviceable to 132, 135 136, defeated and killed at King s Mountain, 131, 142

Ferguson, Thomas, 23, n 162 sequestered estate of, 139

Fishdam ford, Broad river (S C), 12, n 87

Fishing creek (S C), see Creeks

Fitzgerald, Lord Edward, 25

Fitzpatrick, Mary, 53

Fitzsimmons, James, loyalist (S C), land grant in Nova Scotia, 118

Fletchall, Joseph, loyalist (S C), planter in Jamaica, 72

Fletchall, Col Thomas, loyalist (S C), 5, 63, 78, 87, goes with family to Jamaica, 71, career, 66-72, helps form Tory association in Ninety-Six district, 105

Fletcher, Lieut Duncan, of Loyal American regiment, 14, n 107

Florida, Southern loyalists seek refuge in, 117, South Carolina loyalists attempt escape from Gen Williamson's army into, 131 (See also East Florida and West Florida)

Forbes Gen John, 102

Ford, Capt John, 69

Forrester, D, 93

Forts Anderson's (S C), 10, 11, Augusta (Ga), 16, 21, Barrington (Ga) 8, Blackstocks (S C), 20, Charlotte (S C), 67, 107, Duquesne (Pa), 102 Lawsons (S C), 12, n 83, Motte (S C), 93, n 165, Nichols' (Nicholas's or Nochols, (S C), 12, n 82, 131, Ninety-Six (S C) 5 65 69, 70, 90, 100, Pitt (Pa), headquarters of Capt Richard Pearis, 102 Quarter House (S C), 9, n 62, 27, Thicketty (S C) (also called Anderson's), 10, 11, n 77

Fortune, Col William, loyalist (S C), 26, n 185, member, South Carolina loyalists committee, 116

Fralick, Adam, loyalist (S C), land grant in Nova Scotia, 118

Fraser, Dr James, loyalist (S C), 26 n 185, certificate regarding Alexander Chesney, 129 n 6

Fraser, Maj Thomas, loyalist (S C), 13, n 96, at Parker's ferry, 108, brief account of, 111-112

Frazier, Dr James, see Fraser, Dr James

French, war against the, 117, land in Ireland, Aug, 1798, viii, 47, n 323

French and Indian war, 102

Frost, Maj Jonathan, loyalist (S C), killed, 20, 21

Fry, Capt Jacob, loyalist (S C), 71

Fry, John, killed, 115

Fulkes, Lieut _____ _____, loyalist, executed, 95

Fyffe, Dr Charles, loyalist (S C), 62

GALLOWAY, Joseph loyalist (Pa), Letters to a Nobleman, xi, The Examination of, xi

"Gadkin" river, see Yadkin river

Galphin, _____ _____, 65

Garden, Dr Alexander, loyalist (S C), 10, n 69, 94

Gates, Gen Horatio, 13, n 94 defeat at Camden, 91

General Assembly (S. C), fixes date of Philip Henry's banishment, 98

Georgetown (S C), loyal militia commanded by Lieut -Col James Gordon, 115

Georgia, Augusta, 9, Brier creek, 106, Col Bond, loyalist, killed at Kettle creek, 80, Alexander Cameron, loyalist of, 64, Col

Archibald Campbell and British force sail for, 1778, 89, expedition planned against, 106, expedition for relief of Col Thomas Brown, 107, Fort Augusta, 16, 21, Fort Barrington, 8, Georgia Loyalists (Tory corps), 26, n 187, Capt Moses Kirkland accompanies expedition to, 106, 350 loyalists march to Savannah, 80, loyal militia of South Carolina liable to service in, 113, Ogeechee river, 8 Ogeechie, 107, Col Richard Pearis and family settle near Augusta, 103, Col Daniel Plummer at Savannah, 89, Purysburg, 7, n 51, Revolutionists and Indians in, 65, Savannah river, 24, 103, Second Broad river, 14, n 107, William Simpson, chief justice, 99, Whig militia operates against Indians in, 8, 9

Gibbs, Col Zacharias, 11, 132, career, 79-82 in command of regiment of loyal militia, 114, member, South Carolina loyalists' committee, 116, land grant in Nova Scotia, 118, witness for Alexander Chesney 127, testimony regarding Alexander Chesney, 136, 137, certificate to Alexander Chesney, 141-143

Giesondanner, Capt Henry, of Orangeburg loyal militia, 114

Gilbert Town (N C), 15, n 101, 17, 18

Gilkey, Capt _____, loyalist, executed, 86

Gist, William, loyalist (S C), 104

Gledstanes Maj-Gen S Albert, 52, n 346, 53, n 349

Gordon, Lieut-Col James, in command of Georgetown (S C) loyal militia, 115, member, South Carolina loyalists' committee, 116

Grant, Maj Alexander, loyalist, 13, n 89

Grattan, Henry, 47, n 320

Graves, Capt Richard and wife, loyalists (S C), claim and award, 119

Gray, Benjamin Dingley, loyalist (Va), 109

Gray, Col Robert, in command of Cheraws loyal militia, 114

Green, Henry, loyalist (S C), 64 land grant in Nova Scotia, 118

Green river (N C), see Rivers

Great Bridge (Va), see Battles

Greene, Gen Nathaniel, loses siege of Ninety-Six, 90 threatens reprisals, 95

Greenwood William member, South Carolina loyalists' committee, 116, claim and award, 119

Greer, Capt Thomas, 69

Grey, Capt Isaac, loyalist, executed, 86

Grierson, Col James, loyalist, executed, 95

Grimes, Capt ___ ___, loyalist, executed, 86

Grimes, Col _____, 15, n 102

Grindal ford (S C), Gen Daniel Morgan at, 21, n 147

Grindal shoals (S C), 4, 12

Guest, Edward, 37, n 257

HADDON, Col John, 49, n 332

Halifax (Nova Scotia), see Nova Scotia

Hamilton, Mark Kerr, 49, n 334

Hamilton, Col Archibald, loyalist (N C), 49, n 334

Hamilton, Archibald and Co, merchants, 117

Hamilton, John, member, South Carolina loyalists' committee, 116

Hamilton, Lieut-Col John, of Royal North Carolina regiment, recommended for governorship of Bahama Islands, 117, raised 1200 men, 117

Hamilton, Paul, loyalist (S C), is refused payment of note, 121

Hammond, Col LeRoy, 77

Hampton, Col Andrew, 11, n 76, 61, 73

Hampton, Anthony, 79

Hampton, Capt Edward 73, 79

Hampton, Jonathan, 89

Hampton, Noah, 79

Hanging Rock (S C), battle, see Battles

Harling, Aaron, 79

Harper, Robert, 40

Harvey, Capt Alexander, of Colleton county S C) loyal militia, 115

Hayden, Rev Henry, ix, x, 55, 56

Hayne, Col Isaac, 24, 77, 94, 95

Henry Philip, loyalist (S C), v, 28, 30, 34, 36, n, 252, 37, 38 career, 97-99 claim and award, 119

Henry, S M, loyalist (S C), 98

Heyward, Thomas, 100

Hobbs, Lieut Augustine, loyalist, executed, 86

Hodge, Margaret, first wife of Alexander Chesney, 9

Hodge, Robert, 40, n 277

Hodge, William 9, n 64, 128, 133, 134, 138

Hodgson Robert, lieutenant, Prince Edward Island Fencibles, 76

Hodson, Robert, Jr, 76

Holstein river (S C), see Rivers

Holt, Capt Joseph, of Camden (S C) loyal militia, 114

Hopkin Capt David, 12, n 84, 61

Hopkins, Capt John, ix, 39, n 274, 51, 54

Hopton, John 10 n 70 94 member, committee to estimate losses of South Carolina loyalists, 120

Horry, Col Peter, 77

House, Capt Christian, of Orangeburg (S C) loyal militia, 114

House of Assembly (S C), addressed by Capt Moses Kirkland, 105

Howard, Nathaniel, loyalist (S C), 64

Howard, Peter, 8, 127

Howe, Lord Admiral, 91, 92

Howe, Gen Sir William, joined by Capt Moses Kirkland, 106

Hoyt, Eli, loyalist (S C), land grant in Nova Scotia, 118

Huey, Capt John, of Jackson's creek (S C) loyal militia, 114

Huger, Gen Isaac, 77

Hunt, William, loyalist (S C), 5, n 30

Huntingdon, Lord, 32

Hutchinson, Thomas, *Diary and Letters*, xi

INDIANS, presents for, 5, 6, Alexander Chesney marches against, 7, Catawba, 65, 102, Cherokee, 6, 11, n 77, 63, 64, 102, 104, expedition against, 65, William Henry Drayton's alleged attempt to win 66, actions against, 72, Col Ambrose Mills' campaign against, 74, Creek, 6, 8, 63, 65, northern Creek, in rum trade, 103, under command of Capt Richard Pearis, 102, Col Richard Pearis passes through settlements of, 102, 103, Maj Patrick Cunningham takes powder sent to, 104, Capt Moses Kirkland, deputy superintendent of, 106, Indian field company, 115, in the Revolution, 63-66

Inglis, George, 111

Inglis, Thomas, member, South Carolina loyalists' committee, 116

Inman, Lieut George, loyalist (Mass), 36, n 253

Innes, Col Alexander, loyalist (S C), 13, 83, 84 103

Inspector-General of Provincial (loyalist) forces Col Alexander Innes, appointed, Jan, 1777, 83

Ireland, Alexander Chesney and others go to, \ 28, 125, Philip Henry in, 28, 30, 36, n 252, 37, 38, 93, Alexander Chesney in, 29, 30 36, 39, 40, 45, 46, 48, 49, 50-56, 144, smuggling in, vii, x, 41, 42, 52, 53, 55 56, rebellion in, viii, 25, n 181 45, 46, 47, death of Col John Phillip's in, 62 Jane Downs (Mrs Zacharias Gibbs) in, 62 Maj John Robinson returns to, 97, Capt James Miller in, 101, Col Zacharias Gibbs in, 142

Irish board of Customs, loyalists hold offices under, v vi, vii 28, 34, 35, 36, 39, 40, 98 101, 123

Iron works (S C), location, 4, n 22, skirmish near, 10, Maj Patrick Ferguson victorious at 12, Capt Abraham de Peyster marches to 14

Irving, Thomas member committee of South Carolina loyalists in London, 145

Island ford (Saluda river, S C), 87

JACKSONBOROUGH (S C), 23, 39

Jamaica, see West Indies

James Island (S C), 27

Jefferson, Joseph, 88

Jekyll, John, collector of Customs, Boston, Mass, 110

Johnson, Dr Uzal, loyalist (N J), 19, n 129

Johnston, James, loyalist (S C), member, committee to estimate losses of South Carolina loyalists, 120

Johnston, Robert, member, South Carolina loyalists' committee, 116

Johnstone, Lieut James, of Camden county (S C) loyal militia, 115

Jones, E Alfred, editor, *Journal of Alexander Chesney*, xi, xii

Jones, Judge Thomas, loyalist (N Y), *History of New York during the Revolutionary War*, xi

Journal of a Voyage from Charleston, S C to London, 1778, xi

KELLY, Capt Daniel, of Orangeburg (S C) loyal militia, 114

Kempe's landing place (Kempsville, Va), 110

Kennedy's ford (Enoree river, S C), 101

Kettle creek (Ga), see Creeks

Killmorey, Lord, 52, 54, 55

Kilpatrick, Jack, 45

King, Lieut.-Col Richard, in defense of Ninety-Six, 1781, 90, in command of South Carolina loyal militia, 114

King's American regiment, see Tory corps

King's Carolina Rangers, see Tory corps

King's Florida rangers, see Tory corps

King's Mountain, battle of, see Battles

Kingsley, Zephaniah, loyalist (S C), claim and award, 119

Kirkland, Capt Moses, loyalist (S C), 67; career, 105-108, claim and award, 119

Kirkland Richard Bruce, loyalist (S C), planter in Jamaica, 107

LACY, Capt Thomas, 52, n 345, 53, n 351

Lafferty, Lieut _____ loyalist, executed, 86

Landerkin, John loyalist (S C), land grants in Nova Scotia, 118

Land grants, to 56 South Carolina loyalists in Nova Scotia, 118

Lawson's Fort (S C) see Forts

Legge, Lieut Benjamin Smith, of Colleton county (S C) loyal militia, 115

Leslie, Lieut -Gen Alexander, South Carolina loyalists' address to, 94, certificate to Maj Michael Egan, 97, expedition to Virginia, October, 1780, 110

Lewis, Maj Andrew, 102

Lewis John, loyalist (S C), land grant in Nova Scotia, 118

Lincoln, Gen Benjamin, 9

Lincoln's Inn (London, Eng), see England

Lindsay, William, 81

Little river (S C), see Rivers

Lively, Reuben, loyalist (S C), land grant in Nova Scotia, 118

Livingston, John, 85

Lloyd Lieut -Gen Vaughan, 51, n 336

London (Eng), see England

Long, Capt George, in command of company of South Carolina loyal militia, 114

Long Cane creek (S C), see Creeks

Long Island (N Y), Capt Moses Kirkland at capture of, 106

Long Island (S C), Sir Henry Clinton on, 131

Lord commissioners of the Treasury, attempt to suppress smuggling in Ireland, x, 56, John Cruden's letter to, 120

Losses, of Alexander Chesney, vi, 31, 34, 125, 126, 127-130, 133-138, of South Carolina loyalists, 119, 120

Lowndes, Rawlins, 98

Loyal American regiment, see Tory corps

Loyal militia, and Indians attack "rebels," July, 1776, 102, Maj Patrick Cunningham appointed to command corps, 104, Gen Robert Cunningham's brigade, 104, 107, commanded by Capt Moses Kirkland at Brier creek (Ga), 106, Capt Kirkland in charge of regiment, 107, John Fanning joins South Carolina, 108, account of, 113-116, Alexander Chesney appointed captain and adujtant of, 126, 142, Alexander Chesney in command of company, 130, James Miller appointed captain in Jackson's creek loyal militia, 101, Alexander Chesney joins Col Banistre Tarleton with company, 132, Maj Patrick Ferguson, inspector-general of, 131, Zacharias Gibbs colonel of, 142

Loyalist refugees petition the king, v, in East Florida, and Indians, to be sent against Georgia, 106 Alexander Chesney's wife and child driven within British lines, 142, 143, in London, 145

Loyalists, exiled from South Carolina, v, 28, n 197, 61, 98, 117, early activities of South Carolina, 5 piloted by Alexander Chesney, 6 harbored by Robert Chesney, 7, detachment under Maj James Dunlap, 12, n 83, in Charleston, S C, 23, near Long Cane creek, 24, in British Isles, 31, n 83, meet at Crown and Anchor tavern, London, 32 • association in London, 32, n 216, classification, 33, some return to America, 38, detachment under Cols John Phillips and John Fanning defeated, 60, in Charleston, 61, attempt to sieze leading, in South Carolina, 64, in Ninety-Six district, S C, 66; attempt to disarm those of Ninety-Six district, 68 of South Carolina repudiate treaty of Sept 16, 1775, 69 sent to Charleston as prisoners 71, 500 raised by Cols David Fanning and Ambrose Mills, 72, attack camp of Col Charles McDowell, July, 1780, 73, 2400 at Ninety-Six, S C, in 1775, 74, 10,000 in East Florida suffer by cession to Spain, 75, executed at Ninety-Six, 80, enlist in King's American regiment, Dec, 1776, 84 remain in South Carolina after Revolution, 83, address to Governor Patrick

Tonyn, 92, in house of Col Rowland Rugeley, 95, of district of Great Lynch creek, S C, 96, sail for Rotterdam, 98, committee of South Carolina reports on value of their property, 99, of Camden district, S C, refuse to sign Whig association, 100, over 5,000 raised by Col Richard Pearis, 103, take part in Maj Andrew Williamson's expedition against Indians, 104, slay Capt. John Felder, 115, Southern, seek refuge in Florida, 117, send to British commander about exacuation of Charleston, 116, officers of North Carolina suggest Bahama Islands for loyalist settlement, 117, 1200 raised by Col John Hamilton of North Carolina, 117, 500 South Carolina, go to Nova Scotia, 117, land grants to 56, at Rawdon, Nova Scotia, 117, party piloted by Alexander Chesney, 130, 135, 136, 138, forced to serve in "rebel" army, 135, losses and compensation of South Carolina, 118-121 (see Claims and awards), resolution of, 137, n 13, 144, from South Carolina take action in London, 145, United, 92

Ludlow, Gabriel G, loyalist (N Y), holds offices in New Brunswick, Canada, 111

Lusk, Robert, 40.

Luttrell, Gen Henry Lawes, 38, n 269, 39

Lynch, Thomas, 100

McALLISTER, Samuel, loyalist (S C), land grant in Nova Scotia, 118

McArthur, Maj Archibald, 22

McBee, Capt Vadry, 129, n 4

McCrumb, James, 40

McCulloch, Capt James, loyalist of Camden (S C) loyal militia, 86, 114

McCullom, John, loyalist (S C), land grant in Nova Scotia, 118

McDonald, Donald, 76

McDonald, Lieut Angus, loyalist, 60

Macdonald, Sir William Christopher, loyalist descent of, 76

Macdonald College, 76

McDole, Col Charles, see McDowell, Col Charles

McDowell, Alexander, 43

McDowell (not 'McDole"), Col Charles, 11, n 76, 12, 14, n 104, 73

McDowell, John, 40

McDowell, Maj Joseph 11, n 79

McFall, Lieut John, loyalist, executed, 86

McGill University, Montreal, 76

McGuire, John loyalist (S C), land grant in Nova Scotia, 118

McKay, Maj John, loyalist (Va), in battle of the Brandywine 109, settles in New Brunswick, Canada, 110

McKean, Thomas, 100

McKinnon, Capt John, 22, n 164

McLaurin, Lieut.-Col Evan, loyalist (S C), 69 70, 74, 101 lays siege to Ninety-Six, November, 1775 135, n 9

McMahon, Capt. John, loyalist, 27, n 191

McMechan, Rev James, 54

McMillen, Richard, loyalist (S C), land grant in Nova Scotia, 118

McNeilly, Henry see McNully

McNully, Henry, 42, n 295, 45, 46

McWhorter, Capt Alexander, 8, n 59

McWhorter, Robert, iv, 22

Manly, Capt. _____ _____, and American privateer captured, 105

Manson, Daniel, loyalist (S C), 98

Marion, Gen Francis 20, n 133 24

Martindale, Henry, loyalist (S C), land grant in Nova Scotia, 118

Martindale, Henry, Jr , loyalist (S C), land grant in Nova Scotia, 118

Maryland, Capt Richard Pearis serves on borders of, 102 Col James Chalmers in command of Maryland Loyalists (Tory corps), 110

Massachusetts, Sir Francis Bernard governor, 35, n 246 Lieut. George Inman 36, n 253, Capt Moses Kirkland visits Boston, 105, Capt Kirkland, a prisoner in Cambridge, 106, John Jekyll, collector of Customs at Boston 110

Matthews, Joseph, 47, n 324, 48

Mayfield, Capt John, loyalist, 5, n 30, executed, 86

Mayson ('Maysen"), Maj James, 66, 67, 70 74, 77, 135, n 9

Meek, John, loyalist (S C) land grant in Nova Scotia, 118

Meek Samuel, loyalist (S C), land grant in Nova Scotia, 118

Meek, Capt William loyalist (S C), land grant in Nova Scotia, 118

Meigham (or Meighlan), Lieut Brian, 60

Memorial of Capt John Phillips, 62, of Col Thomas Fletchall, 69 of Capt Moses Kirkland, 105, 107, of widows of loyalists, 116, of Sergeant James White 116 of loyalist officers of North Carolina, 117 of Alexander Chesney, v, vi, vii, 30, 31, 125, evidence on Alexander Chesney's 130-138

Meredith, Maj David 51, n 338

Middle Temple (London) see England

Middleton, Arthur 100

Militia see Loyal militia

Millen, Capt Hugh 101 in possession of Capt James Miller's lands, 141

Miller, Capt James, loyalist (S C), 35 n 237, 37, 62, settler in Camden district, 100, 101, witness for Alexander Chesney, 127, 138, confiscation of his lands, 141

Miller, John, 3

Milling, Capt Hugh, see Millen

Mills, Col Ambrose, loyalist (N C), 65, helps raise 500 loyalists, 72 career, 72-74, executed, 86

Mills, Col William Henry, loyalist (S C), 74, 115

Moira, Lady, 39, 41, n 287, 43, 48, 49

Moira Lord, 44, 53, 143

Moncks Corner (S C), 26, n 184

Monckton, Gen Robert, 102

Montagu, Lord Charles Greville, governor of South Carolina, in command of Duke of Cumberland's regiment (or Loyal American Rangers), 59 ,60, 91 commissions Thomas Fletchall, 66 claim and award, 119, 150

Montell, Anthony loyalist (S C), order for wood cutting, 138

Moody Lieut James, loyalist (N J), Narrative of His Exertions and Sufferings, xi

Moore, Lieut -Col John, loyalist (N C), 80

Moore Capt Patrick, loyalist (S C), 11, 131

Moravian Town (N C), see North Carolina

Morgan, Gen Daniel, 21, n 147, occupies Alexander Chesney's land, 128, n 2, 132, 143 n 13

Morgan, Francis L , 36, n 248, 52, n 342

Motte, Jacob and Rebecca, 23, n 165

Moultrie, Maj -Gen William, 65

Murat, Prince Lucian, 112

Musgrove, Edward, loyalist (S C), 13, n 96

Musgrove,'s Mills battle of see Battles

Muster rolls, South Carolina loyal militia, 116

NASSAU (New Providence), see Bahama Islands

Needham Francis Jack 52, n 347

Neils, Ned 4

Nelson Reason, loyalist (S C), 7 ,n 50

Nelson s (Neilson's") ferry (S C), 7, n 50, 23

New Brunswick (Canada), missionary to, 56, Lieut -Col Joseph Robinson goes to, 75, Capt Abraham de Peyster and brother officers find refuge in, 85 Capt John Saunders holds offices in, 110, 111, Col Jacob Ellegood and Maj John McKay settle in, 110, Judge Edward Winslow in, 111, John Simcoe Saunders holds offices in, 111

New Jersey, treatment of Dr Uzal Johnson of Newark, 19 n 129 Lieut -Col Isaac Allen of Trenton, 21, n 145

New Jersey Volunteers see Tory corps

New York, loyalists, 84, Nassau Blues, 84, New York Volunteers, 12, n 89, 13, n 84, 101, Prince of Wales American Volunteers, 90, Queen's Rangers, 73, 86, 109, 110

New York Volunteers see Tory corps

Nicholls Fort (S C) see Forts

Nicholls, James, loyalist (S C), land grant in Nova Scotia, 118

Nicholls John, 78

Ninety-Six (S C), district, 4, 10, jail, 21, Maj Patrick Ferguson in command of Fort, iii, 10, Lord Rawdon relieves, iv, 90, siege of Fort, November, 1775, 5, 69, 70, 74, 76, 80, 100, 102, 135, n 9, Thomas Fletchall's estate, 66, powder and stores removed to court house, 67, attempt to disarm loyalists, 68, Fletchall's attack on Fort, 69, 70, Joseph Fletchall reared in, 72, 2400 loyalists under Lieut-Col Joseph Robinson, 1775, 74, Lieut-Col James Vernon, resident, 78, Col Zacharias Gibbs, resident, 79, prisoners marched to, 80 brigade of loyal militia, 89, Lieut-Col John Harris Cruger's defense, 1781, 90, Col. Richard Pearis active, 102, Capt Moses Kirkland, planter, 105, loyal militia from Dutch Fork, 114, loyal militia under Col Thomas Pearson, 114, loyal militia of lower, 116

Noble, Capt Joseph, of Orangeburg (S C) loyal militia, 114

Norfolk (Va), see Virginia

Norman, Robert, 42, 48

North, Lord, v, 33

North Carolina, 12, 16, Cane creek, 14, Constitutional Convention, 11, n 79 Col David Fanning, 84, 86, 108 116 Col Edmund Fanning, 84, 86, 108-111, Green river, 72, Holstein river, 14, n 105, Col Archibald Hamilton, loyalist, 49, n 334, Lieut-Col John Hamilton, loyalist, 117, loyal militia in battle of King's Mountain, 73, memorial of loyalist officers, 117, men join Maj Patrick Ferguson, 16, Lieut-Col John Moore, 80, Moravian Town, 19, n 131, 132, Royal North Carolina regiment, 117, Second Broad river, 14, n 107, Silver creek, 14, Thomas Loughton Smith, merchant, 111, Maj William Spurgeon, 80 William Tryon, governor, 1765-71, 127, Turkey cove, 14, n 105, Yadkin river, 19, 132

North Carolina Provincials (loyalists), John Cruden, paymaster, 92

Northern Creek Indians, see Indians

North Pacolet river (N C), see Rivers

Nova Scotia, 500 loyalists sail from Charleston, S C, to, 117, South Carolina loyalists in, 117, 118, North Carolina loyalists in, 117, Lord Charles Greville Montagu and 300 Loyal American Rangers settle in, 59, John Cruden, the younger, goes to, 93, Richard Fenton and family in, 82, Col Zacharias Gibbs receives land grant in, 82, 118, land grants to South Carolina loyalists, 118, 119

Nugent, Gen Sir George, 46, n 317

OATH of allegiance, James Barber refuses American, 97, Lieut-Governor William Bull (S C) keeps British, 112, loyalists seek to avoid State, 131, loyalists' committee in London justify taking State, 145-149

Ogeechee river (Ga), see Rivers

Ogeechie (Ga), see Georgia

Ogilvie, Charles, 94, member, South Carolina loyalists committee in London, 145

Ogilvie Charles, Sr, agent, South Carolina loyalists, 116, 117

Old Fields (S C), 21

Oliphant, Dr David, imprisoned, 117

O'Neal, Henry, loyalist (S C), 64

Orangeburg (S C), see South Carolina

Orde, Capt John, loyalist (S C), claim and award, 119

PACOLET river (S C), see Rivers

Palmerston, Viscount, 75

Parker's ferry (S C), see South Carolina

Party divisions, in South Carolina families, 145

Patteson, Brig-Gen James, 61

Pearis, Margaret, land grant in Bahama Islands, 104

Pearis, Col Richard, loyalist (S C), 64, 70, 71, 88, career, 102-104, claim and award, 119

Pearis, Richard, Jr, loyalist (S C), 88, 104

Pearson, Col Thomas, in command of Ninety-Six (S C) loyal militia regiment, 114, land grant in Nova Scotia, 118

Pelham Thomas, 46 n 314

Pennsylvania, Carlisle, 2, n 10 Continental Congress, 100, Fort Duquesne (Pitt), 102, Maj Thomas Fraser in Philadelphia, 112, Capt Moses Kirkland at evacuation of Philadelphia, 106

Pensacola (W Fla), see West Florida

Peronneau Henry loyalist (S C), member, committee to estimate losses of South Carolina loyalists, 120

Petition, of loyalist refugees to king's ministers, v, 32, n 216, of officers of British American regiments, 84, of Capt James Miller, 100

Phepoe, Thomas, 61

Philadelphia (Pa), see Pennsylvania

Phillips, David, loyalist (S C), 61

Phillips, Capt James, loyalist (S C), 6, 61, James Miller joins loyalists under, 100, and loyalists piloted to Pacolet river, 130

Phillips, Col John, loyalist (S C), 3, 4, 9, 13, 37, n 256, 38, 39, 130, 136, 143, in expedition against Cherokee, 65, 72, career, 60-63 commands Jackson's creek loyal militia, 101 114 member, South Carolina loyalists' committee, 116, witness for Alexander Chesney, 125, 127, testimony regarding Chesney, 135, 136 letter to commissioners on American Claims, 140

Phillips, Capt Mitchell, loyalist (Va), boycotted, 109

Phillips, Robert, loyalist (S C), 60, 61, refugee in East Florida, 61

Pickens, Col Andrew, 77

Pickens, Capt Joseph, 77
Pinckney, Capt Charles Cotesworth, 141, n 8
Platt, Capt George, of Camden (S C) loyal militia, 114
Pledger, Capt. Thomas, of Orangeburg loyal militia, 114
Plummer, Col Daniel, 20, 78, 88, 89, in command of (S C) loyal militia regiment, 113, 132
Pollock, Savage Andrew, 56
Ponpon river (S C), see Rivers
Porter, Maj John, 46, n 318, 47
Postell, Maj John, 77
Powell, Robert, William, 94, chairman, committee of South Carolina loyalists, 116, member, committee of South Carolina loyalists in London, 145
Prevost, Col Augustine, controversy with Governor Tonyn, 6, accompanied on expedition to Charleston by Capt Moses Kirkland, 106
Prince Edward Island, Lieut.-Col Joseph Robinson invited to, 76, Legislative Council, 76, Col Edmund Fanning, loyalist (N C), lieutenant-governor, 75
Prince of Wales American Volunteers, see Tory corps
Prisoners, drafted into Duke of Cumberland's regiment (or Loyal American Volunteers), 91
Proclamation, by Revolutionary party (S C), 100
Proctor, Samuel, loyalist (S C), land grant in Nova Scotia, 118
Provincial Congress (S C), Capt Moses Kirkland, member, 1774, 105, Gideon Dupont member, January, 1775, 117
Publications, by loyalists, xi, John Cruden's pamphlet, 92 Col David Fanning's Narrative, 101, John Simcoe Saunders' Law of Pleading and Evidence, 111
Purdy, I, 43
Purdy, James, 48, n 329, 49
Puriesburg (Ga), see Purysburg
Purvis, Maj John, 77
Purysburg ("Puriesburg," Ga), see Georgia.

QUARTER House (S C), 9, n 62, 27
Queen's Rangers, see Tory corps
Quin, John, 4

RANDOLPH, Peyton, 100.
Rawdon, Francis, 2nd, earl of Moira, 41, n 287.
Rawdon, Lord Francis, iv, vi, 24, 26, 27, 82, 33, 35, 39, 41, 61, 62, 81, relieves Lieut.-Col John Harris Cruger at Ninety-Six, 90, offers medals to British Legion, 90, receives apology from Duke of Richmond, 95, certificate to Maj Michael Egan, 97, gives appointment to Alexander Chesney, 125, certificate to Chesney, 132, 140, 143, Chesney carries expresses to, 142

Ray, George, 101
Read, Capt Nathan, loyalist, 17, n 120
Reade, Joseph, 84
Rebellion, in Ireland, see Ireland
Recollections of a Georgia Loyalist, xi
Reedy river (S C), see Rivers
Reese, David, loyalist (S C), 64
Refugees; see Loyalist refugees
Report, of committee of South Carolina loyalists on value of their property, 99, of committee of South Carolina loyalists in London, 145-149
Return, of loyalists to America, 38, one maltreated in South Carolina, 82, of Mrs Abraham de Peyster to New York, 85, of some to South Carolina, who are ordered to depart, 85
Resolution, South Carolina loyalists, 114, 137, n 13
Revoult, John, 49, n 333, 50
Richardson, Col Richard, 5, 6, 64, 70, 71
Ridley, Hannah, 88
Ritzema, Col Rudolphus, loyalist (N Y), 83, 84
Rivers   Altamaha (Ga), 8, 9, Broad (S C), 4, 11, 12, 13, 17, 18, 24, 26, 30, 74, 79, 101, 103, 108, 125, 130, Bush (S C), 128, 137, Catawba (N C), 14, n 105, 16, 61, Congaree (S C), 25, Cooper (S C), 27, n 189, Edisto (S C), 114, Enoree (S C), 13, n 96, 14, 102, Green (N C), 72, Holstein (N C), 14, n 105, 16, Little (S C), 20, 73, 114, Lynnhaven (Va), 109, North Pacolet (N C), 73, Ogeechee (Ga), 8, Pacolet (S C), 3, 4, 8, 11, 21, 126, 128, 130, 133, 135, 136, 137, 144, Ponpon (S C), iv, 23, 24, Reedy (S C), 6, 102, St Mary's (E Fla), 92, Saluda (S C), 16, n 114, 79, 87, 101, Sandy (S C), 4, Santee (S C), 7, 24, 115, Savannah (Ga), 24, 103, Second Broad (N C), 14, n 107, Tiger (S C), 11, 16, 20, 88, Yadkin ("Gadkin," N C), 19
Robertson, Maj Charles, 11, n 76.
Robinson, Capt Elisha, in command of company of lower Ninety-Six loyal militia, 116
Robinson, Elizabeth, 76
Robinson, Maj John, loyalist (S C), 28, n 193, 35, n 238, 95, 96, 114
Robinson, Lieut.-Col Joseph, of South Carolina Royalists (Tory corps), 6, 67, 70, career, 74-78, lays siege to Fort Ninety-Six, November, 1775, 139, n 9
Robinson, Mrs Lilly, flees to Virginia with children, 75, death of, 76
Robinson, Rebecca, 76
Rocky Mount (S C), loyal militia under Col William Vernon Turner, 115
Roebuck, Col Benjamin, 21, 129, n 4
Rogers, Capt Jasper, of Camden (S C) loyal militia, 114.
Rose, George, 32, 33.

Rose, John, loyalist (S C), 94, claim and award, 119, member, South Carolina loyalists' committee in London, 145

Rose, Capt. (later Gen) Alexander, 13, 33

Ross, Robert, 41, n 293, 42

Rotterdam (Holland), South Carolina loyalists sail for, 94

Round O company (American), of Colleton county, S C, 94

Rousselet, Capt John, loyalist, of British Legion, in battle of Hanging Rock (S C), 90

Rowand, Robert, loyalist (S C), 98

Rowe, Capt Samuel, of Orangeburg (S C) loyal militia, 114

Rugeley, Col Edward, loyalist (S C), 95, 97, 97.

Rugeley's Mills (S C), 95

Rumford, Count (Benjamin Thompson), loyalist (Mass), 66

Rutledge, Edward, 100

Ryerson, Capt Samuel, of New Jersey Volunteers (Tory corps), 14, n 107, 85

Ryland, Peter, loyalist (S C), land grant in Nova Scotia, 118

ST AUGUSTINE (E Fla), see East Florida

St Helena, island, ix

Salisbury (S C), see South Carolina

Sally, Capt John, in command of company of loyal militia, 114

Saluda river (S C), see Rivers

Santee river (S C), see Rivers

Saunders, Capt. John, loyalist (Va), 143, n 15, career, 105-111

Saunders, John Simcoe, loyalist (S C), 110, in New Brunswick, Canada, 111

Saunders, Rev Jonathan, 108

Saunderson, John, loyalist (S C), land grant in Nova Scotia, 118

Savage, Francis, 41, n 288

Savannah (Ga), see Georgia

Savannah river (Ga), see Rivers

Scott, Robert, loyalist (S C), land grant in Nova Scotia, 118

Second Broad river (N C), see Rivers

Sequestered property, in South Carolina, iv, 92, of Capt James Miller, 101, John Cruden, commissioner of, 139, services of Alexander Chesney in connection with, 139

Sharp, Capt. James, of Jackson's creek loyal militia, 114

Sharp, Lieut William, of Jackson's creek loyal militia, 114

Shaw, David, 28, n 192.

Shelburne, 32

Shelby, Col Isaac, 11, n 76, 17, n 120

Shepperd, James, loyalist (S C), lieutenant, Indian field company, 115

Shuberg, Capt George, loyalist (S. C.), 71.

Silver creek (N C), see Creeks

Simcoe, Col John Graves, of Queen's Rangers (Tory corps), commends Capt. John Saunders, 109

Simpson, Barbara, wife of James Simpson, 100

Simpson, James, attorney-general of South Carolina, 32, 99, 100, claim and award, 119, member, committee of South Carolina loyalists to estimate their losses, 120, member, committee of South Carolina loyalists in London, 145

Simpson, William, chief justice of Georgia, 99

Skeffington, Hon W. J, 39, n 270, 44, n 303.

Slaves, of Lieutenant-Governor William Bull, 112, of those lost by South Carolina loyalists, 118, 120, one lost by Alexander Chesney, 129, 134, 137

Smith, Anne Loughton, marries Maj Thomas Fraser, 111

Smith, Capt Esaw, 12, n 84

Smith, Capt Hugh, loyalist (S. C), of Camden loyal militia, 114

Smith, Thomas Loughton, merchant of Charleston, 111

Smuggling, see Ireland.

Smyth, J F D, loyalist (Md), Tour in the United States, see also Stuart, Ferdinand Smyth

Smyth, Solomon, loyalist (S C), 28, n 197

Snell, Daniel, David, and George, loyalists (S C), land grants in Nova Scotia, 118

Snipes, Maj William Clay, 24

South Carolina, abuse of returned loyalist, 82, Assembly, General, 98, House of, 105, 111, 113, address of loyalists to Lieut -Gen Alexander Leslie, 97, banishment of loyalists, 61, 98, 117, battles (see Battles); Beattie's Mill, 73, Big Canebrake, 102, Blackstocks Fort, 20, Col John Boyd raises 600 loyalists, 80, British troops, 7, 9, 10, 13, 15, 31, 71, 75, 94, 97, 116, 126, 136, Lieut.-Governor William Bull, 32, n 218; 112, 113, 119, Camden, 13, 14, 60, 80, 91, 96, 97, 114, 115, 117, Lord William Campbell, last royal governor 5, 63, 66, 67, 83, 99, 105, Charleston (see Charleston), Cherokee ford, 11, 17, 131, 133, 136, claims and awards of loyalists, 118-121 (see also Claims and awards), commissioner of sequestered property, 139, loyalists' committee on value of property, 99, 120, committee of loyalists in London, 145-148, committee's warrant, 116, confiscation of loyalists' estates, 26, n 185, 39, n 274, 94, 110, 112, 113, 141, 142, Council of Safety, 63, 68, 191, creeks (see Creeks), Duet's Corner, 8, Fishdam ford, 12, forts (see Forts), Gilbert Town, 17, 18, Georgetown, 115, Grindal shoals, 4, 12, Indian field company, 115, Iron works, 4, n 22, 10, 12, 14, Iron works, Wofford's or "old," 12, n. 83, 14, Island ford, 87, Jacksonborough, 23, 39, James Island, 27, losses sustained by loy-

alists, 119, 120 (see also Claims and awards),
loyal militia, 60, 66, 68, 79, 80, 88, 94, 96,
97, 101, 102, 104, 106, 107, 108, 113-116, 126,
131, 132, loyalist regiments, viz Duke of
Cumberland's or Loyal American Rangers,
26, n 187, South Carolina Royalists, 6, 13,
n 96, 67, 70, 74-78, 80, 83, 102, 111, 112,
loyalists, 68, 74, 80, 82, 85, 88, 96, 98, 99,
116, 117, 119, 120, 131, 137, 145, Monk's
Corner, 26, n 184, Ninety-Six (see Ninety-
Six), Orangeburg, 25, 26, 79, 89, Parker's
ferry, 108, Quarter House, 9, n 62, 27,
Rocky Mount, 115, Round O company, 94,
Rugeley's Mills, 95, Salisbury, 72, seques-
tered property, 92, 101, 139, slaves, 112, 118,
120, Spring Hill, 101, Sullivan's Island, 3,
43, Tacaw, 7, 8, Tory association in Ninety-
Six district, 105, Whig associaition, 60, 67,
100, 101, 130, Whig convention, 109, 145,
Winnsborough, 3
South Carolina and American General Gazette,
98
South Carolina Royalists, see Tory corps
Spain, cession of East Florida to, 75
Spence, Thomas, 45
Spring Hill (S C), see South Carolina
Spring Gardens coffee house (London, Eng),
loyalists meet at, v, 32, n 216
Spurgeon Maj William, loyalist (N C), 80
Stack, Jacob, loyalist (S C), 5, n 30
Stagner, Daniel, loyalist (S C), 5, n 30
Stanwix, Brig -Gen John, 102
Stedman Charles, *History of the American
War,* 2 vols, London, 1794, xi
Stevenson's creek (S C), see Creeks
Stromer, Capt L, of Orangeburg (S C)
loyal militia, 114
Stroup, Capt George, of loyal militia from
Dutch Fork, 114
Stuart, Ferdinand Smyth, loyalist (Md), *The
Case of,* xi
Stuart, Col John, loyalist (S C), superin-
tendent of Indians, 65, commissions Richard
Pearis, 103, appoints Capt Moses Kirkland
deputy superintendent, 106
Sugar Creek (S C), see Creeks
Sullivan's Island (S C), see South Carolina
Sumter, Col Thomas, iv, 7, 13, 14, n 97
Sunbury (Ga), see Georgia
Sydney, Lord, receives memorial from layalist
officers of North Carolina, 117

TACAW ("Tachaw," S C), see South Carolina
Tanner, Mr _____, 100
Tarleton, Lieut -Col Banistre, 14 n 97, 18, n
127, 20, 21, 22, n 148, 33, 34 defeat at
Cowpens (S C), Jan, 17, 1781, iv, 22, 60,
128, appointed lieutenant-colonel of British
Legion, 90, joined by Alexander Chesney
with company of loyal militia, 132, Chesney

serviceable to, 135, certificate regarding
Chesney, vi, 130, 132, 143
Taylor, Herbert, 47
Taylor, Capt John, of New Jersey Volunteers
(Tory corps), 16, n 111, 85
Tennent, Rev William, 68, 100
Tennesee, William Chesney in, ix, x, 20, 43,
54, n 356, 56
Terry, Maj _____, loyalist (S C.), 67
Thicketty creek (S C), see Creeks
Thicketty Fort (S C), see Forts
Thomas, Col John, 77
Thompson, Capt Adam, loyalist (S C), of
Camden loyal militia, 114
Thompson, Benjamin, loyalist (Mass), see
Rumford, Count.
Thompson, Elizabeth, loyalist (S C), 33
Thorney, Miss _____, 98
Thornton, Abraham, loyalist (S C), land
grant in Nova Scotia, 118
Thornton, Eli, loyalist (S C), land grant in
Nova Scotia, 118
Tiger ("Tyger") river (S C), see Rivers
Tonyn, Patrick, governor of East Florida, 61,
address of loyalists to, 92, visited by Capt
Moses Kirkland, 105
Tories, see Loyalists
Tory association, Maj Terry's men sign, 67,
5,000 signers in Ninety-Six district, 105,
proposed by Alexander Chesney, 1775, 137
Tory corps
American Volunteers, under Maj Patrick
Ferguson, 11, n 76, 82, 93, Capt Abra-
ham de Peyster serves in, 84
British Legion, Lieut -Col Banistre Tarle-
ton of, 14, n 97, 18, n 127, 20, 21, 22, n
148, 25, n 182, 85, n 182, 33, 34, 60, 90,
raised by Lord William Shaw Cathcart,
90, in battle of Hanging Rock, 90, later
history, 90, 91, Capt John Rousselet of,
90
De Lancey's brigade, 13, n 96, 16, n 109,
Lieut -Col John Harris Cruger, of 1st
battalion, sails for Georgia, 89, defends
Ninety-Six, 118
Duke of Cumberland's regiment (or Loyal
American Volunteers), commanded by
Lord Charles Greville Montagu, 59, 60,
prisoners drafted into, 91
East Florida Rangers, Robert Phillips, lieu-
tenant in, 61
First American regiment, see Queen's Rang-
ers
Georgia Loyalists, 26, n 187
King's American regiment, Cols David and
Edmund Fanning in command of, Dec,
1776, 84, Frederick de Peyster joins, 84,
in battle of King's Mountain, 86
King's Carolina Rangers, 26, n 187
King's Florida Rangers, 26, n 187

Loyal American Rangers see Duke of Cumberland's regiment

Loyal American regiment, Duncan Fletcher in, 14, n 107, Lieut Anthony Allaire of, 85

Maryland Loyalists, 110

Nassau Blues, organized in New York by Col William Axtell, May 1, 1779, 84, officers and men later join New York Volunteers, 84

New Jersey Volunteers, 14, n 107, 16, n 111, Lieut.-Col Isaac Allen of, 21, n 145, Cap Samuel Ryerson of, 14, n 107 Capt John Taylor of, 16, n 111, 85, in battle of King's Mountain, defends Ninety-Six, May 22–June 19, 1781, 90

New York Volunteers, 13, n 89, officers and men of Nassau Blues join, 84, Lieut.-Col George Trumbull of, 12, n 89, 101

Prince of Wales's American Volunteers, 90 Maj John Cruden of, 90

Queen s Rangers, Maj James Dunlap of, 73; in battle of King's Mountain, 86, Col John Graves Simcoe of, commends Capt John Saunders, 109, moved from Virginia to South Carolina, 110

Queen's Own Loyal Virginia regiment, 109

Royal North Carolina rgeiment, 117

South Carolina Royalists, Lieut -Col Joseph Robinson of, 6, 13, n 96, 67, 70, 74-78, 80, 102, Col Alexander Innes given command, 1779, 83, Dr James Clitherall, surgeon to, 98, 112, Evan McLaurin, lieutenant-colonel of, 102, Thomas Fraser, appointed major, Aug, 1780, 111

Volunteers of Ireland, 25, n 180, n 181, 27, n 191

West Florida Rangers, son of Col Richard Pearis ensign in, 103

Towne, Rev Dr ___ ___ , 49, n 334, 50

Townsend, Thomas, British secretary for war, 31, 32

Trail, Henry, 99

Treaties treaty of neutrality, Sept. 16, 1775, 5, 69, 70, 71, 87, Lieut -Col Evan McLaurin signatory of, 102 treaty with Cherokee Indians, 8, n 58, treatiees between United States and Great Britain disregarded, 120

Tyron, William, governor of North Carolina, 1765-1771, 127

Turkey cove (N C), see North Carolina

Turnbull, Lieut -Col George, loyalist (N C), of New York Volunteers, 12, n 89, 101

Turner, Col William Vernon, in command of Rocky Mount loyal militia, 115

"Tyger" river (S C), see Tiger river

Tyne, Col Samuel, in command of Santee loyal militia, 115

UNITED Irishmen, association of, viii, 25, n 181, 45, n 308

United Loyalists, assembly of, 92

VERNON, Alexander, 79

Vernon, Lieut -Col James, loyalist (S C), 9, n 64, 71, 78, 79

Virginia, Robert Dinwiddie, governor of, 102, Lord John Murray Dunmore, last royal governor of, 1771-1776, 105, 106, 109, Col Jacob Ellegood, 108, 109, 110 Great Bridge, battle of, 109, Benjamin Dudley Gray, 109, Archibald Hamilton and Co, 117, Indians, 102, Kempe's landing place, 110, Capt Moses Kirkland in, 105, Lieut -Gen Alexander Leslie's expedition to, 110, Norfolk, 117 Richard Pearis in Provincial regiment of, 102, Queen's Own Loyal Virginia regiment, 109, Capt. John Saunders, 108-116, 143, n 15, Mrs Lilly Robinson and children flee to, 75

Volunteers of Ireland, see Tory corps

WALKER, Capt ___ ___ , executed, 86

Walker, Capt Jacob, loyalist (N C), 15, n 107

Wallace, William, loyalist (S C), land grant in Nova Scotia, 118

Ward, James, 49, n 107

Waring (Warring"), Rev Lucus, 46

Washington, Gen George, headquarters at Cambridge, Mass, Capt Moses Kirkland a prisoner at, 106

Washington, Col William, 95

Waxhaws (S C), 3, n 8, destruction of Col Abraham Buford's force at, June, 1780, 90 location, 2, n 8, Maj John Robinson, resident, 95

Weir, James, loyalist (S C), 98

Weir, Benjamin and William, loyalists (S C), land grants in Nova Scotia, 118

Wells, Eliza, 4

Wells, Zachariah, loyalist, executed, 19, n 129

Wesley, Rev John, 48, n 328

West, Peter, 55

West Florida, Governor Peter Chester, 106, northern Creek Indians, 103, Rangers, 103, Col Richard Pearis goes to, 102, 103, son of Col Pearis in Rangers, 103, Capt Kirkland on mission to, 106

West Indies, Solomon Smyth takes refuge in, 28, n 197, Francis Rawdon Chesney's company ordered to Jamaica, 53, n 352 Lord Greville Montaku's loyalist corps for service in Jamaica, 59, Col Thomas Fletchall and family settle in, 71, 72, Cols Thomas Edghill and James Vernon settle in, 71, Joseph Fletchall planter in, 72, Lieut -Col Joseph Robinson and family go to Jamaica, 75,

Capt Moses Kirkland takes refuge in, 107, loyalists take refuge in, 79, Col William Vernon Turner and family go to, 115, Southern loyalists seek refuge in, 117, South Carolinians join Duke of Cumberland's regiment in, 91, John Cruden and Co trade with, 91

Whealley, Moses, loyalist (S C), 74

Wheate, Sir Jacob, 28, n 192.

Whig association, opposed in Camden district, July, 1775 60, Maj Terry's men refuse to sign, 67, James Miller and others refuse to sign, 100, William Henry Drayton seeks signers, 101, Alexander Chesney pressed to enter, 130

Whig convention, John Saunders opposes sending delegates, 109, affiliations with, 145

Whigs, Alexander Chesney obliged to side with (see Chesney, Alexander), seek support of Col Richard Pearis and Indians, 102

White, Capt ——————, 15, n 104

White, John 52, n 341

White Oak creek (N C), see Creeks

Williams Edward, 9, n 64

Williams, James, 18, 40, n 281, n 282

Williams, Col James, 18, n 123, 20

Williams, Robert, 94, claim and award, 119 member, committee to estimate losses of South Carolina loyalists, 120, also of South Carolina loyalists' committee in London, 145

Williams, Thomas, loyalist (S C), land grant in Nova Scotia, 118

Williams, Col Hezekiah, in command of regiment of loyal militia, 115

Williamson, Gen Andrew, 7, in siege of Fort Ninety-Six, 69, 70, 74, 76, 80, 135, n 9, expedition against Indians, July, 1776, 65, 104,

loyalists attempt escape from army of, 131, 137.

Wilmington (N C), see North Carolina.

Wilmot, John Eardley, commissioner of American Claims, 37, n 258

Wilson, Capt ——————, loyalist, executed, 86

Wilson, Jane, second wife of Alexander Chesney, 36, n 249

Wilson, John, 40

Wilson, Roger, loyalist (S C), land grant in Nova Scotia, 118

Winder, Thomas, 37, n 255, 38.

Winn, Col John, 3, n 15, 13

Winnsborough (S C), see South Carolina

Winslow, Judge Edward, loyalist (Mass), in New Brunswick, Canada, 111

Withrow, David, Jacob, and John, loyalists (S C), land grants in Nova Scotia, 118

Wofford, Capt Benjamin, loyalist (S C), 5, n 30, 69

Wofford, William, 9, n 62

Wofford's Iron works (S C), see South Carolina

Wolfe, Lewis, agent for loyalists, v, vi, 31, 34, 36, 37, 38, 44, 49, 82, 139

Wright, Alexander, loyalist (S C), claim and award, 119

Wright, Maj James, 26, n 182, of loyal militia from Dutch Fork of Ninety-Six, S C, 114

YADKIN river (N C), see North Carolina.

Yorktown (Va), British surrender at, 110

Young, Lieut -Col William, in command of loyal militia of Little river, S C, 114

Young, Maj William, in command of (S C) loyal militia regiment of Dragoons, 114

DATE DUE

GAYLORD			PRINTED IN U.S.A

CPSIA information can be obtained
at www.ICGtesting.com
Printed in the USA
BVHW040235111220
595469BV00027B/337